# 6500
Jacksonville
Florida 2-96

# Compensation for Teams

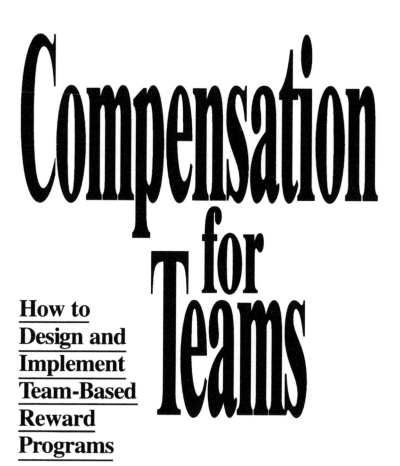

# Compensation for Teams

How to
Design and
Implement
Team-Based
Reward
Programs

## Steven E. Gross

### The Hay Group

# amacom

## American Management Association

New York • Atlanta • Boston • Chicago • Kansas City • San Francisco • Washington, D. C.
Brussels • Mexico City • Tokyo • Toronto

This publication is designed to provide accurate and authoritative
information in regard to the subject matter covered. It is sold with the
understanding that the publisher is not engaged in rendering legal,
accounting, or other professional service. If legal advice or other expert
assistance is required, the services of a competent professional person
should be sought.

Library of Congress Cataloging-in-Publicaton Data

Gross, Steven E.
    Compensation for teams : how to design and implement team-based
reward programs / Steven E. Gross.
        p.   cm.
    Includes bibliographical references and index.
    ISBN 0-8144-0299-2
    1. Incentives in industry.   2. Incentive awards.   3. Work groups.
4. Compensation management.   I. Title.
HF5549.5.I5G726   1995
    658.3'225—dc20                                          95-24748
                                                              CIP

Printing number

10   9   8   7   6   5   4   3   2   1

*To my team members:*
*Barbara, Sara, and Abby*

# Contents

# List of Exhibits

# Preface

*Compensation for Teams* was born out of the fundamental change in the way companies are organizing and paying their employees. In the early 1990s, The Hay Group began documenting alternative internal work cultures, and I began working with several leading companies on organizing, training, and rewarding employees working in teams. Over the next several years, it became apparent to me from my consulting that teams were not a passing fad, but represented a philosophical change in the way work and the workplace would be organized in the future. As with most fundamental shifts, change is not uniform and does not proceed at an even pace across every organization. In fact, teams come in a variety of types, each created to fit a particular work culture—and each having its own characteristics and reward strategy. I've tried to capture the elements that make and sustain team success in *Compensation for Teams* by providing both a conceptual framework and many case examples from Hay's consulting experience.

This book was made possible through the support of my colleagues at Hay and through the support of many clients—named and unnamed—referenced throughout the book.

Preparing this book would not have been possible without Sandy Salmans, who helped guide me through this effort, and Chetta Gofredo from Hay, who patiently assisted us in preparing the manuscript. Other Hay colleagues who helped include: Dan Glasner, Bob Ochsner, Stephanie Leffler, and Tom Flannery, who were especially helpful as the book was being finalized; Katie Cofsky and Debra Olson, who provided case examples from their own consulting work; and Doran Twer and Scott Spreier, who assisted throughout. Survey data supports many of the book's conclusions, with Jeff Harth and John Tracy deserving credit for making that process work.

—Steven E. Gross,
Philadelphia, Pennsylvania

# 1

# Introduction: Aligning Compensation, Culture, and Strategy

There weren't any covered wagons, but in some respects it was a pioneering journey that Unisys made to Bismarck, North Dakota, in 1994. Relocating its back-office accounting function to the prairies, the company took advantage of the new, or greenfield, site to make dramatic changes in the way people worked. In the past, employees had worked and been paid strictly as individuals. Starting with the move, they would work and be paid as members of teams.

Today there are more than 120 people organized into ten teams at the Bismarck office. There are teams that handle the company's accounts payable, teams that reimburse employees who travel on business for Unisys, and teams that are responsible for other accounting functions. Each team takes care of the entire process it is assigned, from opening the mail to issuing the checks. If there are problems, the team seeks solutions—*within* the team. And when it comes to pay, while everybody gets an individual base wage, people also get paid for the performance of the team. If the team meets its goals, up to 10 percent of each member's total quarterly earnings comes from team-based incentive compensation, with as much as another 10 percent of annual earnings based on the greenfield site's overall success.

## A Fundamental Change: The Move to Teams

What's happening in Bismarck reflects a fundamental change in the way work is organized and rewarded. Since the Industrial Revolution, companies have organized work on a functional model: Each job was analyzed into its component parts, and workers became functional experts in a rigid hierarchical setting. The essence of the functional model was the assembly line, in which each man or woman performed one unvarying task, hour after hour. It was possible, even desirable, to organize work this way because the environment in which business operated was nearly as unvarying as the assembly line. Trading patterns and markets were stable; technology was static; customers were passive; speed in getting to market was secondary; competition was limited to sectors and regions; and hierarchies were generally accepted in every walk of life. This was a business environment in which it was possible to develop a long-range plan and follow through year to year with little, if any, deviation.

No more. Since the 1960s, America—and much of the rest of the world—has been almost continually buffeted by change. Customers demand that businesses do it better, faster, cheaper; employees want to control more than the "stop" button on the assembly line. Sweeping change has forever altered the nature of work:

• Organizational designs and strategies are now being determined by the customer. Customers are demanding better service, faster response, higher quality, and a greater sensitivity to their needs. If there was any doubt that business is responding, witness the development of customized production in bicycles and apparel, two products that historically have been among the most resistant to new technology. To ensure that customers are served promptly and efficiently, companies are using integrated teams rather than parceling out the different functions to separate individuals. Planning, execution, and control are integrated as close to the customer as possible; suppliers, teams, and customers are linked through the decision-making process. "Stay close to the customer is the business mantra of the 1990s," a recent issue of *Fortune* magazine noted, and in the 1990s the "customer" has been redefined as virtually anybody inside or outside the company with whom one has a business relationship.[1]

• The increasing sophistication of technology and explosion of information have made it impossible for individuals to perform their jobs alone. Systems are far too complex today for any one individual to have all the necessary expertise; increasingly, they are managed by teams of multifunctional members, with highly specialized work being contracted out to consultants or freelancers. Furthermore, the computerization of the office has encouraged the sharing of information—not only within offices but across oceans—and broken down the lines on organizational charts. And, since knowledge is power, the growing availability of information to anybody with access to a computer has fostered the empowerment of the workforce.

• Speed and simplicity are becoming the key resources of competitive advantage. To survive and compete in a fast-changing, demanding global environment, organizations must move through their product cycles and to the marketplace faster. Companies can no longer tolerate the long delays as a product moves from design (which never communicated well with manufacturing or sales) to the factory (which can't produce the design) and to marketing (which can't sell the product at the predetermined price). To increase speed, flexibility, and efficiency, companies are forming teams that bring together design, manufacturing, and marketing, among other functions. A study by International Data, cited in *The Wall Street Journal*, found that of 200 big companies that were reengineering, 28 percent cited shorter cycle times as their primary goal, compared with 23 percent whose chief target was cutting costs.[2] Nor is the quest for speed confined to manufacturing; paper processing operations like mortgage brokers and insurance companies are also working hard to reduce their cycle time.

• Global economics is establishing the cost of labor. For more and more organizations, the *world* is the marketplace. That means that the cost of labor, as a percentage of a product's cost, cannot exceed a certain range if the product is to compete internationally. Hence the growing pressure for greater productivity. Companies are downsizing, steadily reducing the number of workers needed for a product or service. At the same time, the need is increasing for employees with multiple skills and behavioral competencies—those important underlying motives, traits, and characteristics that, as I'll discuss later in this chapter, are necessary for people to do their jobs well within different work cultures. Organizations are being restructured around teams and processes, rather than individual jobs.

In a 1995 survey of 230 companies on team-based pay, Hay Management Consultants confirmed that these trends correspond to the main objectives companies give for adopting teams: customer satisfaction, quality of the product or service, and productivity (see Exhibit 1-1). As Tom Sevin, the general manager of the Unisys operation in Bismarck, notes, two of his company's motives in deploying teams was to reduce cycle time and eliminate "handoffs" (the way customers were handed off from one employee to another if their invoices weren't completely routine, for example). By increasing everybody's knowledge of the entire operation, so that team members could han-

**Exhibit 1-1.  Why teams?**

## To Improve:

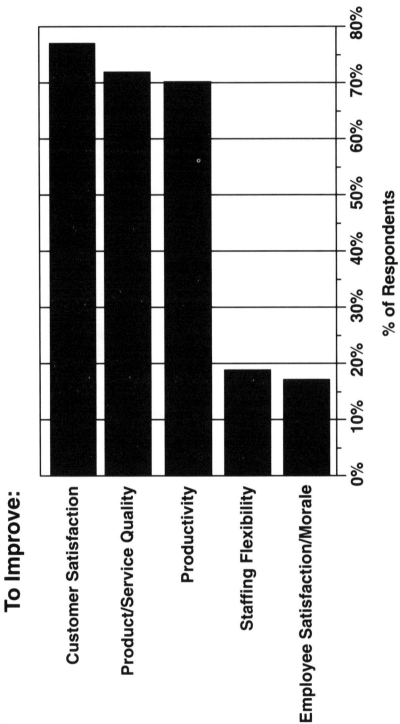

| | | |
|---|---|---|
| Customer Satisfaction | | |
| Product/Service Quality | | |
| Productivity | | |
| Staffing Flexibility | | |
| Employee Satisfaction/Morale | | |

0%  10%  20%  30%  40%  50%  60%  70%  80%

**% of Respondents**

*Source:* Hay 1995 Team-Based Pay Survey (U.S.A.)

dle the process from beginning to end, Unisys was able to look after its customers faster and better.

The two other reasons cited by companies for the need for teams (which trail the first set by a wide margin) concern internal company and employee needs: staffing flexibility and employee satisfaction. The suggestion that teams are good for employee morale is supported by research, including studies by Hay showing that the vast majority of employees—70 to 80 percent—acknowledge that teams are the way to go. However, while morale certainly has a bearing on how well people work, psychic income is one form of compensation outside the scope of this book.

## Paying for Teams

Judging from the numbers—and the trends that led to their development—teams are here to stay. While they aren't the answer to every corporate ill, where they work, they've become an essential part of corporate life. But why do we need to pay for teams?

This may sound peculiar coming from a compensation consultant (and it may not feel quite this way when you get your paycheck), but pay is in large measure a communication device. In fact, pay is one of the loudest and clearest ways a company can send a message to employees. By and large, people tend to behave the way they're measured and paid. If people serve together on teams, they must ultimately be paid as team members or they won't work together as a team. In fact, I'll go further: To ensure that the group works together toward a common goal, some form of assessment of team performance, recognition, shared reward, or team incentive is always necessary. As Sevin of Unisys puts it, making pay an integral part of the team concept "reinforces the team. It definitely works."

At the same time, there must be multiple other communicators. Pay is a punctuation mark within a communication—it's not the entire sentence structure. Organizations must take a holistic approach to teams. A company's business strategy must also be communicated through its work culture (which we discuss in detail below) and the behavioral competencies it emphasizes and rewards, as well as through pay. Work culture, behavior competencies, reward: These must all be aligned with the corporation's business strategy—the way the company differentiates itself in the marketplace—if it is to achieve the results it wants (see Exhibit 1-2).

As a longtime compensation expert, my particular interest is aligning reward strategies with an organization's business strategies,

**Exhibit 1-2. Team effectiveness: alignment.**

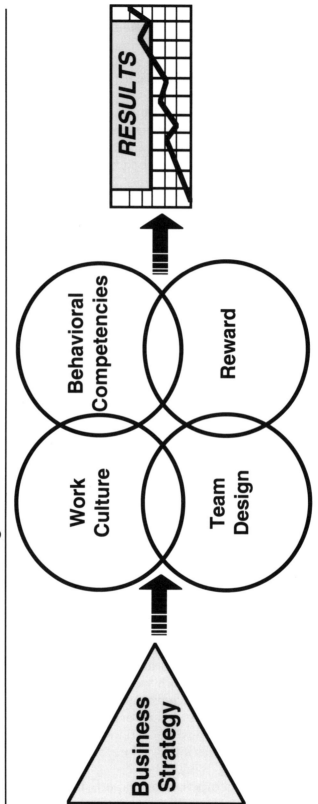

culture, and competencies. At Hay Management Consultants, we call this *dynamic pay*. For complex organizations, developing a workable dynamic pay model can be a complex exercise, incorporating multiple elements of reward. Increasingly, however, companies are acknowledging the need to undertake this exercise. As their work cultures and competencies become more team-oriented, these companies recognize that they must eventually address the most concrete phase of alignment: paying for teams. Just what the specific elements should be, and in what proportion, depends on the particular business strategy and work culture of the organization.

I'll discuss each of the elements of pay in this book. But before the different components of pay can be identified and evaluated, it is necessary to understand the context in which they operate. So while the core of this book is compensation practice, the first few chapters are devoted to furthering a conceptual understanding of compensation. In these chapters, I will describe in detail the types of teams for which different pay systems may be most appropriate, the "competencies" or attributes that are the best predictor of worker success, and the evolving approach to performance appraisal.

To avoid making this discussion entirely theoretical, I will bring in the real world as much as possible through examples and case studies. At that point, having laid the necessary foundation, I will move on to a more tangible discussion of the benefits and drawbacks of different pay systems and how they may best be designed and implemented.

This book does not specifically address the use and compensation of teams in a collective-bargaining environment.

I'll begin here by introducing the work cultures most prevalent in organizations today.

## Work Cultures

Customers. Reliability. Technology. Flexibility and agility. Such are the strategic priorities that shape virtually any business. How a company ranks those priorities, however, accounts for its evolution into one of the four major work cultures described on the following pages: functional, process, time-based, and network. As I show, each culture orders these priorities differently.

In reality, of course, few organizations fit any one of these cultural models exactly; many organizations have different characteristics in different business units or operations. There are hybrid cultures, and hybrid compensation solutions. But a work culture diagnostic, including identification of its specific type of team, narrows the range of solutions, and takes much of the guesswork out of compensation design.

## The Functional Culture

Until the last decade or so, most companies were organized along functional lines. The functional culture was perhaps best exemplified by AT&T, prior to deregulation, and it remains the model today for large government bureaucracies. Although many companies are moving away from this model, it still serves as a very effective structure for companies where high degrees of reliability are critical, or for specialized units—the risk management function, for instance.

In a functional culture, the focus is on what the organization does, and on doing it consistently. Functionally oriented companies are generally not on the cutting edge technologically, but they apply technology reliably and limit risks through reliable production as well as by a heavy emphasis on planning. Performance is measured in terms of size, market share, return on equity, and industry reputation. Strategic priorities, in order of importance, are likely to be:

1. Technology
2. Reliability and quality
3. Customer needs
4. Flexibility and agility

The functional culture is the bastion of the traditional top-down organizational chart. Internal order is strong: Work is designed around clearly defined specialization by individuals, and integrated through deep management hierarchies in which decision-making is clearly set apart from actual execution. The behavioral competencies most valued in this type of culture are self-control and discipline; power comes through the organization, and by being more capable than the next person in one's specialized function or field, that is, the position ranking. For employees, good job security is one of this culture's biggest selling points. Teams in this environment are created to solve specific problems—most common being the cross-functional task force. Employees serve part-time on these parallel teams in addition to their normal job accountabilities. Chapter 2 discusses in detail the characteristics of each type of team with each culture.

## The Process Culture

With the emergence of the total quality movement (TQM) in the 1980s, much of the evolution of work cultures has been toward the process model. Companies conforming to this model design work processes for meeting obligations to customers, and execute through empowered permanent full-time work or process teams that have the mutual goal of customer satisfaction and continuous quality improvement. Team members in process cultures must be able to share influence with others and demonstrate tenacity, team spirit, and helpfulness. TQM gurus have maintained that more than 90 percent of an individual's success is tied to the system of which he or she is a part. The process culture firmly adheres to that view.

In an organization with a process culture, effectiveness is measured through the eyes of the customer. Risk is limited by the ongoing emphasis on continuous improvement. Planning, execution, and control are integrated as close to the customer as possible. Communication—both formal and informal—is constant, and the process team is linked to both suppliers and customers through the decision-making process. Strategic priorities, in order of importance, are likely to be:

1. Customer needs
2. Reliability and quality
3. Technology
4. Flexibility and agility

The process culture is most characteristic of organizations that link service and reliability and that market and deliver consistently improving customized capabilities. Some of the major telecommunications companies stand out as examples of those that have moved at least some aspects of their organizations toward this model.

### The Time-Based Culture

Technical advances in the late 1980s, which placed greater emphasis on the cost of capital and the opportunity of speed, gave birth to the time-based culture in organizations dominated by concerns of finance and manufacturing, such as General Electric. Companies that have a time-based culture seek to maximize their return on fixed assets and dominate their markets through technical prowess during their highly profitable phase, and then use the accumulated internal competencies of their people to move on to new or emerging market opportunities once they reach a mature, lower-return stage.

Organizations that employ this model emphasize a comparatively flat structure. Work is designed around management levels that add value and manage necessary risks, and full-time cross-functional program or project teams for the duration of the activity. Power in this culture comes from one's "gatekeeping" abilities to control both critical resources and access to opportunities. Individuals are encouraged to develop multifunctional expertise and competencies. Team members must be able to direct and persuade others, bring initiative and self-confidence to the effort, and demonstrate a results orientation.

Strategic priorities, in order of importance, are likely to be:

1. Flexibility and agility
2. Technology
3. Customer needs
4. Reliability and quality

## The Network Culture

At the far end of the current organizational spectrum is the network, or "partnership," culture. Ad hoc groups and temporary alliances create an organization that brings together the necessary skills to complete a specific venture and ceases to exist after its goal is achieved. Key performance indicators are cash flow and the uniqueness of the venture. Risk is managed through diversification; priorities are shaped around the need to respond immediately to customers and to first create, and then penetrate, opportunistic market niches. Strategic priorities, in order of importance, are likely to be:

1. Flexibility and agility
2. Customer needs
3. Technology
4. Reliability and quality

The motion picture industry, construction industry, and professional partnerships, along with R&D projects in certain high-tech industries, are the best examples of this model. Filmmaking brings together a production team that includes a variety of skills (direction, sound, lighting, acting, set and wardrobe design) for a single project. The construction industry takes a similar approach: A general contractor links a number of subcontractors with diverse skills and competencies.

Power in this culture comes from being able to perform critical work and bring the right people together to orchestrate successful outcomes—to "do whatever makes sense." Team members must be able to build strong relationships with others, demonstrate a "trail-blazing" spirit, and be both pragmatic and creative.

As you'd expect, however, pay is relatively unstructured, generally negotiated between management and key contributors. Because pay arrangements are highly discretionary, I will not discuss the network culture, partnership teams, or compensation specific to them, further in this book.

## Competencies

"We grossly underestimated the culture change that would take place in having people work in groups to solve problems and make decisions," says Norm Bruening, vice president, residential products, for American Meter, in Nebraska City, Nebraska. About five years ago American Meter, which makes gas meters and regulators for people's homes, moved from a traditional functional organization to one based on teams. As Bruening tells it, it wasn't a smooth transition.

"You can't make cultural change short-term," he notes. "It's very difficult and takes time, day to day, to get in place. We told supervisors their new job was to help employees look for solutions and act as coaches, rather than tell them what to do. Some couldn't adjust, and they're no longer supervisors. They've stepped down, left, or retired. We had to persuade other people to take initiative. Some employees didn't want to be involved, and we're not forcing them." But for new hires, Bruening concludes, the company has had a much easier time finding people "who can fit in our 'world-class concept,' work on a team, handle job rotation, and are more receptive to change."

Not every company has the advantage of launching a new corporate culture on a greenfield site. As American Meter's experience shows, bringing it into well-established operations can be difficult. Although American Meter eventually modified its compensation scheme, pay is only part of the problem or solution. As I noted earlier, behavioral competencies must also be closely aligned with business strategies, work cultures, and teams.

In the traditional functional culture, employees were rated and paid primarily in terms of their skills or past experience. But sometime during the past thirty years, organizational psychologists became increasingly aware that neither skills nor experience was the best predictor of what people will do. Instead, they identified competencies, defined as "what outstanding performers do more often, in more situations, with better results, than average performers." Unlike skills and education, competencies go deeper and are measured purely by observable behaviors. For example, a customer service representative can be taught computer and telephone system skills, but the key to successful performance may be such things as a customer service orientation, flexibility, listening and responding, and self-control. Employees are selected for team assignments primarily for their skills or the functions they represent, with increasing or exhibited competencies (see Exhibit 1-3).

For every culture, there are competencies that are especially appropriate. But there are also competencies that apply broadly to people working in teams in any culture—starting with teamwork and cooperation. In Chapter 3, I describe the competencies that are vital to successful teamwork—what they are and how they vary from one corporate culture to another—and how to develop a competency model. Competencies can be used in every culture for recruitment, development, succession planning, and reward purposes. While promotion and career development are outside the scope of this book, in Chapter 5, I discuss the way competencies are used in performance appraisals as a basis for evaluating the performance of team members.

When it comes to paying for teams, the use of competencies in performance appraisals creates both problems and opportunities. For one thing, the rise of teams, particularly self-managed teams in a process culture, has reduced the role of the supervisors who traditionally conducted performance reviews. Recognizing that fellow team members are probably better informed, companies are introducing multi-rater or "360-degree review"—appraisal by peers as well as managers and (where relevant) subordinates. As I discuss in Chapter 5, many workers are reluctant to have a voice in how their coworkers get paid, and equally reluctant to be judged by their coworkers. As a result, the evolution toward paying for competencies as determined by teams has been slow. But eventually, I believe, competencies judged by and for team members will become aligned with pay.

First, however, people must acquire more team competencies. The ability to work well on teams isn't inherent—and in America, it might be argued, it almost runs against the grain. While more class-conscious societies engender team feeling within a class because they limit mobility, this country has a unique emphasis on individualism. That comes through loud and clear in the workplace. When people give their list of arguments for earning more money, they mention performance, needs, seniority, experience, ability, and so forth. Far

**Exhibit 1-3. Employee selection for team assignments.**

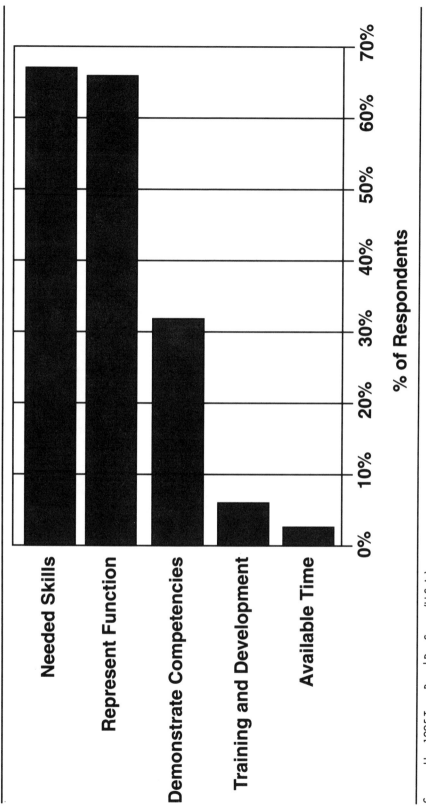

% of Respondents

Needed Skills

Represent Function

Demonstrate Competencies

Training and Development

Available Time

0%  10%  20%  30%  40%  50%  60%  70%

*Source:* Hay 1995 Team-Based Pay Survey (U.S.A.)

In fact, pay may be one important means of encouraging team members to acquire more team competencies. "You can't make more than your teammates" is a message, loud and clear, that—at least for certain types of pay—people are accountable to each other.

# Reward

That leads us to pay or, more elegantly, reward—the last but essential element companies must align with their business strategies to achieve their desired goals. To see where we want to be headed in pay, let's look at where we've been.

In the not-too-distant past, most companies operated as traditional management hierarchies and used traditional forms of pay. Incentives and bonuses were reserved mainly for managers and salespeople, the only employees formally empowered to affect results. For nonmanagement employees, the pay system had a strong base-salary focus. Base pay was designed to attract and retain employees, with little attention to the cost of doing business.

Companies relied heavily on increases in base pay (seniority or merit raises) and promotions as means of rewarding and motivating individuals. The link between pay and performance was, at best, unclear. Generous merit raises were common during the late 1970s through the early 1980s not only because they kept people "whole"— regardless of their performance—in an era of double-digit inflation, but also because fixed increases in the cost of doing business were automatically passed on to the customer. And, because organizations had a traditional pyramid, promotions were nearly as predictable as merit increases.

But with the flattening of the pyramid and downsizing today, there are fewer rungs on the corporate ladder to climb. And merit raises don't make such great economic sense, for several reasons. For one thing, with competitiveness rising in almost every sector, it's harder to pass higher costs along to the customer. Secondly, merit raises, with their explicit focus on the individual, may not be the best way to reward people working in teams. And the low rate of inflation has taken the wind out of cost-of-living adjustments. Already there are signs that companies are breaking from the strict merit-increase mentality of the past few decades. Hay's U.S. Compensation Conference surveys indicate that raises have declined gradually from 5 percent in 1986–87 for clerical/administrative and 4.7 percent for hourly workers, to a projected 3.9 percent and 3.8 percent, respectively, in 1994–95.

Yet in the midst of cultural change, companies are moving slowly to align pay systems with business strategies. The 1994 Hay Conference Survey, for example, found that 39 percent of organizations said they had a substantial reengineering/work transformation project under way, 7 percent had already completed such a project, and another 25 percent were considering this type of change. But of those with a project under way or completed, only one in four indicated that employee compensation played a "primary" part in the change effort, and one-third said the issue of pay remained "unaddressed." Granted, changing pay programs may not be the first thing organizations look at when they transform their work processes. But in fact, upwards of 80 percent of all companies in the survey said they felt they needed to revamp their pay programs.

Other studies, by the American Compensation Association and the Center for Effective Organizations at the University of California, confirm what the companies are indicating: There is no connection between work culture and reward. By and large, pay has not changed to reflect the changing nature of work. In the newer, team-oriented cultures, traditional pay practices are still in use. Initially, the new work cultures and the old reward system seem able to coexist, but ultimately, the combination makes for an unstable situation. Not only is pay not reinforcing desired behaviors in such situations; it's countercultural. When work changes and pay doesn't—for example, when you emphasize quality but pay only for financial results—you'll get inappropriate behavior.

The problem is exacerbated because in the current economic climate the comforts of the traditional culture are being jettisoned. Many organizations, including some of the world's largest and most successful companies, have radically changed the nature and makeup of their workforce through employee downsizing, early retirement, and the increasing use of contract workers. Companies are no longer building up staffs as they once did, and they are unable to live up to the implicit promises of job security and long-term rewards. Without structural changes in pay, many employees, already cynical about business, perceive any reengineering as a proxy for downsizing.

The result: a continuing decline in workers' confidence, commitment, and loyalty to their corporate management, according to Hay's employee attitudinal database of over 500 companies. Hourly employees especially are increasingly disaffected. I believe it's no coincidence that, even though close to half of the employees we surveyed say they're satisfied with their pay in absolute dollars, a sizable majority do not perceive their pay as linked to their performance (see Exhibit 1-4).

jority do not perceive their pay as linked to their performance (see Exhibit 1-4).

Only new ways to compensate people will lead to a more motivated and productive workforce. Team goals should be linked to the organization's strategic plan, and team pay should be linked to achieving team goals. This is not to say that traditional position evaluation of the type pioneered by The Hay Guide Chart®-Profile Method of Job Evaluation nearly fifty years ago, or vehicles such as the merit raise, should disappear in the near future. But I expect companies to blend them with a pay-for-performance approach, focused increasingly on teams. When well-designed, the compensation program will reinforce an organizational culture that significantly advances the company's strategic goals.

What are the components of such a compensation program? Compensation is a function of total opportunity. In this book, I discuss base pay (Chapter 4), increases in base pay or merit raises (Chapter 6), recognition cash and noncash awards (Chapter 7) and incentive compensation (Chapter 8). All are components of how to design a compensation architecture, which I describe in Chapter 9. Companies that have changed their business strategies and cultures to reflect the business challenges of the nineties need to bring all four of these components into alignment. However, I expect that the primary focus for many companies will be the components that allow employers to pay for performance: recognition and incentives. Both of these types of compensation come under the category of variable pay.

## Variable Pay

Although interest in variable pay has grown with the growing appeal of pay-for-performance, it's been around in a number of forms for years. People working in sales, for example, have traditionally been offered *individual incentives*, commissions that often constituted a large part of their total income. And top executives have been awarded stock options and other incentive pay to motivate and reward long-term performance. On a company-wide level, many employers have made their first foray into incentives with *profit-sharing*, an approach in which a share of corporate profits is distributed in cash on a current basis to all employees.

More recently, companies have been offering *gainsharing* to production-oriented workers, giving them a percentage of the value of increased productivity, under a prearranged formula. Unlike profit-sharing, gainsharing is typically driven by operational factors—quality, productivity, customer satisfaction—rather than financial

**Exhibit 1-4. Employee perception.**

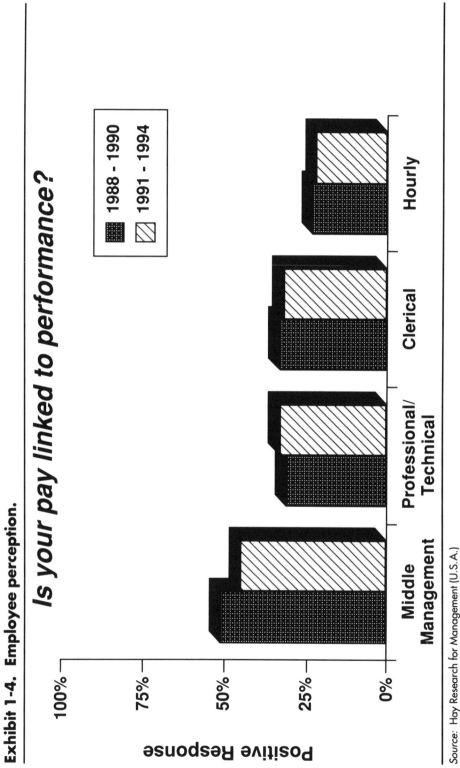

*Is your pay linked to performance?*

Legend:
- 1988 - 1990
- 1991 - 1994

Positive Response: 100%, 75%, 50%, 25%, 0%

Categories: Middle Management, Professional/Technical, Clerical, Hourly

Source: Hay Research for Management (U.S.A.)

results. This type of plan usually appears as an add-on to compensation and thus is easily accepted by employees. However, at times it too has proven far removed from workers' control to affect their performance.

In fact, none of these forms of variable pay is designed specifically to motivate and reward teams. That's the purpose of the two components I mentioned earlier: team incentives and recognition. In the first case, a team of employees receives money based on increased performance against predetermined targets. Spot award/recognition programs are one-time awards for a limited number of employees or groups for performing well beyond expectations or for completing a project, program, or product. As I note in Chapter 9, incentives are better suited to certain types of teams, and recognition programs are better for others.

Our research shows that recognition awards have made greater inroads than other types of pay-for-performance: 38 percent of all companies in the Hay 1994 Compensation Conference Survey. That's at least partly due to the fact that they're the easiest to implement, since they reward results that are already achieved. Only 12 percent of those companies surveyed had special pay programs for teams. However, an additional 39 percent of companies said they were considering implementing team-based pay—more than were contemplating any other type of pay-for-performance.

Does variable pay work? Intuition would say that it must. It forges the connection between work culture and reward. It helps communicate companies' values to employees by defining the range of reward opportunities and the ways performance will be measured. This is noteworthy because people tend to behave as they are measured.

While research is still limited, it tends to support the conclusion that variable pay works. A 1994 study by the Consortium for Alternative Reward Strategies Research (CARS), sponsored by the American Compensation Association, of performance-based pay plans for non-management employees at more than 600 companies—large and small, service and manufacturing, union and nonunion—concluded that variable pay plans "clearly provide an organizational tool to improve performance through people. . . . They make good business sense."[3] As for group- or team-based variable pay, it's still too new to provide much more than anecdotal evidence. Still, a review in 1994 of the literature by George T. Milkovich, Catherwood Professor of Industrial Labor Relations at Cornell University, concluded that "group-based performance plans have had dramatic and positive influences on firm performance."

Why, then, has team-based variable pay lagged so far behind team-based cultures? There are many reasons, not least of which is the normal resistance to change. In addition, as we mentioned earlier, just as people tend to resist thinking of themselves as team members, they also resist being paid as such. Some employees are afraid they won't be recognized for their contributions. Finally, it's risky; most variable pay programs put some base pay at risk in return for a potentially higher reward. Getting employees to accept risk isn't easy, especially for a workforce that has become accustomed to the annual base-pay increase. The entitlement mentality of the U.S. workforce over the last thirty years has been the single largest roadblock to innovative pay plans.

Until recently, companies have been reluctant to rock the boat. But if the alternative is for the boat to go under, companies will have to change their approach to compensation.

## Finding the Proper Alignment for Your Work Culture

The functional culture is not obsolete; the network culture is not inevitable. It is a mistake to assume that only certain work cultures will prevail, or are better suited to these times than others. Each type of culture still has a clear place in the world of work, and each offers specific opportunities for success, given the right mix of market and competitive factors. However, it seems clear that no one culture will attain the dominance of the function model in the future.

The key issue is alignment. An organization must come to grips with where it currently stands in relation to where it wants to go, and then identify the missing values, skills, and behaviors that help close the gap between the two. Only then can the organization bring its structure, training and development efforts, compensation approaches, and all other manifestations of its new strategic thrust into proper alignment with the new work culture that it seeks to create.

When the culture includes teams, as is often inevitable, compensation should focus on strengthening team building, boosting performance levels, and achieving desired business results, and fundamentally changing team members' behaviors to meet organizational goals. Rewards can be cash or noncash. They can be linked to the team's performance through the use of merit pay based on team performance appraisal, by providing special awards for excellent performance, or through incentive compensation plans that provide payouts for achieving or exceeding predetermined objectives.

One rule of performance-based pay, however, is that the goals should cover areas that team members can directly affect. Otherwise the team is disempowered. Compensation won't motivate employees unless there's a direct line of sight between performance and results. And for most nonexempt workers, that's not the case. When incentives are tied only to the final profit of a company or group, which can be affected by all sorts of market forces, the connection between performance and reward is weakened. At the same time, pay should bear some relationship to the company's bottom line. If the company is in the red, team rewards appear nonsensical—unless management is confident that ultimately the team's superior productivity and quality will help turn the company around.

Unfortunately, many employees and even some managers believe that a successful program is one that always pays out. On the contrary, these programs are specifically designed not to pay out when performance is below par. The key is to create a plan that equitably shares risk, offers a potential gain that makes the risk worth taking, and gives employees a fair shot at making more by working harder, smarter, and better. The key is to find the right amount of pay at risk so that employees on the team feel adequately rewarded when the team performs adequately, but can feel handsomely rewarded when performance soars.

For some teams, a carefully crafted mix of individual and group incentives may be most appropriate. Other approaches may be oriented exclusively toward the achievement of mutual goals. In between an almost infinite number of combinations of base and variable pay can be employed to motivate and reward both the team as a whole and its individual parts.

Whatever arrangement it chooses, the company needs to realize that making the change to team-based pay demands great care. In Chapters 10, 11, and 12, I describe in detail the thirteen steps that I believe are necessary to develop and implement a successful compensation plan. This is the crucial "how to" of paying for teams. While the theory is helpful, the best-conceived plan in the world is irrelevant if it doesn't align compensation with the company's business strategies, culture, and competencies. It will not be effective if the company's internal culture is not ready to accept change—if, for example, middle managers and supervisors become roadblocks—or if the company's communication is not consistent, honest, and complete.

Wherever possible, team members who will be affected should be consulted. We can expect that employees will be concerned about the fairness of compensation based on a team approach. Is it fair relative to other teams or other people? Is it externally competitive? Does it seem to be tied to performance? Are the appraisal systems that judge team performance fair and accurate? Do they aim to help people perform better? If there's an incentive plan, is it simple enough to understand and calculate? At the end of the day, is there enough of an incentive on an absolute basis to motivate anybody? Does it recognize the individual as well as the team? People still need an outlet to express themselves and to excel as individuals—and, in fact, business teams, like football teams, do have Most Valuable Players (MVPs). At the same time, let's not exaggerate the role of the individual. It may truly be lonely at the top, but closer to the bottom, where most people work, they work in teams.

From the first, I've presumed that changes in compensation follow, or support, cultural change. But should compensation ever lead? This is a "cart before the horse" issue. In general, compensation plans should not be expected to lead a cultural change; that will only prompt the workforce to focus on the wrong message. When the right values, behaviors, and results have been promoted, compensation should then be used to *reinforce* the change. In fact, organizations can use compensation as a "reinvigorating" element to be introduced just as interest in the new culture change process is beginning to wane, as it inevitably will. Used this way, the new approach to pay can serve as a welcome, and highly effective, reinforcement mechanism that can strengthen the culture change process even more.

However, there are times when pay can lead. Incentives can be pivotal in jump-starting and easing the integration of quality initiatives into an organization, for example. They can serve as a sort of "pump-priming" function, getting employees' attention for the impending cultural change and reinforcing its credibility. But if pay leads, it cannot be by much, just as it shouldn't lag too far behind cultural change. Ideally, the two should be in sync.

A final, cautionary note: Before they study the matter closely, many companies don't really understand what they're trying to accomplish with pay, or how best to motivate employees. The danger is that they'll jump to the latest trend in compensation (currently pay-for-performance) without knowing where precisely they want to land.

My advice is, don't start out by saying, "I want to pay for teams." First, ask yourself, "Do I need teams? If so, what kind of teams? And what do I want them to accomplish?" Only after you've answered those questions can you address the central question of this book: "How should I pay for them?"

# Notes

1. Kenneth Labich, "Why Companies Fail," *Fortune*, November 14, 1994, p. 64.
2. William M. Bulkeley, "The Latest Big Thing at Many Companies Is Speed, Speed, Speed," *The Wall Street Journal*, December 23, 1994, p. 1.
3. "Organizational Performance & Rewards," Consortium for Alternative Reward Strategies Research, American Compensation Association, 1994, p. 35.

# 2

# The Many Forms
# Teams Take

So you're interested in paying for teams. But before you can even begin to tackle that issue, there are at least two basic questions you've got to address. First, does your workplace have teams or does it have work groups? Second, if they *are* teams, what *kinds* of teams are they?

## What Is a Team?

The word *team*, as Jon R. Katzenbach and Douglas K. Smith observe in *The Wisdom of Teams: Creating the High-Performance Organization* (McGraw-Hill, 1992), tends to be loosely applied. Because teamwork has come to epitomize many of the values and virtues we seek in business—the corporate equivalent of apple pie and motherhood—many executives see teams where, in fact, none exist. Good teamwork—sharing information and decisions—does not necessarily make a team. "Groups do not become teams simply because that is what someone calls them," Katzenbach and Smith note. Nor, wishful thinking aside, can an entire workforce of a large corporation be a team; regardless of the name, Team Xerox, an agglomeration of some 30,000 people, is not a team.

We have thus established what a team is not; but what, then, *is* a team? Here is the definition, crafted by Katzenbach and Smith, that has been widely adopted within management circles:

> "A team is a small number of people with complementary skills who are committed to a common purpose, set of performance goals, and approach for which they hold themselves mutually accountable."[1]

23

How small is small? Who defines the common purpose, the goals, and the approach? Obviously, answers to such questions depend on the corporation and the specific team. A team may be as small as two people, like the rare partnerships of coequal chief executives or presidents that head some corporations. More typically, the number of members is closer to five or ten; at the upper limits, it may be as large as thirty-five or forty. Beyond a certain number, however, it's likely that the "team" loses its common purpose and disintegrates into subteams. To be effective, teams need to be small enough to allow employees to make a significant contribution to the team's goals, and to see the impact of what they've done.

As for defining the team's goals, that's a variable, too. As we use the term here, a team consists of people who *do* the work, i.e., not the managers; the possible exception is a time-based team, which may cut across the entire hierarchy of a corporation. That doesn't mean, however, that the team sets its own direction. How a team is led or supervised is one of its distinguishing characteristics.

In recent years, as *empowerment* has entered the lexicon of U.S. industry, "self-directed" or "self-managed" teams have become the latest goal toward which to strive. But to a large degree, the notion of self-management by teams remains more wishful thinking than reality. Teams typically engage in a lot of problem-solving, but evidence of significant decision-making is scarce. It is rare for teams to decide, for example, how they should be treated, how they should be equipped technologically, or who their members should be. So far, such decisions are usually made at a supervisory level, and that has important ramifications in terms of paying for teams. At the same time, many corporations, notably those with process or time-based cultures, are beginning to truly empower their teams. I discuss specific cases later in this book.

Returning to the definition for a team then, what remains is *mutually accountable*. Here there are no variables. In teams that are truly teams, members are accountable to each other. They cease to operate strictly as individuals interested solely in their own particular performance and results and instead function as team members whose value will be judged at least in part by how well the team performs overall.

## Types of Teams

So now you've established whether your organization has teams rather than groups of individuals who happen to be sitting around the same table. That raises the second basic question: What kind(s) of teams does your company have?

Teams, like corporate cultures, can take many forms. At Hay, we have defined three types of teams—the parallel team, the process team and the project team—that correspond to the three main corporate cultures described in Chapter 1. However, just as companies are often a blend of cultures, they may have a blend of teams. They may have all three types of teams for different purposes, and they may have employees serving on multiple types of teams. Finally, they may have "hybrid" teams that represent a blend of the characteristics of two or three of the main team types.

Below, I describe the three main types of teams, with a case study for each. See Exhibit 2-1 for a graphic analysis of the prevalence of the three types.

## The Parallel Team

Parallel teams can and do arise in any kind of corporation. What distinguishes them from every other kind of team discussed here is that they are part-time. They may be temporary, such as a team assembled to solve a particular problem within a matter of weeks or months, after which it dissolves itself. Or they may be permanent, requiring their members to convene periodically, year in, year out. They may be cross-functional, representing different skills within the organization and thus permitting a holistic approach to a problem. Or, less typically, they may be composed of employees who perform the same function in their regular jobs.

In either case, the parallel team represents only a partial and limited use of its members' time. The members have other jobs within the company that, as a rule, make greater demands on their time. As a result, members of parallel teams typically have at least two bosses—one who leads or supervises their team, and another to whom they regularly report and who typically conducts the employees' performance review. In fact, in some companies—notably the process culture described in Chapter 1—the employee's "full-time" job may be a role on a different type of team.

Inherent in this arrangement are both the benefits and drawbacks of parallel teams. Before we look into those pros and cons, however, let's first examine their uses.

What are examples of parallel teams? In the sports world, they may be gymnastics or skiing teams. Most of the time, the members of such teams work very much as individuals, perfecting their mastery of their sport. Often they compete against each other. But for a rela-

**Exhibit 2-1. Team-type prevalence.**

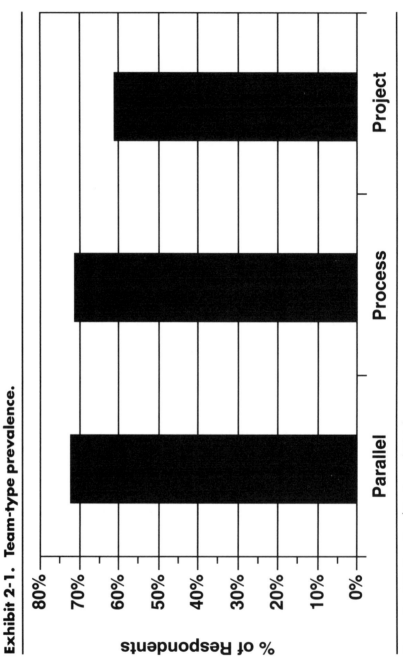

*Source:* Hay 1995 Team-Based Pay Survey (U.S.A.)

tively small but important part of the time, these athletes are united as a team, working together to produce the highest possible aggregate score at, say, the Olympics or other sporting competitions.

In the world of the corporation, parallel teams may be formed to serve a variety of purposes. In a factory, such a team may be chartered to meet periodically to monitor and address safety issues. Factory or white-collar teams may work on quality issues, on redesigning a work process, or on product development. In the upper reaches of the hierarchy, they may be permanent steering committees that meet quarterly to review communications policy or compensation design. Or they may be ad hoc teams formed to bring their cross-functional skills and perspectives to bear on a specific short-term problem or situation.

At some companies, participating in parallel teams is almost as much of a "given" as doing the job for which one was hired. At Hallmark Cards, a company that has moved aggressively in recent years to internalize a process culture, virtually everybody in the risk management services department, secretaries included, is on one or more teams, working on such areas as workers' compensation. At the Upper Merion, Pennsylvania, factory of SmithKline Beecham, the British-headquartered healthcare company, 87 percent of the 225 people who work at the plant participate in at least one team. "It's hard to work here and not be involved," says Bobbie Thompson, the facility's manager.

## Parallel Teams: A Case Study

One example of a parallel team is a team proposal system—an updating of the old-fashioned employee suggestion box with the addition of such important elements as employee empowerment, pay-for-performance, and total quality management. Increasingly, many companies are initiating team proposal systems in an effort to contain costs and become more competitive. In 1991, when St. Joseph Hospital—a 300-bed facility located in Lancaster, Pennsylvania, and part of the Franciscan Health System—used a team proposal system with volunteers, teams came up with more than 200 suggestions that generated millions of dollars in savings over the next four years.

How does a proposal team work? In my experience, the best configuration is seven members from different departments within the organization. Seven is a critical mass, providing enough people to collect ideas from a variety of perspectives while allowing for a group small enough to guarantee that everyone gets involved. For a period that usually lasts between twelve and twenty-four weeks, teams meet, submit proposals, and then await a determination of their acceptability. Management plays an important role. Although the teams generally include only employees below the management level, management must agree on the ground rules—including how much, if any, of the savings should be passed along to the team—and the process for proposal evaluation and implementation. How the teams and individual members are rewarded for their contribution is discussed in Chapter 8.

### Pros and Cons of Parallel Teams

When well-planned, well-communicated, and well-monitored, proposal teams and other kinds of parallel teams are an excellent means of getting employees involved and participating. They can change the corporate culture as well as reflect it, introducing a cross-functional approach to a company that otherwise still operates in traditional silos. They also provide an opportunity for individuals, both as a form of personal development (especially important in a flat organization) and a means of exposure to higher management levels. Serving on a team allows people to interface with the rest of the corporation, to have greater visibility, and to shine in a different light—and for management to evaluate them accordingly. But parallel teams have their drawbacks as well as their advantages.

The main problem can be accountability, which we identified earlier as the critical characteristic of a team. For people who work on parallel teams, there is an inherent conflict. They are pulled in two opposing directions—toward their regular job and toward their team job—and the tug can be considerable, especially when, as is often the case, it's the busiest people who get chosen to serve on teams. How that conflict is resolved depends on the individual and the demands of each job. Some people, feeling that their boss and their performance evaluation will recognize only what they do in their regular job, may give the team short shrift. Others may find the work of the team so engrossing or potentially rewarding that they neglect their regular job.

For that and other reasons, parallel teams can fall apart more easily than other teams. Because they're peripheral, in terms of time, the danger is that they may be treated as a low priority; team leadership may be lacking, and management may not provide the members with sufficiently strong sponsorship or adequate resources. If the team's task is to look at new computer applications, for example, members may find themselves overtaken by changes in the technology before they've completed their assignment. Exacerbating this problem is the fact that parallel teams are sometimes used as a cheap means to an end. All too often, managers may shove a problem off onto a parallel team instead of dealing with it themselves or hiring outside experts who are better trained to do the job.

To keep parallel teams running in parallel, not on a collision course, management needs to structure the team environment carefully. Every team must have a charter: a defined set of goals, or objectives; assumptions about what may be out-of-bounds—activities outside of the team's scope; clearly specified resources, including the amount of time members are expected to allocate; and a timetable, with interim milestones. To cultivate a sense of accountability, it must be clear to all members that their performance will be evaluated holistically. Thus, if one member fails the team, that is reflected in the evaluation of his overall job performance. If there is a conflict in the time devoted by members, management must resolve it for low-level employees; higher-level employees must resolve it themselves. To do so, the question they need to ask themselves is, "What best serves the customer?" Admittedly, that's a short-term consideration. But, as it's often said in business, there's no long term if there's no short term.

## The Process Team

The process, or work, team is the workhorse of corporate teamwork. It may be self-managed, although, as I already indicated, that is still more an ideal than a reality; probably it has limited authority. In either event, it is a full-time, permanent team whose function, as the name suggests, is to carry out the work or process, by having its members work together. Such teams are rarely cross-functional. In the vast majority of cases, process teams consist of employees in the same job family doing similar work with comparable training and education. Their goals are also more uniform than those of other types of teams: They are working to maximize productivity and customer satisfaction, often by providing goods and/or services cheaper and faster than the competition. Like the culture that produces it, the process team is driven by an emphasis on quality. Measurement of these teams must be built around group results, such as units produced or transactions processed by the team *as a whole* per day, and not around individual counts.

What are examples of process teams? In the sports world, they are represented by soccer or basketball teams. In the corporate world, process teams can be found as assembly "cells" in a manufacturing operation, or as semi-self-directed work units that process orders or claims in a service organization.

The process model was a natural, for example, for the U.S. factory of LEGO Systems, Inc., the Danish-headquartered company that makes the plastic toy "bricks" that have become an international classic. There are more than 1,300 types of molds used to make over 3,000 LEGO elements, and each mold is accurate to five one-thousandths of a millimeter. It is a such a high tolerance standard that a LEGO brick made in the 1960s is likely to fit with one made today. At its Connecticut factory, LEGO Systems, Inc., has found that process teams help it achieve the consistency that differentiates the company from competitors.

The desire to increase customer satisfaction and speed fueled the development of process teams to handle accounting at ARCO Products. In an effort to improve efficiency and the quality of the information given to customers in the refinery, the team leader engaged members in a process of cross-training and goal-setting. As a result of the enhanced teamwork and communication, the teams' customers in the refinery have been able to make decisions faster and more accurately, and to manage their budgets more effectively.

## Process Teams: A Case Study

At Cigna's Customer Service Center in Bethlehem, Pennsylvania, the operation's organization chart fills a thirty-foot wall. What it shows, complete with photographs of some one hundred individuals, is a matrix of customer teams and the specific corporate clients they serve. Aside from the team leaders, there is only one box for a higher authority, the center director.

Until 1992, Bethlehem, home of Cigna's group universal life division, had a more traditionally hierarchical organization chart. The division's three main functions—customer service (including claims), accounting and new business—were in three discrete departments. This created multiple handoffs when staff members dealt with customers: corporations, which purchased group packages on behalf of their employees, and the individual employees themselves, each of whom is represented in Cigna's files with a "life contract." This functional organization not only created communication barriers between areas; it also limited access to and understanding of information and restricted the center's ability to give the client quick service. For example:

- A customer inquiry about a billing/payment history would require the customer service representative to contact the billing/reconciliation area.
- The billing/reconciliation representative would research the accounting data provided from the group client.
- The billing/reconciliation representative would then get back to the customer service representative.
- Finally, the customer service representative would communicate the answer to the customer.

So in early 1992 Cigna set about reengineering the division to meet one mission: satisfying the customer with *one* contact. The result was the teams on the thirty-foot wall. Cigna created a number of customer representative teams with members from each of the three main functional areas. Now, when a client calls the 800 number, it reaches any of the five representatives dedicated to its business. Because those five can answer any question about its policies, from the amount of the last recorded deduction to the current status of its billing, there is no longer a need to transfer the client to someone with greater expertise.

Backing up these frontline teams are a handful of support teams for specific functions: finance, claims, underwriting, mailroom, and long-term care (a relatively new product line for Cigna). Except for their handling of claims, a function that Cigna decided was best separated from general customer service, the support teams are mostly invisible; the frontline teams hear from them only when there is, for example, a discrepancy in the balance statement.

The movement to teams wasn't entirely painless. Approximately one quarter of the customer representatives then employed left the company. For many, the reason was that, as specialists in certain functions, they felt they couldn't fit into the team environment. "It was a recognition thing," says William Faris, assistant vice president, compensation design and education. "They felt they wouldn't be as important as they were before." They also feared that, because supervisors were being eliminated, there would be less room for advancement. In fact, because the teams required process, development, and administration coordinators, Bethlehem still has at least as many upper-level jobs, but it wasn't widely perceived that way.

Before the reorganization, the center's productivity was about 2,700 certificates per employee per month. Two years into process teams has increased productivity to 3,600 certificates per employee per month with a comparable reduction in unit labor cost. Customer satisfaction levels, measured by periodic surveys by Cigna, has remained generally high and has improved in some areas. Each team has a weekly staff meeting to talk about workloads and other issues. "It takes a while to build a good team," says Faris. "Bethlehem is the perfect example of teamwork working well."

### Pros and Cons of Process Teams

The Cigna example indicates the advantages of process teams at their best. Cycle times become shorter, quality improves, and the operation is more customer-sensitive. Because members share work, process teams offer great flexibility; productivity rises and overhead costs decline as the layer of supervision is reduced. At the same time, there are also significant drawbacks or potential problems associated with process teams, which corporations must address if they are to succeed.

As with parallel teams, accountability can be a problem—but with a difference; while people on parallel teams may be torn between their two jobs, people on process teams may have trouble accepting the reality that they are accountable to their team rather than to their personal self-interest. On process teams, accountability is diffused. So is recognition: Even if a team is getting good results, it may be difficult for management to know who is responsible, especially when all the members have similar assignments. By the same token, it can be hard to identify those who aren't contributing to the team. At its worst, accountability can take on a negative edge: Just as there can be peer pressure to perform up to the team's standards, there can be peer pressure to do less, to "not work so hard."

Management can do much to enhance a team spirit, through team reward and recognition and, ultimately, paying for teams; people, as noted in Chapter 1, perform as they're measured. Another way for management to surmount the accountability issue is to have team members evaluate each other (for a discussion of performance appraisals and multi-rater, peer, or 360-degree reviews, see Chapter 5). At the same time, to some degree team members are born, not made; if people are rugged individualists, it may be hard for them to work within teams. As discussed in Chapters 1 and 3, management in companies with process teams will want to select employees with team-oriented competencies to be team members, instead of trying to convert those not so inclined. After all, life is too short. To use my favorite analogy: If you need tree climbers, select a squirrel; it's easier then trying to train turkeys.

At their best, members of process teams feel highly accountable to each other. When teams work, members can sit down and tell each other, "This is what I expect from you; this is what you should expect from me." Members know what to expect from every member of the team. With a well-established team, quality is consistently high because everybody is checking.

As such examples suggest, introducing process teams changes the way work is performed. People who were previously highly specialized become generalists, so they can share the work, rotating assignments and filling in for each other as needed as a means of improving productivity and ensuring consistent quality. For most corporations, that will change significantly the approach to development of personnel. The corporation that uses process teams will have to invest in more training, or cross-training, to ensure that all members are qualified to handle many if not all the tasks assigned to the team. People may also need even more training in behavioral competencies, such as interpersonal skills: problem-solving, conflict resolution.

Most people welcome the variety allowed by process teams as an alternative to the tedium of the assembly line. But variety isn't the spice of life for everyone and in fact many people like routine. A car manufacturer that once sought to diversify the workday found that some workers wanted to do nothing but install glove boxes eight hours a day. Such workers may need to be reoriented to the way work will be performed in the future or transferred to other areas of the company that remain narrowly functional.

### Self-Managed Process Teams

The need for more training is arguably greatest for self-managed teams, whose members have unprecedented responsibility. It follows that if knowledge is power, then—at least when it comes to teams—power, or empowerment, requires knowledge. Starting up self-managed teams involves a substantial investment in training and education. At LEGO Systems, Inc., as soon as the teams were put together, they began receiving information about downtime, safety problems, scrap. Before they went to self-managed teams, they could train people in all the required skills in about ten hours. Now it takes one hundred hours or more for skill as well as competency training and is an ongoing commitment by the company.

In a recent article in *ACA Journal*, Edilberto F. Montemayor of the School of Labor and Industrial Relations at Michigan State University listed the most important functions that may be handled by self-managed teams:[2]

- Dealing directly with customers
- Dealing directly with suppliers
- Setting priorities and goals
- Preparing and managing budgets and schedules
- Developing and choosing work methods
- Assigning tasks to members
- Vacation scheduling
- Performance appraisal
- Training
- Hiring and firing

It is an impressive list, and even if it is still more a wish list than reality, team self-management is changing the way U.S. industry functions. At General Motors' Saturn factory, for example, there are no time cards; workers who come in late are dealt with by their teams. (At Chrysler's Neon plant, by contrast, everyone clocks in and out, and while teams discuss a tardiness problem, the personnel manager deals with it.[3]) Still, as you go farther down the list, the less likely you are to find that power has been delegated—particularly if the workplace is unionized. At the end of the list, hiring and firing are also at the end of companies' team agendas.

LEGO Systems, Inc.'s, "self-managed" teams, for example, participate in interviews of applicants and voice their opinion, but they don't do the hiring and firing. In addition to using permanent teams, LEGO Systems, Inc., allows lesser-skilled employees to move to different teams on a day-to-day, as-needed basis. If the "floater" works well with the permanent members, they have the right to invite him or her to come on board when a vacancy arises, but the last word is management's. And at PPG Industries, which has three plants using self-managed work teams (one of them since 1980), the company is only starting to involve the team members in the selection system, training them to conduct job interviews to give them "more of a voice" as to who is brought onto the teams.[4]

Notably missing from the list is pay. Of the relatively few companies that currently pay for teams, fewer still allow the teams to allocate the pay. However, some companies do submit to the teams for approval the method of measurement they plan to use in pay. Pay is the last holdout for self-managed teams, and corporations are treading cautiously. For example, a fertilizer company that is developing self-managed teams plans to certify its teams as capable of effective self-direction within one year after they're formed, and recertify them annually after that. Only after the second recertification will the team be expected to take responsibility for base pay of its members—*with* guidance from the "steward" team that helps guide and support it.

### The Project, or Time-Based, Team

This team type supports the time-based work philosophy: Whether the object is a new product or service, a process that needs to be reengineered, or another company project, the emphasis is on speed to gain a competitive advantage. It is the antithesis of the parallel team. Members of a time-based team are committed to it full-time, but only for the duration of the project. Work processes are collaborative and outcomes are shared. Team membership is composed of individuals from different functions, and the team receives direction from multiple or diverse sources. Levels of management hierarchy are limited, but the team isn't as "flat" as, say, a process team.

Project teams may also be more fluid than parallel or process teams. As their needs change over the course of the project, their membership may also change. Charles Savage, author of *Fifth Generation Management* (Digital Press, 1990), talks of "virtual" teams that break up and form again with new members as the product-development cycle requires. Such teams may include not only a firm's employees but even members recruited from customers and suppliers.

The project team that developed the production facility for Motorola's successful Bravo pager, for example, included a software expert from Hewlett-Packard.[5]

What are examples of project or time-based teams? Harking back to the sports world again, it's hard to find an instance of a full-time but temporary team. One case would be the basketball dream team of the 1992 Olympic Games, maybe the greatest assemblage of basketball players ever for a limited duration—one Olympiad. The performing arts offer more-common examples: an orchestra or an opera company gathered from around the world for just a few performances.

In the corporate world, such examples are less exotic. One thinks immediately of the "skunk works" undertakings common to Silicon Valley—at Apple Corporation, for example, when Steve Jobs assigned a team to create the personal computer that would revolutionize the industry. Or teams in Detroit to design new cars—one of the pioneering uses of cross-functional teamworking in this country. Or teams to reengineer an activity anywhere in the organization, or to design or redesign an information system. In fact, preliminary Hay data shows a 33 percent increase in project teams due to corporate reengineering.

## Project Teams: A Case Study

At Mobil's U.S. Marketing and Refining division headquarters in Fairfax, Virginia, the traditional walls on one floor of the office building have been knocked down. In their place are numerous small cubicles, all of them around a conference center. This is the home of four teams that, since mid-1994, have been part of a process reengineering program launched by the division in an effort to cut costs and improve the company's focus on consumers.

The four teams consist of some one hundred people from virtually every area within the division—Refineries, Sales, Finance, Human Resources—whose full-time task for at least the next eighteen months is to evaluate and redesign some fifty different processes at Mobil. An example is "order fulfillment," a rather understated term by which Mobil refers to its total effort to serve the consumer, from buying the real estate on which to build a service station, to delivering the gasoline.

The teams are temporary but, because it was expected that the assignments would last for about eighteen months, members' former positions are filled, and there is no guarantee of returning to them when the project is completed. Despite this uncertainty, the appointment to a team was widely regarded as an honor. In fact, of those who have already completed their assignments, most have returned to the areas in which they previously worked. However, some employees have become involved in running the redesigned processes, and still others have gone on to assignments on a new project team.

## Pros and Cons of Project Teams

In both their benefits and pitfalls, project teams have lots in common with parallel teams, on the one hand, and with process teams, on the other. Having representatives of various functions on a single team can be an extremely effective way to get important input. A project team to redesign a company's information system, for example, may be dominated by systems people but should also include users. By the same token, a project team chartered to reduce costs at a steel mini-mill should include employees from both the production and rolling-mill parts of the plant.

The problem with such arrangements is that they may bring together people with the wrong mix of skills as well as competencies. Management must be careful to ensure that the teams have an appropriate mix of skills and knowledge. Selecting people with the necessary competencies is more problematic. Training may be necessary to help people work as a team. But at the start, as the Mobil example suggests, Human Resources needs to make sure the people it chooses for the team are *project-oriented*, can live with some degree of job uncertainty or insecurity, and recognize that serving on such a team is an opportunity to excel rather than something that could handicap their career.

A related issue is the level of employees on the team. In their book *Revolutionizing Product Development* (Free Press, 1992), Harvard Business School professors Steven Wheelwright and Kim Clark draw a distinction between the "heavyweight" product-development teams used by Japanese carmakers and the "lightweight" teams favored by American companies. While the Japanese give their teams a senior manager, access to the best of the firm's people and resources, and "ownership" of the whole project, the authors say, the more hierarchy-bound U.S. firms emasculate their teams by putting junior managers in charge. To enhance their limited resources, these "lightweight" teams then spawn numerous satellite teams and advisers. A study by Clark and Tokyo University's Takahiro Fujimoto found that, on average, the American manufacturers needed a total of 1,500 employees to staff their product-development teams, while the Japanese employed just 250 people—and completed the task in less time.[6]

Accountability is an issue, as it is with any other team type. But project teams begin with an advantage: a sense of euphoria about the team adventure on which they're embarking. ("Let's build a new computer!" "A new car!") The task for management is to ensure that the team continues to bond as weeks and months pass, and that the grueling work does not flatten the team spirit. Establishing milestones is a valuable tool for keeping teams on track. The flip side is that the team may function so well, and the experience prove so exhilarating, that the members become more bonded to each other and to the project than to the corporation. When the project is completed, they may leave the company to seek similar challenges elsewhere.

Finally, the team may have to struggle with problems endemic to corporations that basically have a functional culture. Often, says Savage, the incompatibility of a company's various computing systems or the inability of its existing management-accounting systems to cope with cross-functional projects can be real obstacles to cross-functional teams. Management doesn't need to regard this as an overwhelming obstacle. In fact, it can use the introduction of such teams as an opportunity to break down these corporate silos and create more efficient services that the entire company can share.

## Hybrid Teams

Just as most companies have more than one culture, a company may have multiple kinds of teams and a given employee may serve on more than one type. There may be "hybrid" parallel, process, and project teams composed of full-time and part-time team members or, as in the Motorola example cited earlier, of full-time employees and suppliers. Teams can also have rotating membership. For example, DuPont has even used teams that combine staff researchers and temporary employees—typically people with college or graduate degrees—to develop and test instruments for its food-quality systems. According to Vinay Chowdhry, the general manager for the food-quality management systems business initiative, such inclusion is a way of bringing temporary workers up to speed as well as changing the pool of people working on the project as it evolves.[7]

In describing the various teams here, I've tried to indicate in broad brush strokes how they are most commonly used and how they differ from each other. Exhibit 2-2 summarizes the various team characteristics and the work cultures in which they are most likely to appear. While each team type is unique, they also share many similarities, the most important of which is teamwork. Whether parallel, process, project, or hybrid, the team must consist of individuals who have the competencies, personal characteristics, and technical skills that will make them productive members. These characteristics —the qualities that make teams work—are the subject of the next chapter.

**Exhibit 2-2. Team-type characteristics.**

| Work Culture | Functional | Process | Time-based |
|---|---|---|---|
| Team Type / Attribute | Parallel | Process | Project |
| Commitment | Part-time | Full-time | Full-time |
| Duration | Short/Long-term | Permanent | Long-term |
| Process | Individual | Collective | Collaborative |
| Outcome | Individual | Shared | Shared |
| Direction | Diverse | Consolidated | Diverse |

# Notes

1. Jon Katzenbach and Douglas K. Smith, "The Discipline of Teams," *Harvard Business Review*, March-April 1993, p. 111.
2. Edilberto F. Montemayor, "A Model for Aligning Teamwork and Pay," *ACA Journal*, Summer 1994, p. 18.
3. Marc Hequet, "Work Involvement Lights Up Neon," *Training*, June 1994, p. 23.
4. "Self-Managing Work Teams at PPG," *Self-Managed Work Teams Newsletter*, Center for the Study of Work Teams, University of North Texas, Winter 1993.
5. "The Team Dream," *The Economist*, September 5, 1992, p. 69.
6. Ibid.
7. "Temporary R&D employees in unique roles at DuPont and Henkel," *Chemical & Engineering News*, February 28, 1994, p. 26.

# 3

# Team Environment and Competencies

The premise of this book is that, to be effective, teams must ultimately be paid for teamwork and team performance. But pay is arguably the last of the building blocks that must be in place for teams to succeed. Before organizations can pay for teams, they must first ensure that they have laid the foundation on which teams can build, namely, the internal environment that is favorable for teams to operate effectively and the behavioral competencies people need to perform successfully within teams. As I discuss later in this book, these competencies can be linked into any or all of the components of pay—base salary, salary increases, and incentive compensation—that make up an organization's total reward package. Sustaining team performance is impossible without the link of team expectations to reward.

In this chapter, I describe in detail the competencies that are vital to successful teamwork: what they are and how they vary from one corporate culture to another. I also explain how to develop a competency model and how to ensure that the competencies are well represented on your company's teams. But because not even the most "competent" team members can operate in a vacuum, I will first review the environmental requirements for effective teams.

## Enhancing Team Effectiveness

Long before teamwork became the Holy Grail of American industry, a significant amount of research had been devoted to developing a conceptual model for group or team effectiveness. Richard Beckhard, in his now classic model of team effectiveness ("Optimizing Team-Building Efforts," *Journal of Contemporary Business*, 1972), defined four factors that influence team performance:

1. Setting goals or priorities
2. How work is allocated (roles)
3. The way the team is working (its processes)
4. The relationships among the people doing the work

The sequence of factors—goals, roles, processes, and relationships—is intentional. Many people assume that a good working relationship among team members is the first prerequisite for good team performance, but this is actually the last factor that organizations should address when they build teams. While it's true that the quality of human interactions is critical, fostering sound relationships is generally the most elusive of human resources' targets. Relationships cannot be forced; they develop over time as people work together with clear goals, roles, and processes. For that reason, most of the team-effectiveness consultations Hay performs focus on those three elements.

We can illustrate all four factors using the example of the accounting team at the Cherry Point refinery of ARCO Products, the West Coast refining arm of the oil company. ARCO, which had traditionally operated along strict functional lines, had recently moved nine accounting staffers into a cross-functional team. It was a difficult transition, partly because all of the team members except the supervisor had worked there for a number of years, had fixed notions of how to do their jobs, and were very comfortable with their level of expertise. The presenting issues included: little or no credibility with the customer, no team allegiance, low team self-esteem, poor relationships among members, inefficient systems to process the volume of information flowing through the department, and resistance to change.

1. *Goals.* Because teams exist to meet goals, setting those goals may be the most important step of the team-building process. Teams fail to meet expectations when the goals are not clearly defined or when the objectives change frequently or without warning. The ARCO team, which performs all the accounting functions for the refinery, had numerous goals and deadlines for accounts payable, accounts receivable, and customer service. The supervisor worked with team members to establish goals and gain members' commitments. Committing the team to common and consistent goals is critical, as it fosters the members' commitment to the team itself.

2. *Roles.* Once goals are defined, the next step is to establish the roles to be undertaken by team members. In some cases, when indi-

viduals already have areas of expertise, they gravitate to certain roles in the team; sometimes one person emerges as the team's natural leader, and others follow. In the case of ARCO, the team was already led by a supervisor who had initiated all these changes. Her objective was to have all team members cross-trained so that they would essentially be interchangeable; each person would be able to handle all the accounting functions.

3. *Processes.* Every team must agree on its processes, or the way it works—for example, it must decide how much involvement members will have in making decisions. Using consultants, the ARCO team collaborated and developed processes to achieve its targeted goals. It then defined six required team behavioral competencies necessary to support process goals: team relationships, team cooperation, continuous improvement, initiative, work achievement, and communication.

4. *Relationships.* Once team members are committed to the goals, roles, and processes, team commitment can follow. As defined by Hay/McBer, Hay's human resources planning and development consulting practice, there are four dimensions of team commitment:

1. *Congeniality*—the feeling of amiability and trust among co-workers
2. *Cooperation*—the extent to which people help each other get a job done
3. *Dedication*—the degree to which people give extra effort when needed
4. *Group pride*—the feeling of pride people have in their work group or organization

At ARCO, relationships were a particularly problematic aspect of the team development process; members did not see themselves as a team. To improve team relationships, thirteen ground rules for team behavior were adopted, which were designed to foster a sense of shared responsibility, recognition and appreciation, and respect for each other. They were as follows:

1. All feedback is discussed directly with the person involved.
2. We take others' feelings and time constraints into consideration when giving feedback.
3. We confront and "process" issues as they arise within forty-eight hours.

4. We recognize and acknowledge others for the help they contribute.
5. We will actively solicit participation from everyone on the team.
6. We will encourage, support and be positive with each other.
7. We realize that it is as difficult to give feedback as to receive it.
8. We respect others' need for privacy.
9. We give each other the benefit of the doubt when working together.
10. We will listen fully to each other.
11. We will have fun and enjoy working together.
12. We will take initiative to bring up problems to resolve and prevent.
13. We will each take initiative to improve our reputation with our customers.

Over the year and a half that the Hay consultant worked with the team, relationships were the area which showed the most improvement (starting from the lowest base).

## Stages of Team Development

Once they have identified goals, roles, and processes, teams typically pass through four stages of development. Using the words coined by Bruce W. Tuckman in 1965, in his classic model of developmental sequence in small groups, the stages are widely known as forming, storming, norming, and performing.

1. *Forming.* The initial stage of team formation, forming is a period of confusion, testing, and orientation. Management has chosen team members because of their skills or knowledge, functions they represent, or behavioral competencies they exhibit, which I'll talk about later in this chapter. But initially they're unsure why they were chosen, let alone what role they will play. Members may be confused about the goals and the processes to achieve them. They do not yet have a team orientation; they tend to think in terms of ''me,'' not ''we.''

2. *Storming.* As the name indicates, storming is a period of conflict and turmoil. Members' different work styles are becoming more apparent and contentious; while such differences predated the formation of teams, they were better tolerated when people weren't ex-

pected to work together. Most members, still lacking a team orientation, are promoting their personal agendas more openly, perhaps seeing the team as an opportunity to prove themselves as leaders or to gain power.

3. *Norming.* The stage at which individuals are accepting their roles as members of the team—when they are finally thinking in terms of "we," not "me"—is known as norming. Members now have accepted and internalized the goals and roles, share information openly, and recognize the importance of relationships in meeting those goals.

4. *Performing.* In the last developmental stage, called performing, individuals become fully committed members of the team, cooperating with each other—regardless of formal assignment—to improve overall team performance. In this stage, team members have created a sense of mutual accountability among themselves. All members have at least an average level of competencies, and some have progressed to the excellent levels characteristic of leaders, which can be exhibited individually or collectively. At this point, the team perceives it has the power to meet its goals and objectives.

If teams *don't* progress through these steps, they are less likely to be effective and, in fact, will probably fail. Exhibit 3-1 lists the reasons why teams fail to meet their objectives.

## Exhibit 3-1. Why teams fail.

|                                   | % Responding |
| --------------------------------- | ------------ |
| **Goals Not Clear**               | 35%          |
| **Changing Objectives**           | 35           |
| **Inadequate Management Support** | 26           |
| **Ineffective Team Leadership**   | 20           |
| **Inadequate Team Member Priority** | 19         |
| **No Mutual Accountability**      | 17           |
| **Lack of Team Pay**              | 5-21 *       |

*Range based upon year of team initiation. The longer the team was in place, the more important "lack of team pay" was as a factor for failure.*

*Source:* Hay 1995 Team-Based Pay Survey (U.S.A.)

# Competencies

How do competencies fit into team success? To reach the "performing" stage, a team needs a set of behavioral competencies that are appropriate to both its mission and the corporate culture in which it operates.

The recognition of the importance of competencies is a relatively recent development in U.S. industry. Historically, most managers and human resources professionals have focused on those skills and knowledge they believed workers needed to do their jobs. Psychologists identified the tasks required for the job (e.g., the motor skills needed for operating a drill press or assembling a car), then constructed tests to measure the skills needed to perform these tasks. In essence, traditional industrial/organizational psychology started with separate analyses of the job and the person, and tried to fit the two together.

It is only in the past twenty to thirty years that psychologists and others have been publishing studies showing that traditional academic aptitude and knowledge content tests did not predict job performance or success. Studies have also shown than many of these tests were biased against minorities, women, and people of lower socioeconomic status. It was in this context that human resources specialists began seeking other characteristics as a means of differentiating superior from average workers, or effective from ineffective workers.

Among those doing pioneering research in this area was David McClelland, professor emeritus of Harvard, the cofounder of Hay/McBer. McClelland set out to identify variables that predicted job performance more successfully. The best predictor of what a person can and will do, McClelland said, is what he or she spontaneously thinks and does in an unstructured situation, or has done in similar past situations. He defined these characteristics as an individual's competencies.

In his approach to understanding people McClelland broke new ground. Where traditional job analysis had looked at elements of the *job* (for example, following people around with stopwatches), McClelland undertook competency assessment studies of the *people* who did the job well. He then defined the job in terms of the characteristics and behaviors of these people—their "competencies."

What precisely is a competency? Using the iceberg metaphor (Exhibit 3-2), skills and knowledge are competencies that are obvious

**Exhibit 3-2. Behavioral competencies.**

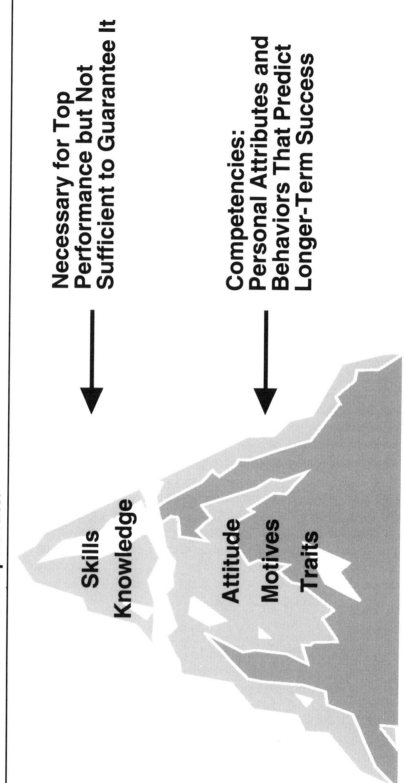

Necessary for Top Performance but Not Sufficient to Guarantee It

Competencies: Personal Attributes and Behaviors That Predict Longer-Term Success

Skills
Knowledge

Attitude
Motives
Traits

characteristics, easy to identify but relatively minor in their overall impact. Well below the surface are the other set of competencies, the underlying individual qualities, partly in the subconscious, that are closest to the person's "core." These competencies include motives (recurrent thoughts that drive behavior); traits (a general disposition to behave in a certain way); and self-concepts (attitudes, values, and self-image). If skills and knowledge shape one's formal role on a team, these other competencies shape the informal role—the style one adopts in interfacing with other team members.

Although less easily discerned than skills and knowledge, this set of behavioral competencies can also be assessed and documented. And in growing numbers of organizations, this set of competencies has been found to describe what outstanding performance is in a given job. In brief, competencies are what outstanding performers do more often, in more situations, with better results, than average performers. It is these competencies that I will discuss in the balance of this chapter.

## Designing a Competency Model

Originally, competency models were used to evaluate individual managers. Increasingly, however, they are used to recruit people for teams, identify training and development needs, and evaluate the performance of team members.

To build a competency model, there are two primary sources of data:

1. *An expert management panel.* Managers define what they want people to do. If the operation is a start-up, with no history or employees, they define what they expect people to do. The potential problem with this is that, when the operation actually gets going, no one can measure up to the expert panel's wishful expectations.

2. *Behavioral event interviews (BEIs)* with a sample of high-performing and average-performing employees. (Management and other team members generally agree on who fits those categories.) As developed by McClelland, the BEI uses careful probing by a trained professional, often a psychologist, to ferret out concrete information about how the individual approaches his or her job.

The interviewer asks people to think of several important on-the-job situations in which things turned out well or poorly and then to describe these situations in exhaustive narrative detail. The interviewer asks: What led up to the situation? Who was involved? What did you think about, feel, want to have happen in the situation? What did you do? What was the outcome? The transcripts of these interviews are analyzed and "scored" by a coding system that enables investigators to measure and test statistically for the significance of differences in the characteristics shown by superior and average performers in various jobs.

The limitation of both the BEI and the management panel is that they set up as the ideal those individuals who are performing best under the rules of the day. If the company is in the process of changing the rules—which often coincides with its desire to develop a competency model—then the model may be partially out of date even before it's finalized.

As a result, the best way to develop competency models is the hybrid approach: integrate information from the BEIs with input and validation from the expert management panel.

## The Twenty-one Team Competencies

Competency research studies conducted by human resources planning and development consultants at Hay/McBer have identified twenty-one competencies for teams. (See Exhibit 3-3.)

The competencies are grouped into five clusters, listed on the following pages. The letters *L* and *M* indicate those competencies that are most important to team leaders and members, respectively; eleven of the competencies, indicated by *A,* are required equally by all members of the team.

### Exhibit 3-3. Team competencies.

| All Members | |
| --- | --- |
| • Developing Others<br>• Customer Service Orientation<br>• Interpersonal Understanding<br>• Oral Communication<br>• Organizational Awareness<br>• Organizational Commitment | • Teamwork and Cooperation<br>• Achievement Orientation<br>• Initiative<br>• Analytical Thinking<br>• Continuous Improvement |
| Members Only | Leaders Only |
| • Influence<br>• Adaptability<br>• Personal Growth<br>• Self-Control | • Directing Others<br>• Empowerment<br>• Team Leadership<br>• Self-Confidence<br>• Planning and Organizing<br>• Conceptual Thinking |

### Influence

1. *Developing others (A).* Strives to improve the skills of subordinates or others by providing clear, behaviorally specific performance feedback, effective coaching and mentoring, and development experiences and opportunities.
2. *Directing others/holding people accountable (L).* Develops and issues effective strategies and interpersonal styles and uses the power of the leadership position to set expectations for others, enforce rules, confront others about problems, and tell others what they must do toward the accomplishment of identified objectives and goals.
3. *Empowerment (L).* Empowers individuals and groups by sharing responsibility so that they have a deep sense of commitment and ownership, participate and contribute at high levels, are creative and innovative, take reasonable risks and are willing to be held accountable, and demonstrate leadership.
4. *Influence (M).* Uses appropriate interpersonal styles and methods and logical arguments to convince others to accept an idea, plan, activity, or product.
5. *Team leadership (L).* Able to develop cooperation and teamwork while leading a group of people; working solutions that generally benefit all involved parties.

### Interpersonal/Organizational Effectiveness

6. *Customer service orientation (A).* Demonstrates concern for meeting internal and external customers' needs in a manner that provides satisfaction for the customer within the resources which can be made available and anticipates additional needs of customers.
7. *Interpersonal understanding/sensitivity (A).* Acts in a way that indicates understanding and accurate interpretation of others' concerns, motives, and feelings; recognizes strengths and limitations in others.
8. *Oral communication/honest and open communication (A).* Demonstrates the ability to effectively transfer thoughts and express ideas through speaking in individual or group situations.
9. *Organizational awareness/resourcefulness (A).* Demonstrates a comprehensive sensitivity to power and influence relationships in own organization. Able to identify key people who influence particular decisions.

10. *Organizational commitment (A).* Demonstrates an understanding of the link between own job responsibilities and overall organizational goals and needs, and performs the job with the broader goals in mind.
11. *Teamwork and cooperation (A).* Able to develop cooperation and collaborative work efforts toward solutions which generally benefit all involved parties.

**Personal Effectiveness**

12. *Adaptability/flexibility (M).* Adapts easily to change, sees the merits of differing positions, and adapts own positions and strategies in response to new information or changes in a situation.
13. *Personal growth/attention to learning and development (M).* Desires to improve and develop self; sets own development challenges and volunteers to learn.
14. *Self-confidence (L).* Demonstrates a strongly positive image of self and own skills, capabilities, and judgment.
15. *Self-control/maturity (M).* Maintains stable performance and emotions when faced with opposition, pressure, and/or stressful conditions.

**Task-Related**

16. *Achievement orientation/work achievement (A).* Demonstrates desire to set and meet challenging objectives, to find a better or more efficient way to do things, and to compete against a self-defined standard of excellence.
17. *Initiative (A).* Evaluates, selects, and acts on various methods and strategies for solving problems and meeting objectives before being directed or forced by events; self-directed rather than passively complying with instructions or work orders.
18. *Planning and organizing/project management (L).* Establishes a systematic course of action for self or others to assure accomplishment of a specific objective. Determines priorities and allocates time and resources effectively.

**Thinking/Problem-Solving**

19. *Analytical thinking/troubleshooting/information seeking (A).* Scans own knowledge and experience base and calls on other references and resources as necessary, building a logical approach to solve problems or manage the situation at hand.
20. *Conceptual thinking (L).* Recognizes connections or patterns

between situations that are not obvious to others, and identifies the key or underlying issues in complex situations.
21. *Continuous improvement (A).* Constantly looks for incremental improvements in work processes and results.

Obviously, it is an all-encompassing list, and it is not intended to be applied, line by line, to every member of every team in every organization. Certain competencies are more relevant to some corporate cultures than to others; similarly, certain competencies are more relevant to some jobs than to others. "Achievement orientation" (competency 16) may be most relevant to the time-based culture's project team, for example, while "continuous improvement" (competency 21) may be most relevant to the process culture's process or work team. The team that designs the competency model needs to consider the entire list in concert with its desired work culture and team types, expert panel, and behavioral event interview results. Of course, senior management always reserves the right to exercise its line-item veto power over applying any selected competency.

Exhibit 3-4 shows how key factors in a competency-based approach can be matched with the different work cultures. For example:

• In a parallel team common within a *functional* environment, competency models are used primarily for selection and development of "stars" who can constitute the present and future leadership. This type of organization pays particular attention to differentiating key competencies in core jobs.

• Process teams in a *process* culture emphasize spurring excellence and pushing competencies to higher levels. The variance between baseline (the minimum required to do the job) and differentiating competencies is minimized, because too much focus on baseline competencies will hinder the team thrust of the organization. Team competencies are integrated with individual roles.

• In a project team within a *time-based* environment, time pressures emphasize superior performance. However, these organizations develop people with the broadest range of skills and capabilities. Thus, competencies for specific jobs are subordinate to acquiring a general group- and individually oriented competency set that moves the enterprise forward.

## Establishing a Competency Model: Case Study 1

To see how individual corporations may customize the list to their particular needs, let's look first at the case of a service company that recently initiated a

**Exhibit 3-4. Comparison of competency models for work cultures.**

| Work Culture | Functional | Process | Time-based |
|---|---|---|---|
| Competency Focus | • Individual | • Individual and/or Team | • Individual and/or Team |
| Orientation of Competency Model | • Baseline- All Jobs<br><br>• Differentiating- Core Jobs | • Minimize Variance Between Baseline and Differentiating | • Differentiating |
| Job vs. Person | • Competencies Separate from Jobs | • Competencies Integrated in Roles | • Competencies Separate from Jobs |

new back-office operations center—a move that involved hiring some 300 new employees. Having organized its initial workforce into quasi-self-managed process teams, the company wanted to establish a competency model to be used in recruitment of additional workers and development of all staff. Eventually it would also become the basis for a "pay for competencies" program to increase base pay, which would focus on assessing and rewarding each individual's performance as part of an integrated individual base pay and team-based incentive compensation program. Complicating the task was the fact that each process team consisted of two levels of employees: "associates," high school graduates who handled clerical assignments; and "analysts," college graduates whose work was more sophisticated. While they worked together as teams, there was little if any movement between the two groups.

To build the competency model, there were two primary sources of data: an expert management panel and nine behavioral event interviews (BEIs) with a sample of high-performing and average-performing employees. In a four-hour meeting, the expert panel identified the "baseline" and "outstanding" requirements for each position and the key situations they regularly faced. They were also asked to identify those competencies that may be more relevant in the future, as team members share more functions and job requirements change. Each BEI was conducted on-site and took between one and one and a half hours. These two sources of information were blended together.

The competency model that eventually emerged from this process included ten competencies critical for associates. In addition, it identified two other competencies—"developing others" and "initiative"—for analysts. A third, "continuous improvement," was to be included in the model at some later date. The model also identified various "levels" or behaviors within each competency.

Essentially, the company's list includes thirteen of Hay/McBer's twenty-one competencies. In part, this paring-down reflects the company's view that not all twenty-one competencies pertained to these two job types. But there was another factor as well. While some competencies, such as "self-confidence" and "self-control/maturity," were frequently observed during the BEI process as being critical for success in both positions, they were not included in the model because they did not differentiate between average and outstanding employee performance. In essence, these competencies became job requirements for all team members.

On the following pages are listed the twelve initial competencies selected by the company. Also included are excerpts from the nine BEIs to convey a real-life sense of how each of the competencies plays out on the job. These statements are used only to support the various behaviors—states of performance associated with each competency—and would not appear in the final competency model rolled out to employees.

Each competency is calibrated, or scaled, into multiple levels of complexity—that is, level 4 indicates a higher state of behavior/performance than level 1. Each behavior is typically rated into four grades referring to the frequency or quality of the behavior in terms of being exhibited "often," "occasionally," "seldom," or "not observable." The application of competencies as part of a performance appraisal process is discussed in Chapter 5 and the linkage to base pay increases in Chapter 6.

*Associate and Analyst*

1. **Teamwork and cooperation.** To do this job, the associate or analyst typically:

   *Level 1:*      Cooperates as a good team player and does his/her share of the work.

   > He said, "Would you like to do it? Would you like to do one part?" And I thought, "Well, no, not really, but it probably wouldn't hurt me to try this." So I decided that, sure, I would.

   *Level 2:*      Contributes by sharing data and information with other team members.

   *Level 3:*      Takes extra effort to encourage, coach, and support peers.

   > And then, when we'd start training again, and the other people would start talking and going off, and I was understanding what they were saying and he wasn't, I'd try to slow them down and say, "Wait a minute, you've got to explain this to him because he's new at this."

   *Level 4:*      Looks beyond the requirements of own job to offer suggestions for the improvement of team performance and overall business operations.

2. **Adaptability/flexibility.** To do this job, the person typically:

   *Level 1:*      Adjusts workload with ease in light of changing priorities.

   *Level 2:*      Works around obstacles that prevent the completion of projects.

   > Managers were all in meetings and we were supposed to have all the work done by 10 A.M., so I just kind of took the initiative and told them how to do it, hoping that I was right and that we wouldn't have to delete them. And luckily, I was right.

   *Level 3:*      Maintains effectiveness during stressful circumstances.

   > I got the stuff at one-thirty and had to leave at two, so I was getting a little nervous when she was taking all my time to explain how to do each thing. I was taking very close notes, and writing in pencil on each document. We got done with the phone

> *call at two minutes to two, and I was handing stuff off and talking to her. I had everyone lined up at my desk and I said, "This is this, and this is how you do this," and I handed it to each one with all the notes on.*

*Level 4:*    Adjusts behavior to suit new procedures, systems, or responsibilities.

3. **Achievement orientation/work achievement.** To do this job, the person typically:

*Level 1:*    Pays attention to detail.

> *So, I set up the lab, made sure that all the PCs could be signed on, and then I set up some more examples. There were some other details, we had to set up more users because we had more people. And then I got the overhead working.*

*Level 2:*    Checks accuracy and researches account.

> *Then I would go to the next item and say, "This one has not been processed. This is an open item." And I would go through line item by line item, and tell him. So, then at the end of the conversation, what he needed to do was go and re-process the item.*

*Level 3:*    Works to meet standards of excellence as defined by the team or the company.

*Level 4:*    Sets high personal standards for self which are higher than those of the team or the company.

4. **Analytical thinking/troubleshooting/information-seeking.** To do this job, the person typically:

*Level 1:*    Asks questions of people who are directly available or who are supposed to answer questions, such as people who are directly involved or have relevant knowledge, even if they are not physically present.

> *Anyway, I called him and asked him about why they were torn off and why his name wasn't on it.*

*Level 2:*    Personally investigates the problem or situation, when normally would not do so.

> *And then I'd give it a few days to get to them, and then I would dig for a telephone number and go on the phone and call them, and at least get a particular person to contact.*

*Level 3:*     Understands the company's informal structure and can identify specific individuals who would be able to provide assistance with account or situation resolution. Recognizes and calls on these people outside of normal reporting relationships and established procedures in order to achieve goals.

*Level 4:*     Develops a network of contacts in key positions, both internal and external to the company, to facilitate account resolution. Expands this network whenever possible and continually builds rapport.

5. **Organizational commitment.** To do this job, the person typically:

*Level 1:*     Returns calls and completes required tasks on specific dates and times, despite obstacles and competing deadlines.

*Level 2:*     Persistently follows up, based on established time frames and commitments. Calls back repeatedly.

> *And I was filing through them, trying to find these people's transactions, and pulling them out. And I found them all except for this one. So, I am running through these again and again and again, and just came to the conclusion it wasn't processed.*

*Level 3:*     Demonstrates unflagging energy in pursuing a problem. Is willing to work extra hours to accomplish a goal. Keeps trying to achieve a goal despite encountering obstacles.

> *Tuesday night I stayed with them and we worked as late as we possibly could, because I wanted to get all the work done and have it in the system. Something bombed the run out and we had no idea what it was, so we were trying to figure out what was wrong with it.*

*Level 4:*     Sticks with a problem until it is resolved. Stays with a position or plan until the desired objective is achieved or is found to be not reasonably attainable.

6. **Oral communication/honest and open communication.** To do this job, the person typically:

*Level 1:*      Presents rational arguments based on data and factual information. Draws on reason and logic in making a case.

*Level 2:*      Speaks assertively about what is needed or expected from others. Speaks with authority to communicate expectations and to convey a sense of urgency regarding the situation.

> *There was a big problem with one of the team members who was constantly on the phone with personal calls. And she'd be sitting at her desk on the phone, and I'd walk by and say, "Get to work, what are you doing, get off the phone."*

*Level 3:*      Maintains rational focus when confronted by customers. In a difficult situation, focuses on the problem, not on the person. Looks for a "win-win" solution.

*Level 4:*      Confronts others when appropriate to achieve successful business results. Speaks forcefully but tactfully and in a no-nonsense manner. Willing to say "I don't believe you" to resolve issues.

> *And so, anyway, at that point, I got a little bit abrupt: "I want those Fed-Exed to me; I want them on my desk by tomorrow."*

7. **Customer-service orientation.** To do this job, the person typically:

*Level 1:*      Follows up promptly on customer inquiries, requests, and problems. Keeps the customer updated on progress of issues resolution.

> *I always end conversations with my internal and external customers with, "OK, that's fine, and if you have any questions or concerns please do not hesitate to call me," and then I give my phone number at the end. I also ask them at the time, the buyers, if they would like anything faxed or mailed to them so they have the hard copies to look at.*

*Level 2:*      Takes personal responsibility for correcting customer problems. Corrects problems promptly and undefensively.

> *I was processing and I had to call him because he had not provided the necessary detail. So I called him right away and, as he gave me the information over the phone, I cleared the ones that I could.*

> *I think he just didn't understand the process of what he was supposed to do.*

*Level 3:*    Represents customer needs to the appropriate people in the organization and pushes them to help resolve customer-related account or systems problems.

*Level 4:*    Uses a long-term perspective to address customer, vendor, or buyer problems and needs. Looks for longer-term benefits to the customer and ways for the operation to add value to the customer.

8. **Interpersonal understanding/sensitivity.** To do this job, the person typically:

*Level 1:*    Listens for both emotion and content, and picks up clues relating to underlying feelings and meanings.

> *Well, I felt bad for her because I normally feel bad for her. I think she's lonely. And she probably was a lot more nervous than I was.*

*Level 2:*    Understands unexpressed or poorly expressed feelings or meanings. May ask questions for clarification to help define the underlying issue.

*Level 3:*    Listens with empathy and shows genuine commitment and caring toward others' issues and concerns.

> *She said, "You know, I was expecting that transaction to be processed this week, and it won't be." And so I said, "Well, we could provide an alternative." I gave her that option.*

*Level 4:*    Can reflect the other's point of view in conversations, and is able to remove emotional or underlying obstacles to resolution of issues by addressing them using this insight.

9. **Personal growth/attention to learning and development.** To do this job, the person typically:

*Level 1:*    Quickly understands what new tasks and jobs require. Learns unique job-related vocabulary, systems, and processes.

> *And then I reformat my spreadsheet so that everything will balance by the end of the month.*

*Level 2:*    Easily learns and uses knowledge of new and changing operating systems, processes, practices, and technologies.

> *When I was on-site, I was trying to help input the work into the database. I also made a point of meeting with the people that were doing this work in the first place, and watched what they were doing just to have an idea of how the work was coming to us.*

Leve      Exhibits expertise. Is seen by others as a technical expert or is sought after due to expert knowledge or skill in a particular area.

Level 4:    Offers technical help and acts as a "floating" consultant, offering personal experience to improve performance or resolve technical problems.

10. **Conceptual thinking.** To do this job, the person typically:

Level 1:    Makes sense of information by organizing it efficiently. Breaks problems down into simple lists of tasks or activities and considers pros and cons before making decisions.

Level 2:    Performs calculations and combines quantitative information in order to diagnose and solve a problem.

> *I kind of looked through all the questions they had and tried pulling up different things they had on the computer, to see what was wrong with them. And I tried fixing some of the errors, if there was something I could go back to in the system and fix. If not, I made very detailed notes of it, and the second time around we were able to go in and fix them.*

Level 3:    Recognizes patterns. Observes trends, relationships, and discrepancies when reviewing accounts and related information. Quickly identifies "gaps" and missing information in account records.

> *Well, I kept my list going because I wanted to get through the entire report, and then I sat down and tried to analyze what was causing the problem, what I could do to correct it. Maybe there was something that was beyond my control that needed to go back to division headquarters again.*

Level 4:    Understands a problem in terms of the bigger picture and considers alternatives in solving an account or systems problem.

*Analyst Only*

11. **Developing others.** To do this job, the person typically:

*Level 1:*      Displays a leadership style in line with the desired corporate culture. Expresses positive belief in team members' abilities and initiates two-way communication and sharing of information and knowledge.

*Level 2:*      Develops and trains team members. Gives how-to directions or demonstrations with reasons and rationales included as a training strategy. Gives practical support or assistance to make job easier for subordinates.

> *So the next two days I spent developing what I thought was a way to proceed with the training we had done that day and a way to go on. I published it, made a schedule, and then I would call the associates to see how it was going. I said, "I don't care if you go down to the lab or you don't. The main thing is to learn the software as best you can. And the reason we want to do that is to make our job easier when we have to do it."*

*Level 3:*      Supports the team to management. Acts as liaison between accounting management and associates to ensure a two-way flow of relevant information and to obtain needed resources. Suggests to management appropriate assignments or formal training for the purpose of fostering team members' learning and development. Is able to make effective oral presentations when appropriate.

*Level 4:*      Inspires the team and adds significant value. Gets team members to buy into the team mission, leading to a measurable improvement in performance.

12. **Initiative.** To do this job, the person typically:

*Level 1:*      Addresses current opportunities or problems. Works independently and completes projects or responds to problems in a timely manner without constant supervision.

*Level 2:*      Is decisive in a crisis and takes action in areas for which he/she is not directly and personally responsible.

*Level 3:*      Anticipates and acts ahead. Creates opportunities or minimizes potential problems by anticipating them and acting accordingly.

> *I thought it would be a really good idea for me to do it because, when all is said and done and the*

> *consultant is gone, I thought it would be good to have somebody for the associates that they remembered from the first time that they got introduced to this new system, and who would then be able to help them.*

Level 4:      Is highly proactive. Looks ahead for specific opportunities or problems that are not obvious to others and takes action to maximize opportunities and minimize problems.

*To Be Added to the Model at a Later Date, for Analysts*

13. **Continuous improvement.** To do this job, the person typically:

Level 1:      Originates alternative responses to a problem. Presents ways to overcome obstacles that are new to the team or operation.

> *The main objective was to get the process working here, and it seemed like nobody was getting the ball rolling. So all I did, one day, was to just sit down at my PC, get as much information as I could, and write down a way to do that. And I faxed it to the gentleman and it worked.*

Level 2:      Provides clarity in complex situations by using knowledge of current issues, past trends, and technological information to provide innovative alternatives.

Level 3:      Offers suggestions for continuous improvement of processes and systems. Thinks of innovative ways to effectively manage customer requests, work processes, or systems flaws, and communicates these ideas to management.

Level 4:      Uses understanding of the business to produce imaginative or unique approaches. Improves performance of the team by using business savvy to conceive and successfully instigate the implementation of new approaches to problems or work processes.

## Establishing a Competency Model: Case Study 2

The automotive parts manufacturer in the Midwest had process teams in place for several years. But factory management still sensed that something was missing. For example, on the second shift management took four people with good skills and put them together as a team to improve productivity and quality. One month later, however, each was still functioning on his or her own. The reason, management determined, was that while the four individuals had the skills necessary for the job, they weren't interacting appropriately as a team—

either because they didn't know how to do it or because they weren't willing. In its next effort, on the same shift and line, the company put together people who were good at working together but didn't have the full set of skills. While that effort was much more successful, there were concerns about the group's ability to do the job.

Traditionally, basic manual dexterity had been the main criterion the company looked for in hiring its 1,000-odd production workers. What few skills employees needed to make the component parts, they received in various training sessions. The company recognized it had to do a better job of selecting people for a team-based environment. Without understanding team dynamics precisely, it also recognized that some people had team potential while others, who were excellent individually, could never be trained for teams.

The company was also running into problems in the way it evaluated employees. Because it had implemented self-managed work teams, it had eliminated the layer of supervisors who had traditionally evaluated workers and was relying instead on presentations by the teams themselves to assess and reward performance. It started hearing comments from people on the floor, such as "I can't believe that person got promoted. I work with him every day. He's the worst person in the world to work with. He doesn't help anyone." Or, "The first chance he gets, he talks about how bad it is to work here."

So the company decided to develop a competency model. Unlike the company in Case Study 1, this company had a veteran workforce, so it was possible to hold focus groups of employees in which they identified the best workers in the plant. Based on those findings, the company conducted fifteen behavioral event interviews of competent and superior production personnel, at the end of which the fifteen employees completed a competency assessment questionnaire. Consultants reviewed tapes of the interviews, coded them, and analyzed the questionnaires for patterns. The company also conducted two half-day expert panels with senior managers, human resources managers, production coordinators, and consultants.

In the end, the final list was a matter of negotiation between management and employees. They agreed that because the jobs under consideration were low-skilled, technical skills should play a minor part in the assessment. Accordingly, the company came up with a total of nine competencies, which it grouped into three clusters:

Team Orientation

1. Team commitment/teamwork and cooperation
2. Interpersonal understanding/sensitivity
3. Adaptability/flexibility

Team Achievement

4. Initiative to help performance
5. Developing others
6. Being direct with respect to standards/quality

Personal Effectiveness

7. Achievement orientation
8. Self-control/maturity
9. Personal growth

What was striking was that all the competencies that emerged had an interactive, people-oriented theme, and six were explicitly team oriented. Presumably because the work was low skilled and organized by team, there was a strong emphasis on cooperation and teamwork. "Developing others," for example, was central to distinguishing superior from competent performers. "Self-control/maturity," which didn't make it into the operation center's list in Case Study 1, was rated high here; management and workers agreed that it was important to restrain strong emotions such as anger.

At the same time, some of the competencies were a specific reflection of the company's culture. While "adaptability/flexibility" is likely to be a competency for most corporations, especially those employing teams, in this case it was particularly critical because the company sees itself as a "change" culture. Any team may be shifted to a different area the next day, so everybody has to be cross-trained.

Because quality is among the highest priorities for this manufacturer, it too was built into the competency model. Even average performers were expected to show "initiative" when it came to quality. When there were problems with a high reject rate for its auto parts, teams were expected to investigate the problem—measuring different parts, for example, to explain discrepancies—rather than complain to a supervisor or technician. In short, it wasn't enough for team members to say, "I like quality"; they had to take action. People who were to get ahead had to show more initiative, learning how to analyze the quality data and address problems at a higher level. They were expected to come up with a method to do the rework, if necessary, and communicate directly with industrial engineering and the quality assurance department.

The company adopted the competency model as one of its four "core values" that defined performance management. (The others were safety, attendance, and growth and use of skills.) It became a part of its selection, development, and evaluation processes. Recruiters who had previously sought only basic mechanical skills now sought to determine whether would-be hires had team commitment, flexibility, and a desire to grow. The emphasis on competencies made the job interviews longer because they involved more probing. However, the company has found that its newest hires have precisely the traits and attributes—the competencies—it wants.

The company's next step was to redesign its compensation system to reflect roles, skills, and competencies. "Your competencies are going to be just as important as your skill level," says a manager. "I think that's going to work out really well because it's your personality and how you adapt to change and how you deal with others that's half of being a team. The skills will always be there, if you're willing to learn them. But you have to know how to get along with each other. That's just as important as anything else."

# 4

# Determining Base Pay

During the 1980s, in a futile effort to remain aloft, the now defunct Eastern Airlines persuaded its unions to adopt a two-tier pay scale. Flight attendants who had joined the airline during Eastern's high-flying days were grandfathered in at the comparatively high base pay negotiated at that time; newer recruits were paid on a lower scale. Not surprisingly, this "separate and unequal" pay system strained relations between the two groups. Shortly before its demise, I was on an Eastern flight when the call bell rang nearby, and I happened to overhear an exchange between two harried flight attendants. "*You* get it," one snapped at the other. "You're paid more."

It was a perfect illustration of how a bad pay system can harm the workplace. Here were two people doing essentially the same job and doing it on a time-based team. (Few teams, by our reckoning, are of more finite duration than an airline flight crew.) Yet one was paid significantly less than the other, on a scale that mandated such inequity. Clearly, the second attendant's testiness underscored the importance of ensuring that base pay—perhaps especially for people working in teams—be fair and equitable.

But what is fair and equitable for the members of a team? Should all team members have the same base pay?

At one extreme is the view that everybody on a team, at least a process team, is cross-trained to perform the same tasks and should receive the same pay. While that sounds good, it may have little relationship to the real or perceived contributions by team members. At the other extreme is the view that every job should be individually evaluated and compensated. But not only is that terribly labor-intensive, it makes for the sort of trouble I overheard on the Eastern flight: The more differentiation there is in pay, the greater the sense of inequity or unfairness among team members and the greater the hindrance to teamwork. If employers cannot justify a difference in pay on the basis (or content) of the work, they must have the same rate, or scale, or pay opportunity. (This isn't the same as pay levels or increases in base pay, which may be based on seniority, skills, competencies, and innumerable other factors, as I discuss in Chapter 6.)

Amid all the talk about performance management and incentive pay, you may wonder why I'm devoting so much time to base pay. The answer is that the base pay system still delivers most of the pay for most people, so the messages it sends stand out. If you believe that money is at least one motivator—and most of us do—then you have to look closely at what message your company is sending in its pay envelopes. If you pay one group of flight attendants at one level and a similar group on a different scale, the newer recruits will inevitably feel shortchanged. If you tell your employees that you want quality and customer service, but you pay on a strict piecework basis (the number of units produced), you're sending a mixed signal; and, as a rule, the message that rings clearest is the one that shows up in the paycheck.

It's no different when people work in teams. If you tell people that you expect them to work in teams but you continue to pay them as individuals, the message they may pick up is that teams don't count. At the same time, I am not advising every company to change its pay structure every time it forms a team. Because of the time, expense, and potential for disruption, usually only those companies with dedicated permanent teams—the process or work teams described in Chapter 2—need to change the base-pay system to support them. However, if teams do much of an organization's work, that organization in order to be effective should seriously consider changing its base-pay system to support those teams, or at least change those elements that are likely to clash with the team environment, to maximize return.

In determining base pay, there are a number of elements to be taken into consideration. First, assuming you're not paying a single or different wage for every member of the team, you will want to consider the number of pay grades, or "bands," in the team. As I indicate later in this chapter, the trend to "broadbanding"—encompassing more jobs in fewer bands—is an important component of the move to teams.

Once you have your bands, you'll need to establish the parameters for paying for every job. There are two key methods: market pricing (what the market will bear), and job evaluation or work comparison (how the company rates or values the job). In this chapter, I discuss both those methods and their relevance to teams. Finally, you will need to decide how much of the total pay is to be allocated to base pay, how much to variable pay. That discussion is reserved for Chapter 8, Incentive Compensation, and Chapter 9, The Architecture of Team Pay.

Before I embark on the mechanics of base pay, I'll make one more point. Whatever pay system is established, every element—except what individuals are earning—should be communicated to all employees. The team needs to know the number of and criteria for each band. They should know how jobs and roles are being evaluated. It is difficult if not impossible to motivate employees with a secretive pay plan that can be easily misunderstood and that might communicate the wrong messages of what it takes to be successful. Communication is a matter of U&A, understanding and acceptance. It's not satisfactory when an employee says, "I understand your lousy plan." That's a *U* without an *A*.

## Broadbanding

Broadbanding is a relatively new pay concept of creating pay opportunities for a given job or role encompassing several traditional salary grades. In this process, an employee's pay will be administered in different segments of the band based upon contribution—for example, learning stage, competent performance, and leadership role—without the notion of salary grade midpoint. Midpoint control, or compa-ratio (actual salary divided by salary grade midpoint), analyses tend over time to drive base pay to the midpoint by granting larger increases to those earnings below the midpoint while increasing pay for those above the midpoint at a slower rate. Broadbanding can create greater equality of base-pay opportunities by having most if not all team members in the same band.

Bands can be narrow or wide. The narrower the band, the fewer differences, or the greater equality of pay opportunity among the people within it. On balance, however, the broader the banding, the better—up to a point.

Broadbanding has a number of advantages. It simplifies salary structures by consolidating numerous pay grades into a series of broad bands, transferring the weight of the pay decision from the grade to the position in the band. (Even a huge employer can use a few bands. General Electric, for example, has managed to put all its exempt people into essentially five bands.) Broadbanding minimizes hierarchy, facilitates career development, and gives management more flexibility in making annual adjustments based on each employee's personal value or contribution relative to the position or organization. Paradoxically, broadbanding actually facilitates differentiation of pay. The wider, or broader, the bands, the greater the opportunity for differentiation and the more flexibility for management.

Broadbanding is especially well suited to teams. On process teams, where members generally have similar backgrounds and expertise and the work is shared, broadbanding makes obvious sense. It allows employees to be in the same pay band or range, thereby creating a sense of equality among team members. But because it has the potential to minimize differentiation, it's also suited to other teams that bring many types of employees together with a diversity of pay histories and prior work assignments. The more differences in pay that you encourage people to perceive, the harder it is to get them to work in teams. In fact, my experience is that members of most process teams prefer a flatter structure, particularly when it comes to incentive pay. When there is a bonus to be awarded, it's typically management that wants to create differentiation while employees want a more egalitarian distribution of incentive awards. (See Chapter 8, Incentive Compensation.)

Broadbanding has proven most successful in organizations that were already changing, or planning to change, their culture or structure. It can be an ideal vehicle for change for companies that are trying to empower their employees by increasing their decision-making and responsibilities, and companies that are reengineering work, flattening structures, introducing cross-training, and eliminating functional boundaries.

A case in point is the U.S. factory of LEGO Systems, Inc., which adopted broadbanding shortly after it went to process teams two years ago. Until then, the company listed fifteen production jobs, with a different title and wage for every job. Whenever an employee was assigned to a different job, even for an hour, he or she got an adjustment in pay; LEGO Systems, Inc., accountants were wrestling with minutiae like ten-cent increases. When it moved employees into teams, such differentiation seemed doubly absurd. So LEGO Systems, Inc., eliminated most of the layers, cutting the fifteen positions to three that encompassed all production activities.

Are three bands too few for your company? Are five too many? In general, the answer is, "Less is more." But I'll add a cautionary note. If you sacrifice real-world differences in favor of a uniform ideal, you may be managing dangerously (or foolishly, at least). The bands must be legally defensible and accepted by the team. From the strict standpoint of teamwork, you might think it's equitable to put the winning quarterback of the superbowl in the same band as the rest of the team, for example. But just try to do that, and watch what happens to team performance. Some team members are clearly more equal than others.

For a company that has used traditional job evaluation and salary grades for years, making the transition to broadbanding requires far more than the collapsing of several pay grades into bands. It involves taking a dynamic, carefully aligned, multidirectional approach to blend the fundamentals of market pay (pay for the job) with the contribution or output of individuals and their continued growth in those competencies I discussed in the previous chapter. These individual elements must be aligned with those of the organization: its competencies, strategies, and economics. Finally, both the individual and organizational elements also must be aligned with issues of shareholder value and the organization's continued success. (For discussion of an actual application of bands, see the case study in this chapter "Setting Base Pay.")

## Broadbanding: A How-To for Process Teams

Let's say you've designed the roles of members of your team around core activities or jobs. To establish bands:

1. Think about how work gets done, and then about the jobs. Don't think yet about the roles, or about all of the capabilities of each team member in his or her role. It may help to have a written list or summary of the activities of each job, and of the activities that most team members share.

2. Identify the relative contributions of jobs in terms of differences in skills, competencies, physical and mental effort, responsibility, and difficulty due to unusual and undesirable working conditions. Remember, though, that many different jobs can be in the same band. Don't think that jobs have to be in different bands just because you can see distinctions between them.

3. Start with the most common job, the one with the most incumbents, and compare it to the job with the next greatest number of members. Ask yourself, "On an overall basis, which one makes a greater contribution?" If there is general agreement on a significant difference in level of contribution, then the jobs may be *one band* apart. If there is *no such consensus,* the jobs are probably in the *same* band.

Then apply a "noticeable difference approach." If aspects of two jobs aren't different enough to be detected by 75 percent of people, there's no noticeable difference, and they're probably in the same band.

Follow the same procedure for comparing jobs until you have considered them all. Most process teams have only one or two bands.

4. In structuring pay, there should be an overlap between bands to reflect the comparative value of a newcomer who enters in a higher band and the veteran who, because of limited capability or other factors, will remain permanently in the lower band. Initially, the veteran will be of more value to the team and company than the newcomer, who has a steep learning curve. However, within a short time, perhaps a year, the newcomer may leapfrog ahead.

# Setting Base Pay

As I stated earlier, there are two main methods for establishing the parameters for base pay: market pricing and work comparison, or job evaluation. The first method is purely external, the second is internal, and together they enable companies to arrive at fair and impartial base-pay structures.

## *Market Pricing*

This is based on one of the simpler notions in economics: supply and demand. You want to pay what the market will bear. That means finding out what the market is paying for the same or similar work. Then, depending on a variety of factors—not least of which is the structure of your total pay-and-benefits package—you can set your scale accordingly: higher than the market, the same, or below market.

But it's not quite as simple as it sounds. First, what *is* your market? Is it your immediate community? Your region? Is it the competition in your industry, anywhere in the country? How you answer that depends partly on the level of job that you are trying to price. If you are pricing the jobs of lower-skilled employees, who tend to work close to home and who have skills that are readily transferrable within the immediate area, you may define your market narrowly as, for example, the area with a ten- to twenty-five-mile radius from your facility. In that case, state data on comparable jobs or a survey of large employers in your area will give you the going rate. That formula is fine, as long as you're in a low-wage area. If local wages are higher than those of the competition in your industry, however, you will have to underprice your jobs (which hurts your ability to compete for workers), seek additional productivity gains, provide greater employment security or benefits (e.g., daycare center, flextime), or settle for lower profitability and take the consequences.

If, on the other hand, you are pricing higher-level jobs, you need to redefine your notion of your market. If you are pricing a professional job, such as an accountant, your market may be the region. Or, if you're competing with other companies in the U.S. for a talented plant manager, your market is national. The more skilled or industry-specific the job, the closer you must pay to regional or national, rather than local or community, going wage. In pricing jobs, companies need a hybrid approach.

Market pricing is relatively simple as long as there are other companies whose workforce is organized in the same way as your own. If that is not the case, you have to use "job slotting," comparing those "benchmark" jobs that you can compare and slotting the other jobs in between. For example, secretaries with a sophisticated grasp of computer technology may represent a new category to be "slotted" somewhere above secretaries doing more-traditional work. But that approach becomes more problematic when organizations have no comparable jobs in their market, or when a company is using teams in a market where most employers are organized along functional lines.

A case in point is a large insurance company that, for its medical malpractice policies, has adopted a team approach with, in essence, two bands of workers: underwriters, who assess risk, and assistants, who process the paperwork. Until recently, the word processing was farmed out to another unit within the company. Now, however, the company is moving to bring word processing within the team and have it done directly by underwriters and assistants. Should the team members be paid more because it's additional work; less because it requires relatively less skill? Because other companies don't operate that way, it's difficult to find a direct market comparison.

In such a case, one way to estimate market pay is to evaluate several jobs that represent the mix of work the team member does and weight the result for these narrowly defined jobs or roles according to the mix of responsibilities in the position. That approach may become more necessary as growing numbers of companies move to teams.

## Job Evaluation

In job evaluation, the company looks inside, comparing work or jobs in terms of their internal value. Using the concept of comparable worth (which states that jobs requiring comparable skills and accountabilities be paid the same), the employer should compare *all* jobs, like and unlike, within a company.

There are a great many approaches to job evaluation or work comparison, the most common of which I discuss in this chapter. Depending on the specificity of the approach, the jobs may be assigned rankings, classifications, or points. If points are used, they become the universal yardstick by which the company can compare its own jobs with those at other companies in setting base pay. In any event, the better the company describes the work, the better the results that are likely to be achieved from any one of these methods.

### The Guide Chart-Profile Method

Since World War II, the dominant system using points to assess jobs has been the Hay Guide Chart®-Profile Method of Job Evaluation. Conceived in the early 1940s, it is used today by more than 7,000 for-profit and nonprofit organizations in some thirty countries. While it is applied most often to exempt positions, it is also used widely for nonexempt clerical/office positions and, increasingly, for blue-collar jobs. Without getting into the details of the approach, I describe the method generally below.

The Hay Guide Charts involve a systematic evaluation by points that allows each job to be compared with every other. They are based on four key premises:

1. While there are many factors that can be considered in evaluating jobs, the most significant can be grouped as representing the knowledge required to do a job, the kind of thinking needed to solve the problems commonly faced, and the responsibilities assigned. I describe those in more detail below. A fourth factor, working conditions, may be considered for those jobs where hazards, an unpleasant environment, and/or physical demands are significant elements.

2. Not only can jobs can be ranked in the order of importance within the structure of a team or organization, but the distances between the positions can be determined.

3. The factors described above appear in certain kinds of patterns that seem to be inherent in certain kinds of jobs.

4. The focus of the process of job evaluation must be on the nature and requirements of the job itself, not on the skills or background or characteristics or pay of the job holder. This requirement, dating back some fifty years, was unusually farsighted. There was never any consideration of the job holder's talent or education, let alone his or her sex, age, ethnic origin, physical condition, or any other physical attributes that are now explicitly forbidden by law as grounds for

discriminating against an individual. It is noteworthy that the reference in the Equal Pay Act of 1963 to job-to-job comparisons based upon "skill, effort, and responsibility" parallels closely the 1951 Hay Guide Chart factors.

The further stipulation, also from the start, was that the pay of the job holder and the market for such positions were irrelevant to job evaluation. Judgments were to be made only for the purpose of rank-ordering jobs and delineating the distances between ranks—for example, to establish the relative importance of positions, top to bottom, within an organization's structure.

Having defined the three most significant factors in valuing jobs, Edward N. Hay, the initiator of the Guide Charts, and his colleagues ultimately codified them as follows:

1. *Know-how.* The sum total of every kind of capability or skill, however acquired, needed for acceptable job performance. Its three dimensions are requirements for:

- Technical depth. Practical procedures, specialized techniques and knowledge within occupational fields, commercial functions, and professional or scientific disciplines.
- Managerial breadth. Integrating and harmonizing simultaneous achievement of diversified functions within situations occurring in operating, technical, support, or administrative fields. This involves, in some combination, skills in planning, organizing, executing, controlling, and evaluating.
- Human resources skills. Active, practicing person-to-person skills in working with other people.

2. *Problem-solving.* The original, self-starting use of know-how required by the job to identify, define, and resolve problems: "You think with what you know." This is true of even the most creative work. The raw material of any thinking is knowledge of facts, principles, and means. For that reason, problem-solving is treated as a percentage of know-how. It has two dimensions:

- The environment in which thinking takes place.
- The challenge presented by the thinking to be done.

3. *Accountability.* The answerability for action and for its consequences. It is the measured effect of the job on end results of the

organization. It has three dimensions, in ascending order of importance:

1. Freedom to act—the extent of personal, procedural, or systematic guidance or control of actions in relation to the primary emphasis of the job.
2. Job impact on end results—the extent to which the job can directly affect actions necessary to produce results within its primary emphasis.
3. Magnitude—the portion of the total organization encompassed by the primary emphasis of the job. This is usually, but not necessarily, reflected by the annual revenue or budget associated with the area in which the job has its primary emphasis.

Admittedly, these are broad descriptions of the elements that go into job comparison. Compensation experts have refined them by adopting fifty common work-comparison considerations that fit into the four categories (know-how, problem-solving, accountability, and working conditions) and twenty-five more individual characteristics and additional influences that may also need to be taken into consideration in evaluating jobs. For the complete list, see Exhibit 4-1. At Hay, we believe that a company or business unit should use the same factors when it evaluates all its jobs, but not every company needs to apply every factor.

In addition to placing all the jobs in an organization in a sequence representing their relative importance and difficulty, the Hay Guide Chart-Profile Method can also be used as the basis for what Human Resources calls a "reality check": comparing one company's pay practices with those of other organizations. To do that, job evaluation points must first be converted to a standard scale, a task usually carried out by consultants. Given a standard scale, compensation practices are converted into lines specifying the average pay per point that produces direct comparisons from one company to another.

As the number of users of the Guide Chart-Profile Method has grown, so has the market database. As a result, companies that use the method can more easily position themselves strategically in the market for people. By graphing its position, the company will see whether it has *internal equity* (how salary midpoints and salary levels relate exactly to job evaluation points) and *external competitiveness* (how actual pay levels compare against the appropriate labor markets).

(text continues on page 76)

## Exhibit 4-1.  Work comparison: seventy-five common considerations.

*Specific Work Requirements Generally Considered in Valuing:*

<u>Skill</u>

| | |
|---|---|
| Numeracy and literacy | Multi-language ability |
| Manual skills | Motor skills |
| Perceptual skills | Physical coordination |
| Specific knowledge or experiences | Specific certification |
| Specific training or education | Learning ability |
| Analytical ability | Creativity |
| Decision-making ability | Judgment and perspective |
| Working with other people | Influencing other people |
| Specific relationships or contacts | Adaptability |
| Initiative | Resourcefulness |

<u>Effort</u>

| | |
|---|---|
| Immediate physical strength | Stamina |
| Attention to details | Attention to multiple matters |
| Concentration | Patience |
| Tolerance for work volume or pace | Tolerance for monotony |
| Tolerance for uncertainty | Complexity of coordination |

<u>Responsibility for</u>

| | |
|---|---|
| Safekeeping (records, property, cash) | Security or confidentiality |
| Exposures to errors, losses, or risks | Safety |
| Facilities, material, equipment | Effectiveness of other people |
| Financial effectiveness | Quality |
| Organizational policy | Organizational effectiveness |

<u>Working conditions</u>

| | |
|---|---|
| Hazards | Pressure or stress |
| Physical demands | Sensory demands |
| Mental demands | Emotional demands |
| Lifestyle demands | Unusual individual qualities |
| Physical context | Emotional context |

## Desirable Individual Characteristics, Associated with Outstanding Outcomes, Frequently Found In:

<u>Cognitive capabilities</u>
Technical expertise
Innovative thinking

Analytical thinking
Conceptual thinking

<u>Helping and human services</u>
Empathy

Service orientation

<u>Impact</u>
Relationship building
Awareness of social context
Helping and collaboration

Influence
Assertiveness
Team Leadership

<u>Achievement orientation</u>
Focus on outcomes
Information seeking

Concern for clarity
Action orientation

<u>Personal effectiveness</u>
Self control
Flexibility and resilience

Self confidence
Mission orientation

## Additional Influences on Work Comparisons May Be:

<u>Context</u>
Industry, field, or geographic patterns
Labor supply/demand and impact
Contractual commitments and legal/regulatory mandates

<u>Outcomes</u>
Specific work outcomes

General economic conditions

## Other Work Comparison Approaches

The Hay Guide Chart-Profile Method leads a crowded field of work comparison approaches. In Exhibit 4-2, we list the major approaches, with an assessment of each in terms of specificity, cost, complexity, and other elements.

Listed in ascending order of precision, the major approaches are:

1. *Assignment ranking.* Each assignment (job or role) is considered in terms of *any* aspects believed relevant and significant, and placed within a ranking of relative contribution with all other assignments at the company. While this is a more affordable and accessible approach, assignment ranking is far too qualitative, subjective, and imprecise for organizations of any size.

2. *Factor ranking.* Each assignment is considered in terms of specific factors—generally the seventy-five on Exhibit 4-1—and placed within a ranking of all assignments for each factor. The factor rankings are combined into an overall ranking of relative contribution. This shares many of the drawbacks of assignment ranking.

3. *Classification.* The organization establishes a framework of "classes" that includes all recognized work levels in each field of work that is significant, aspects of work that are particularly salient, and relationships of relative contribution of each level of each field of work to all others. Actual jobs/roles are then plugged into these classes.

The classification approach is a favorite of the U.S. government at all levels; civil servants, for example, exist in classes typically from GS (General Schedule) 1–15. It is predictable—engineering is always one level above accounting, for instance—but by the same token it is extremely rigid. If a new field emerges that doesn't fit into one of the classes, an organization such as a government agency must write a description that parallels the classification to which it wants it to correspond.

4. *Factor rating.* Each assignment is rated on specific scales for factors that are perceived as relevant. The combined scale scores represent relative contribution. Such exercises tend to produce the grades—for example, 1 to 22—that many companies have. The approach is reasonably objective, precise, and reliable, and far more flexible than the classification approach; if a job changes, it can be upgraded.

5. *Point factor comparison.* The Hay Guide Chart-Profile Method is in this category, which is based upon the value the company places on jobs.

**Exhibit 4-2. Major work comparison approaches.**

| CRITERIA | APPROACH | | | | | |
|---|---|---|---|---|---|---|
| | Assignment Ranking | Factor Ranking | Classification | Factor Rating | Point Factor Comparison | Statistical Component |
| *Type of Scale* | *Qualitative* | *Qualitative* | *Qualitative* | *Numerical* | *Numerical* | *Numerical* |
| Objectivity | Low | Moderate | Moderate | Moderate | High | High |
| Precision | Low | Low to Moderate | Low to Moderate | Moderate | High | High |
| Reliability | Low | Low to Moderate | Low to Moderate | Moderate | High | High |
| Defensibility | Low | Low to Moderate | Low | Low to Moderate | Moderate to High | Moderate to High |
| Administrative Load | Low | Low | Moderate to High | Moderate | Moderate | Low |
| Ease of Explanation | High | Moderate to High | Moderate to High | Moderate | Low to Moderate | Low |
| Complexity | Low | Moderate | Moderate | Low | Moderate | High |
| Organizational Adaptability | Low | Low | Moderate | Moderate | High (if not customized) | High |
| Cost of Installation | Low | Low to Moderate | Moderate to High | Moderate | Moderate to High | High |

6. *Statistical component.* Highly specific common assignments are identified and placed on a scale of relative contribution (or market value). Statistical analysis identifies the minimum set of weighted objective characteristics of assignments that relate strongly to contribution or value. Actual assignments are scanned for component presence, and for the extent of selected characteristics of the components, and placed on scales of relative contribution (or value) by use of a multiple regression formula.

Due to its complexity and cost, this approach is rarely used. In theory, however, it has great potential for evaluating team assignments, because of the numbers of jobs that combine various components.

## Teamwork Implications of Work Comparison

All of these work comparison approaches, including the Hay Guide Chart-Profile Method, are attuned to the traditional functional model of the organization. For years, compensation experts thought that these approaches were the only way—or at least the very best way—to evaluate jobs. In 1992, however, Hay looked at the world of work again and concluded that, where the corporate culture and values have changed, the company may want to communicate this to employees partly by comparing work using dimensions other than traditional Guide Chart factors of know-how, problem-solving, and accountability.

Accordingly, Hay developed three sets of work comparison charts, for each of the three main cultures: functional (the basic Guide Chart I've already discussed), process, and time-based. As you'll see from Exhibit 4-3, these sets use somewhat different dimensions to reflect the differences between individual and team work, and also order them to reflect different emphases. Thus, functional cultures emphasize specialization within know-how; process cultures, in which employees are expected to cross functional barriers, emphasize complexity and diversity.

To date, these alternative approaches have not been widely accepted. The experience of our consultants has been that, even in different work cultures, management continues to identify with the traditional three factors I discussed previously. And there may be an understandable reluctance to tamper with a formula that's tried and true. "If it ain't broke, don't fix it," as the saying goes. Switching to the culture-customized charts is likely to be disruptive. It produces

**Exhibit 4-3. Work comparison alternatives.**

| WORK CULTURE — Team Type / Emphasis<br>FACTORS | FUNCTIONAL*<br>■ Parallel<br>Position | PROCESS<br>■ Process<br>Role | TIME BASED<br>■ Project<br>Mission |
|---|---|---|---|
| PRIMARY | KNOW-HOW<br>• Specialized<br>• Management<br>• Human Relations | PROCESS<br>• Complexity<br>• Diversity<br>• Centrality | IMPACT<br>• Leverage<br>• Magnitude<br>• Control |
| SECONDARY<br>(Percentage of Know-How) | PROBLEM SOLVING<br>• Thinking Environment<br>• Thinking Challenge | IMPROVEMENT<br>• Importance<br>• Challenge | OPPORTUNITY<br>• Empowerment<br>• Risk |
| SUPPORT | ACCOUNTABILITY<br>• Freedom to Act<br>• Impact<br>• Magnitude | SCOPE<br>• Empowerment<br>• Role Impact<br>• Process Impact | CAPABILITY<br>• Amount<br>• Diversity<br>• Integration |
| SUPPLEMENTARY | WORKING CONDITIONS<br>• Physical Effort<br>• Attention<br>• Environment<br>• Mental Stress | CONDITIONS<br>• Mental Demand<br>• Physical Demand<br>• Change<br>• Unusual Circumstances | SPECIAL CHALLENGES<br>• Physical<br>• Mental<br>• Environment |

*Traditional Hay Guide Chart Factors

somewhat different results and involves recalculation of pay, as any system change creates perceived winners and losers.

Over time, however, as these nontraditional work cultures become standard, the dichotomy between the functional factors and the organization's goals will become more pronounced. At that point, we expect the other culture-based factors to come into play.

A brief description of the work comparison dimensions for process and time-based teams follows.

## Work Comparison for Process Teams

In comparing work on process teams, the focus is the employee's *role* rather than, as in functional cultures, his or her position. There are three key factors. (Like the functional approach, this approach also includes working conditions, but defines it more broadly to include the role's special demands on the employee's attention and acuity.) The factors are:

1. *Process capability.* The total of all proficiencies (knowledge, skills, or abilities) and competencies ("best practice" ways of using proficiencies) of any kinds that are likely to support effectiveness and progress. This corresponds to the functional "know-how." It has three dimensions:

- *Complexity.* The needs for skills ranging from basic capabilities for the simplest work routines to unique and authoritative mastery of combinations of the most complex disciplines and fields of information and technology.
- *Coordination.* Balancing and harmonizing priorities and resources with differing sets of obligations, both within and across processes. This may be exercised through facilitation as well as by direct action, and involves combinations of capabilities for planning, organizing, monitoring, and improving progress.
- *Centrality.* Involves the capacity to meet obligations that are critical to satisfying the company's end-use customers.

2. *Improvement opportunity.* Measures the intensity of effort to identify, define, and enable better ways of doing things or ways to accelerate progress. This is critical in a continuous improvement operation, whether the work is highly creative or somewhat routine. After all, "you are what you think." Major categories of improvement opportunity that are used in comparisons are:

- *Importance.* The emphasis on typical areas for improvement, as demonstrated by collaboration with teams and customers for identifying and implementing improvements.
- *Challenge.* The difficulty in finding and implementing improvements for both the more common and the more unusual elements of roles and processes.

3. *Scope.* Reflects effects of actions and their consequences on effectiveness and progress. It addresses linkages of roles and processes with the overall enterprise and with the broader world. Major categories of scope that are used in comparisons are:

- *Empowerment.* Opportunities within one's role for committing effort and energy.
- *Role impact.* The extent to which specific roles are given priority in decision considerations for the process.
- *Process impact.* The relationship of effectiveness and progress of the process to the satisfaction of end users. This is measured in tandem with role impact. The same role may be seen as making greater contributions to the satisfaction of more-immediate customers than of the end users. The best combination to use is the one that most clearly represents the basic purpose of the role and process.

## Work Comparison for Project Teams

In evaluating the jobs performed by members of project teams, the focus is the team's *mission.* As with process teams, there are three key factors (in addition to working conditions) that correspond loosely to those used in the functional work comparison approach, although the priorities differ. The three factors are:

1. *Impact.* Measures the actions to change conditions and events and the consequences needed to achieve success. Major categories used in comparisons are:

- *Leverage.* Ranges from the simplest and most direct actions to the most intricate chains of action involving manipulation of time, energy, information, or social relations needed to effect change.
- *Magnitude.* The total scope of the mission, relative to the full scope of the operation and enterprise. Magnitude is usually stated in dollar figures, in terms of revenues or expenses within

a specified time frame, or assets or liabilities to be managed and controlled. A valid alternative is to consider the percentage of the breakup value of the enterprise that the mission controls or affects.

- *Control.* The extent of certainty that actions will produce intended results.

2. *Opportunity.* The extent to which value can be added to impact through initiative and managed risk. If external standards or strictures limit such opportunity, the emphasis on impact alone increases. Major categories of opportunity used in comparisons are:

- *Empowerment.* The extent of freedom from direction that comes from outside the immediate operational situation.
- *Risk.* The extent to which the mission can encumber or endanger the resources available to the program or the enterprise.

3. *Capability.* The total of all proficiencies (knowledge, skills, or abilities) and competencies ("best practice" ways of using and exploiting proficiencies) of any kinds that may be needed as a foundation for effective action within a mission. Capability has three dimensions:

- *Amount.* All required proficiencies and competencies, from basic literacy to mastery of multiple disciplines.
- *Diversity.* The dissimilarities within capability, from simple, repetitive activities (low diversity) to a wide array of disciplines (substantial diversity).
- *Integration.* The extent to which the mission involves tasks that are highly specific and limited, at the one extreme, or the integration of the total enterprise, at the other extreme. Integration and diversity are measured in tandem. The same mission may permit greater coordination of more similar fields, or less coordination of more varied fields. The best combination to use is the one that most clearly represents the essential focus of the mission.

To be sure, what characterizes all these approaches is their focus on the individual job. Despite their orientation to different cultures, even the two approaches just described—for process and time-based cultures—still look at jobs, not teams.

Comparing the work of teams, rather than the work of individual members of teams, may be the next frontier. But at this point, frankly, it's one that few companies are inclined to cross in order to structure base pay. Managers still tend to think of a team's performance as the sum or average of the work of its individual members, and so they compare individual jobs. And although they may work in teams, people live and budget as individuals and expect their base pay to be calculated accordingly.

If work comparison did focus on teams, how would it be done? The obvious way of framing the issue would be to compare teams with teams, using any of the work comparison methods described here, with some modifications. Let's say a company has process teams, each with only one role, in which everybody does the same assignment and the only differentiation is in skill level (if that). In that case, the question becomes: Is the work of the members of one team more/less important or difficult than the work of the members of another team? If the answer is yes, then the employer should allocate more resources to that team. (That's precisely what happens on time-based teams, which may be bidding for talent to work on projects.)

Over time, as more companies reach the point where teams are integral to the way they operate, management will have to ask, "What's the relative value of the team?" It's like comparing the price of a car to the price of all its individual components. And while that approach has yet to affect base-pay calculations, as you'll see in Chapters 6 and 8, it is starting to affect the way companies determine base pay increases and incentive compensation respectively.

## Setting Base Pay: A Case Study

To study in detail the way an organization goes about setting a base-pay scale, let's return to the company that, back in Chapter 3, was establishing a new back-office operations center. As we noted, the company had already determined that its operations team consisted of two broad bands: the job of "associate," filled by high school graduates who handled clerical assignments, and the job of "analyst," filled by college graduates whose work was more sophisticated. For example, whenever the company purchased a new piece of equipment, the analysts had to decide whether it should be expensed or depreciated and over what time period. Once the decision was made, it generated a substantial amount of paperwork that was processed by people in both bands.

How should each group be paid? How much more should analysts receive than associates? Should experienced associates be allowed to outearn new analysts? Should analysts and associates have different levels of pay within their assigned bands? And how to pay the "co-op" students who held temporary jobs as associates? To resolve these issues, the company used the two key methods described earlier in this chapter:

**Exhibit 4-4. Salary bands.**

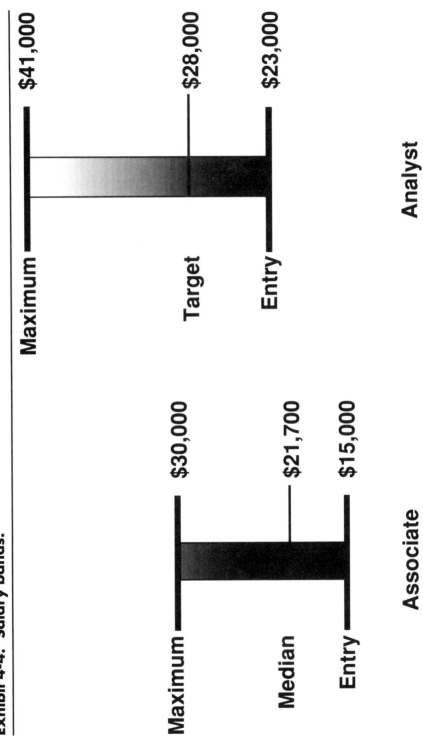

1. *Market pricing.* The operations center was located in one of the lower-wage parts of the United States—a factor that was a primary attraction for the company in expanding its work force.

In this case, it was clear that the immediate community was the relevant labor market. The company obtained local market data from the state on pay for clerical jobs comparable to its own jobs. It also surveyed a few other sizable employers of clerical workers. Its decision: In general, base salaries would target a market position at slightly below median. (That would not only give the company a competitive edge within its industry; it would also permit additional or incentive compensation opportunities based on performance or results to allow higher-than-average total compensation.)

2. *Job evaluation.* Although these jobs had been evaluated previously, the organizational change to teams necessitated a reevaluation. The company had eliminated five salary grades and created two bands. In doing so, it upgraded the clerical jobs. As a result, the company had to determine the value of the associate and analyst jobs respectively.

As Exhibit 4-4 shows, the company established two base salary bands that, on average, valued the analyst job approximately 33 percent higher than the associate. But at the same time, it established a broad range within each band. Associates could expect to start at a minimum of $15,000 a year, to reach a median of $21,700, and to peak at $30,000. The minimum for analysts would be $23,000 and the target would be $29,000; but their base pay, depending on the competency model discussed in the previous chapter, could go as high as $41,000. The bands overlapped, allowing a veteran associate to outearn some analysts, at least temporarily. Co-op students would be paid at a lower rate that would be flat as long as their jobs lasted.

Technically speaking, overtime is not considered part of the base-pay calculation. However, because analysts and associates worked so closely on the same team, it's worth addressing here. Historically, clerical workers at the company had been paid the usual time-and-a-half for overtime, while analysts—as "exempt" employees—received no extra pay. But that differentiation opened the door to conflict when the department ran into inevitable pileups and analysts balked at putting in unpaid extra hours. In the end, the company compromised: overtime for both job bands, with time-and-a-half for associates, straight time for analysts for company-scheduled overtime (i.e., working on Saturdays, but not staying late, which is unscheduled overtime). Reducing the differentiation in pay improved teamwork.

I'll return to this company in Chapter 5 to discuss the way it uses performance appraisal ratings to determine increases in base pay.

# 5

# The Role of Performance Appraisal

Probably few management processes are as universally practiced and at the same time as generally despised as the annual performance review. Employees dread it. And the managers who administer it tend to agree that this yearly ritual of criticism and praise, often followed by a raise, doesn't do much to boost performance levels. More likely, it just increases anxiety levels.

Today, growing numbers of companies are changing the way they go about appraising the performance of employees. Much of that change is due to the advent of teams. It's difficult for a supervisor to conduct a traditional performance appraisal of an individual who's serving at least part-time on a team. And when the individual is a member of a self-managed work team, it's virtually impossible. The "supervisor," if there is one, may play only a nominal role in overseeing the team's activities and may be only marginally aware of how well or badly individual members do their jobs.

In an article in *Inc.*, John Puckett, the manufacturing vice president of XEL Communications, says he discovered that the usual review system wouldn't work when Human Resources gave him a pile of forms "and I had no supervisors to give them to." Puckett couldn't do them himself, *Inc.* reports, "because he wasn't close enough to individual workers. The reviews had to be done by team members themselves."[1] Although XEL, a GTE spin-off based in Aurora, Colorado, is on the cutting edge, the use of peer review is becoming increasingly common. Often it is part of a novel approach to performance appraisal sometimes known as multi-rater or 360-degree feedback, in which a number of sources around the individual provide input on performance.

Another change in the traditional performance appraisal, also precipitated partly by the rise of teams, has to do with *what* is measured. As noted in Chapter 3, companies increasingly are coming to the recognition that *competencies*, rather than skills or objectives, may be one of the better measures of the way people work and the best predictor of whether they'll succeed. That is particularly true of teams, where underlying traits such as flexibility, adaptability, and the ability to get along with others are so critical to the job.

Finally, for many companies seeking a competitive advantage, the performance appraisal is only part of a total process called performance management. As the name suggests, performance management encourages the active *management* of employees, in lieu of criticism after the fact. The process is also designed to stimulate the active involvement of the employee—a goal that, if achieved, should go a long way to changing the "us versus them" nature of the traditional performance appraisal, in which the manager often plays an authoritarian role and the employee is the passive recipient.

At Hay, the performance management process is described in three steps (see Exhibit 5-1):

1. *Performance planning*, a process carried out jointly by employee and manager
2. *Performance coaching*, an ongoing formal and informal interaction
3. *Performance review*, an activity that emphasizes development needs and provides a "final rating"

This chapter focuses on step 3, the performance review, although a how-to section also offers guidance on the first two steps. First, however, I discuss the main criteria for measuring performance, whether for individuals or teams, and describe the review processes that I believe work best for different types of teams. Next I offer a practical guide to the performance appraisal, including a look at various ways to score and some possible answers to the question, Who appraises? Finally I conclude with case studies of companies that have adopted innovative, team-oriented approaches to performance appraisal.

## Performance Criteria

If you don't know where you're going, all roads can take you there. To review performance, you must define how you expect the person to perform—in other words, your performance criteria.

**Exhibit 5-1.  Performance management process.**

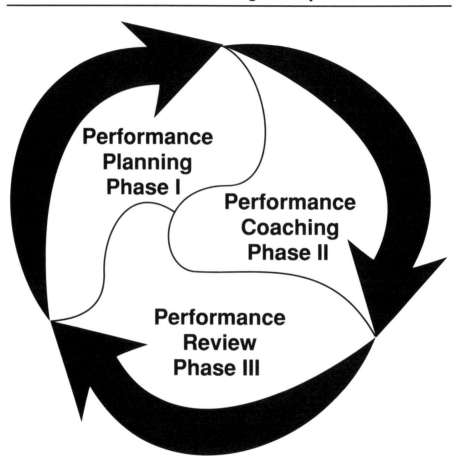

There are four major criteria for measuring the performance of individuals or teams:

1. *The demonstration of behavioral competencies.* Usually in combination with other measures of performance, competencies are becoming more widely used in performance appraisal. (For a discussion of competencies, see Chapter 3.)

2. *The acquisition and/or demonstration of skills and knowledge.* As I discuss at greater length in the following chapter, this is a popular measure for evaluating and rewarding employees. Like competencies, it is typically used in combination with other criteria in performance appraisals. Opponents of the use of skills and knowledge for assessing performance note that these are inputs, not outputs. They

are not a measure of performance, only an indication of what level of performance is theoretically possible. Advocates argue that the skills, once acquired and recognized, will ultimately be put to use to the benefit of the organization.

3. *The achievement of specific objectives within a specified period of time—best known as MBOs, or management by objectives.* Although somewhat out of vogue, MBOs remains a highly efficient approach to evaluating employees' performance. Whenever possible, goals should include measures of quantity, quality, timeliness, and cost. However, depending on the specific job, objectives can take a variety of forms:

- Short-range objectives can be accomplished within the performance cycle, often within a few weeks or months.
- Long-range objectives may require a full performance cycle or longer to complete.
- Routine or maintenance objectives maintain performance at current acceptable levels.
- Organizational objectives may involve establishing a new work unit or new procedure within a unit.
- Problem-solving objectives improve performance that has slipped below acceptable levels.
- Innovative objectives stimulate creativity.
- Development objectives ensure an employee's continual training and development.

Because they are individually oriented (fewer shared accountabilities), MBOs arguably work best in functional organizations—particularly for individuals on parallel teams, who have multiple demands on their time and for whom setting priorities can be critical. The use of explicit MBOs can facilitate a performance appraisal process which must incorporate both the full-time regular job and the part-time team job. A criticism of MBOs is that they can be self-limiting: The goal becomes the ceiling or cap. One of the challenges for management, which sets MBOs, is to ensure that employees continue to strive for improvement once an objective has been met.

4. *Results (quantitative or qualitative).* At a glance, results would seem to be the obvious choice for assessing performance. And it is true that for certain cases, such as the explicitly results-oriented project teams in time-based cultures, results may be the best measure of performance. In other cases, however, the use of results may be more problematic. For example, results may not be within the control of

members of a process team—even those members who rate high on competencies and skills—if other imponderables, such as the performance of other teams, drag them down. Results, without sophisticated measurement, can be misleading. If results aren't within a team's control, another measure should be substituted.

Most performance appraisals are a hybrid of two or more of these approaches. As Exhibit 5-2 shows, different types of teams need to be evaluated by different performance criteria once members progress from the entry-level or basic skill-acquisition period.

## A How-to Guide to Performance Appraisal

As I've indicated, there are numerous approaches to performance appraisal. In this practical guide, I'll use a performance appraisal based on a hybrid of goals, or MBOs, and competencies. In this example, I give you (the manager or supervisor) a key role in shaping employee goals, providing regular feedback, and communicating the results of the appraisal—in other words, performance management. A central managerial role in performance appraisal is still the norm. However, if you're an enlightened manager—as I trust my readers are!—you'll also get feedback from the employee's peers and others. While performance reviews are common to salaried employees, they are still rare when it comes to hourly workers—a trend I see changing as workers (especially teams) at all levels are increasingly valued.

In our hypothetical and ideal world, you meet at the beginning of the year or planning cycle with the employee, individually or as part of a team, to communicate the big picture of the company's business strategy and department goals, and to show how he or she can contribute to the company's success. The idea is to let employees know what's expected from them and why. With help from management, the employee—again, individually or as part of a team—sets challenging but realistic performance goals, similar to the MBOs described above. The number of goals may vary with the corporate culture and the job level, but a total of three to five seems reasonable.

These goals describe *what* results are expected. But it's also important to identify *how* results should be achieved. To a degree, that's done through the competencies. Using your company's competency model (I hope you have one), you review each competency and discuss how it can contribute to meeting the performance goals. To make it real, you describe specific observable behaviors—for example, customer service in terms of returning phone calls promptly with an-

**Exhibit 5-2. Performance appraisal criteria.**

| Priority / Team Type | Primary | Secondary |
|---|---|---|
| Parallel | Management by Objectives | Competencies and Results |
| Process | Competencies | Skills, Knowledge, and Results |
| Project | Results | Competencies* and Management by Objectives |

*Competencies would also be primary when team members are in project-oriented positions, for example, information technology.

swers to customer requests—that demonstrate each competency. You should also identify which competencies are most critical to the employee's and team's success in the year ahead.

In our example, the goals and competencies together provide an up-front, objective, and mutually understood and accepted basis for discussing performance results at the end of the year. But in the intervening months, to help employees achieve their goals, there's informal and formal "performance coaching." In informal coaching, you may have short but frequent day-to-day discussions with individual employees or teams about their progress. This gives workers feedback on the results achieved and how they were achieved. It's here that management can help people develop around critical competencies.

At midyear, you may conduct a more formal "update review" to discuss the employee's or team's progress against performance goals, to discuss the individual's demonstration of competencies, and to identify what, if any, changes need to be made in the performance goals.

By the time the annual performance review rolls around, there shouldn't be any surprises. However, there are a few more preliminary steps. Unless a peer or team feedback procedure is already in place, you may at that time determine who (besides yourself) is knowledgeable about the employee's performance, such as suppliers and customers. Contact those people for additional input. If there's a conflict between the peer reviews and your own, that should be an eye-opening experience.

The review itself is the culmination of a yearlong process designed to reinforce continuous improvement, build teamwork, and motivate constructive behavior. Its main purpose is to facilitate discussion, face-to-face. The review focuses on assessing past results and on developing the employee for the future. Thus, it should concentrate on the employee's performance over time, rather than making a snapshot comparison with other team members. And while the link is stronger at some organizations than at others, the review may also help determine compensation.

## Designing the Performance Appraisal Form

There are many ways to design a performance appraisal process. To illustrate, let's refer to the company that was developing a competency model back in Chapter 3 (Case Study 1).

The company has decided upon some dozen competencies for

the team overall. In designing the performance appraisal form, it includes four behaviors, arranged in order of complexity, for each of the competencies. (Other companies may have a more extensive list, although for simplicity's sake an upper limit of seven is advisable.) Remember that the company's seventh competency was "customer-service orientation," with the following behavior levels:

 a. Follows up promptly
 b. Takes personal responsibility
 c. Represents customer needs
 d. Uses a long-term perspective

In conducting a performance review, evaluators are asked to rate the frequency or quality of each behavior. The form may provide guidance for each item on the list. Under b, for example, it may suggest, "Responds to customer requests . . ."

## The Rating Scale

All performance appraisals should have three states or levels of performance (with a possibility of a fourth—"not measurable," "not observable," or "no opportunity to observe"—as needed). If, as in the example above, the rater is being asked to rate the frequency of each behavior, then the form should offer these options: often/occasionally/never. If the rater is being asked to assess performance or demonstration of a competency, then these measures are more applicable:

 1. Substantially exceeds standard. Performance is exceptional. Employee exceeds expectations.
 2. Achieves standard. Fully meets expectations for performance goals and competencies.
 3. Does not meet standard. Performance is below standard. Failed to meet most performance goals and has not demonstrated acceptable performance on the relevant individual/team competencies.

Either way, a scale of three is recommended. Nonetheless, most companies use performance appraisals that employ five or more ratings. The result is that most organizations rate their employees "above average"—a condition similar to that of radio personality Garrison Keillor's Lake Wobegon, "where all the children are above average." Statistically, of course, that's impossible. Often the companies' fond defense is that "all our employees are above average or they wouldn't work here," but that begs the question. The appraisal is meant to evaluate people as a population within the company, not relative to other companies.

## Scoring

There are a variety of approaches to scoring an individual against the competency model, from simple to complex. Here are three elements to consider:

1. Some competencies are more relevant to some jobs than to others. In designing the form, the company may simply ask the rater to note whether a specific competency is "not shown in this job." Or it may ask the rater to assess the importance of this competency, on a scale of 1 ("not important") to 5 ("critical"). Having done so, the company must decide whether it wants to assign different weights to different competencies.

2. As I noted in the example of customer-service orientation, the behaviors making up each competency are "arranged" in order of complexity—that is, d is a more complex behavior than c, c more complex than b. Management may want to reflect the greater value to the company of more complex behavior by weighting the behaviors accordingly, for example, giving more points to the "often" score on d than on b or a.

3. Earlier I recommended a rating scale with three levels, referring to frequency or quality of behavior. Should these ratings also be weighted? That is, should it be worth more to be scored "often" than "occasionally"? Such weighting rewards desired behavior. On the other hand, any weighting makes the rating system—and ultimately, the pay design—more complex.

### Examples

In the following examples, assume that twelve competencies with four behaviors each are identified for members of a given team. However, not every competency may be observable for each team member. Therefore, the score is based on the maximum achievable points averaged for the number of competencies observed. (See Exhibit 5-3.)

*Illustration 1: Nonweighted Scoring*

1. Weight all behaviors within each competency the same $(a = b = c = d)$; each behavior has the same value to the company.

2. "Credit" a behavior with 1 point if the rating is "occasionally" or "often," zero points if "never," and "nonapplicable" if "no opportunity to observe."
3. Determine performance rating: (maximum average score = 4.0)

Per observable competency:

$$\frac{\text{4 behaviors} \times \text{1 point ("often" or "occasionally")}}{\text{number of observable competencies}}$$

| Average score | | Performance rating |
|---|---|---|
| 3.2–4.0 points | = | superior |
| 2.5–3.19 points | = | competent |
| <2.5 points | = | needs improvement |

*Illustration 2: Weighted Scoring by Observation*

1. Weight the observation of each behavior differently. In this case a behavior rated "often" has more value to the company than one rated "occasionally."
2. Credit a behavior with 2 points for a rating of "often," 1 point for "occasionally," zero points if "never," or "nonapplicable" if "no opportunity to observe."
3. Determine performance rating (maximum average score = 8.0)

Per observable competency:

$$\frac{\text{4 behaviors} \times \text{2 points ("often")}}{\text{number of observable competencies}}$$

| Average score | | Performance rating |
|---|---|---|
| 6.4–8.0 points | = | superior |
| 5.0–6.39 points | = | competent |
| <5.0 points | = | needs improvement |

*Illustration 3: Weighted Scoring by Behavior and Observation*

1. Weight the behaviors and frequency of observation within each competency differently. Each behavior has a different value. In this case the highest-level performance d has more value to the company than c, and c has more value than b (a = 1, b = 2, c = 3, d = 4). At the same time, a behavior observed "often" has greater value than "occasionally."
2. Credit a behavior with 2 points for a rating of "often," 1 point

*(text continues on page 98)*

**Exhibit 5-3. Performance appraisal competency rating example.**

| Competency Weight | × | Behavior Weight | × | Often | Occasionally | Never | Not Observable | = | Maximum Score* |
|---|---|---|---|---|---|---|---|---|---|
| | | | | | **Observation Weight** | | | | |
| *Illustration 1* | | | | | | | | | |
| 1 | | A(1) | | 1 | 1 | 0 | N/A | | 1 |
| 1 | | B(1) | | 1 | 1 | 0 | N/A | | 1 |
| 1 | | C(1) | | 1 | 1 | 0 | N/A | | 1 |
| 1 | | D(1) | | 1 | 1 | 0 | N/A | | 1 |
| | | | | | | | | | 4 |
| *Illustration 2* | | | | | | | | | |
| 1 | | A(1) | | 2 | 1 | 0 | N/A | | 2 |
| 1 | | B(1) | | 2 | 1 | 0 | N/A | | 2 |
| 1 | | C(1) | | 2 | 1 | 0 | N/A | | 2 |
| 1 | | D(1) | | 2 | 1 | 0 | N/A | | 2 |
| | | | | | | | | | 8 |

## Illustration 3

| | | | | | | |
|---|---|---|---|---|---|---|
| 1 | A(1) | 2 | 1 | 0 | N/A | 2 |
| 1 | B(2) | 2 | 1 | 0 | N/A | 4 |
| 1 | C(3) | 2 | 1 | 0 | N/A | 6 |
| 1 | D(4) | 2 | 1 | 0 | N/A | 8 |
| | | | | | | 20 |

## Illustration 4

| | | | | | | |
|---|---|---|---|---|---|---|
| 5 | A(1) | 2 | 1 | 0 | N/A | 10 |
| 5 | B(2) | 2 | 1 | 0 | N/A | 20 |
| 5 | C(3) | 2 | 1 | 0 | N/A | 30 |
| 5 | D(4) | 2 | 1 | 0 | N/A | 40 |
| | | | | | | 100 |

*Maximum Score = Competency Weight $\times$ Behavior Weight $\times$ Observation Weight for "occasionally," zero points if "never," and "nonapplicable" if "no opportunity to observe."

3. Determine performance rating (maximum average score = 20.0)

Per observable competency:

$$\frac{[4 \text{ behaviors} \times 2 \text{ points ("often")} \times \text{value of behavior } (a = 1, b = 2, c = 3, d = 4)]}{\text{number of observable competencies}}$$

| Average score | | Performance rating |
|---|---|---|
| 16–20.0 points | = | superior |
| 12.5–15.99 points | = | competent |
| <12.5 points | = | needs improvement |

*Illustration 4: Weighted Scoring by Competency, Behavior, and Observation*

1. Weight each competency differently, from "critical" to "not important" on a 5–1 scale along with weighting behaviors and frequency of observation within each competency, as indicated in illustration 3 above.

2. Determine performance rating (maximum average score = 100.0)

Per observable competency:

$$\frac{[\text{Number of "critical" competencies} \times 5 \text{ points} \times 4 \text{ behaviors} \times 2 \text{ points ("often")} \times \text{value of behavior } (a = 1, b = 2, c = 3, d = 4)]}{\text{number of observable competencies}}$$

| Average score | | Performance rating |
|---|---|---|
| 80–100 points | = | superior |
| 62.5–79.99 points | = | competent |
| <62.5 points | = | needs improvement |

The key to deciding on the degree of complexity revolves around the maturity of the process and the need for precision. I strongly suggest that an organization begin with a simple system since the value of using competencies in a performance appraisal process lies in identifying the behaviors associated with success and encouraging/motivating employees to exhibit these behaviors. The goal is not to have employees focus on the weightings and measurement at the expense of behaviors that drive success. Over time, there is generally the need to increase complexity and focus on measurement as an organization increases its experience and knowledge. That's consistent with a progressive continuous learning environment.

# Selecting the Appraiser

A number of years ago, there was a television program called "*You Be the Judge*" in which the viewer was presented with the conflicting evidence of a crime and invited to sit in judgment. Judging from the show's rating, people enjoyed that role. But in the real world of performance appraisal and pay, passing judgment is a bit more problematic.

Who should be the judge? For an individual worker in a functional culture, the answer is the same as it's been since the industrial revolution: the boss. But in a team environment, evaluations can come from several sources, typically falling into two broad categories: (1) the employee's supervisor and/or team leader, and (2) the employee's supervisor, peers, and customers. This latter approach is better known, with some geometric license, as 360-degree or multi-rater evaluation. (See Exhibit 5-4.)

Below, I discuss the main options in selecting a performance appraiser.

## *The Supervisor or Team Leader*

For all the cultural change in corporations, the "boss" is still the linchpin of performance appraisal. And while there's the opportunity for favoritism or unfairness when one individual is conducting the review, in traditional corporate cultures that individual is unquestionably the one in the best position to judge his or her subordinate's performance.

How well does this approach work with teams? Project teams are arguably most amenable to review from the top. For these teams, there is generally a project "owner" or "sponsor," as well as a team leader who is typically at a higher level in the corporation than the other members. Thus there are ample layers of supervision for a conventional performance appraisal. If the team members have been "seconded" to the project from their "regular" jobs, then they may also have performance appraisals from their "regular" bosses. If, on the other hand, the individual's job is to serve on a series of time-based teams—the sort of assignment characteristic of people in information

**Exhibit 5-4. 360-degree/multi-rater performance appraisal.**

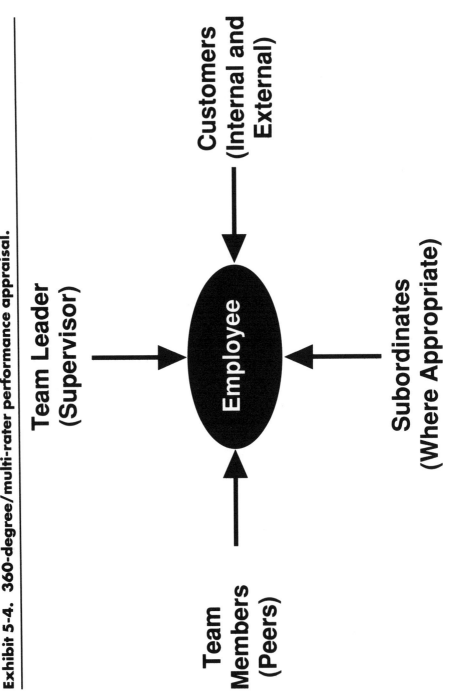

technology who are continually deploying new systems throughout a company—then the performance appraisals by the teams' sponsors or leaders are that much more critical.

With occasional exceptions, traditional performance appraisal from the top also works well for people serving on parallel teams. And for better or worse, there's no shortage of supervisors. The parallel team worker has not one but two bosses: the person to whom he or she regularly reports, and the team leader or supervisor. To be fair, the company must get a performance appraisal from each and integrate them into a single report.

There's no problem when the parallel team commitment is relatively minor—a half day or so each week—or when the appraisals are complementary. The difficulty arises when the individual is required to spend a substantial percentage of time on the team and his or her performances from the two jobs are at odds. This may reflect the individual's trouble in juggling the two tasks or, conceivably, the disproportionate demands of one or both supervisors. As a rule, the last word belongs to the person's full-time supervisor. In rare cases, however, the next layer of management may have to step in to reconcile the two appraisals.

## 360- (or 270- ) Degree/Multi-Rater Review

Particularly on process teams, the people best qualified to evaluate a member's performance are his or her peers. There are two other categories whose input may also be valuable: the team's supervisor and the team's customers. Usually these are internal customers, other people within the company who depend on the team's output. However, they may also be external customers. An example would be a team of claims processors and the people who file claims.

There are various ways to apply this more encompassing approach to performance appraisal. You can conduct a true 360-degree review, getting appraisals from the employee's peers, supervisors, and subordinates (and, where relevant, customers). In many cases, of course, the employee, particularly a member of a process team, has no subordinates. That may narrow your arc to 270 degrees: supervisors, peers, and, if desired, internal and external customers. Finally, if the team is so truly self-managed that there is no supervisor, coach, or even team leader, you may limit the employee's review to peers. (Again, customers may be included if you want additional input.)

Once you've determined which categories you'll be using to conduct the review, you must then decide how you'll weight each category. For example, you may have decided that a team member should be appraised by one supervisor, three fellow team members, and two internal customers. Among other possibilities, you could:

- Give each reviewer equal weight. On the surface, that appears to be the most equitable formula. However, that would mean that five-sixths of the individual's evaluation comes from his fellow workers. Management may be understandably reluctant to turn that much authority over to workers.
- Give each category equal weight: one-third to the supervisor, one-third to coworkers, one-third to customers. That formula may provide a better balance. However, a department's manager may be unwilling to give customers outside the department or company such a large role in appraising his or her subordinates. And if the customers are *within* the department, that means that employees dominate the review.
- Give management and fellow team members equal weight, while sidelining the customers' contribution to perhaps 10 percent of the total or a qualitative "gloss" on the subject. Although input by customers can be valuable, there are many arguments for limiting their role in a performance appraisal or taking measures to ensure that their contribution is properly understood.

External customer evaluations, especially, may require reading between the lines. Take the real-life case of an insurance company whose claims processors were making a flat-out effort to please customers by processing claims faster and more accurately. The only problem was that, at the same time, management had raised premiums. So when customers were surveyed as to their overall satisfaction, ratings dipped precipitously. To prevent appraisals from being distorted by such factors, the human resources function or whoever sponsors the process must clearly establish the difference between customer service, which is within employees' control, and customer satisfaction, which often is not.

While peer review is most appropriate for process teams, peer input can also be important in appraising the performance of members of parallel and project teams, particularly if management is considering reappointing those members to other teams in the future. For these other types of teams, however, the other categories of appraisers—management and customers—should probably be weighted far more heavily. In other words, there's a continuum along which appraisals need to be placed.

## Fairness and Accuracy

Opening up the performance appraisal to new raters usually raises concerns about fairness and accuracy. To a degree, such concerns are unwarranted. Personality conflicts and favoritism can intrude on traditional supervisor-supervisee appraisals as well as on peer reviews. Furthermore, opening up the process to several raters helps ensure that the appraisal isn't distorted by the grudge or friendship of one individual.

On the other hand, any change raises legitimate concerns that need to be addressed. People who work together on teams typically have no experience in rating others (other than the offhand remark), and management must provide training. If competencies are being assessed—the likeliest subject of peer review—the company needs to create a model of what outstanding behavior looks like that is validated by outstanding employees. The behaviors must be communicated to the "raters" so they know what they're measuring against. Some companies may use written descriptions; others opt for videos. To learn the way, companies may first ask the new raters to rate themselves. That's also useful because once there's team feedback they can see how their own self-appraisal compares with the way others see them.

People who work closely on teams have a natural tendency not to criticize each other to management—the "us versus them" mentality—and that's particularly true when money is at stake. While people may critique each other frankly at workshops, the purpose there generally is team-building and personal development rather than performance appraisal, and the exercises are usually professionally facilitated. So, unless management takes precautions, there's a danger that all the peer reviews will be glowing.

One obvious answer is anonymity: People must believe that the confidentiality of their ratings is protected. To guarantee anonymity, there must be a critical mass—at the minimum, three individuals—participating in the appraisal. The design of the performance appraisal form can also help ensure anonymity or, if personal remarks are included, violate it. Check-a-box style forms are not only a better "fit" for hourly workers; they're clearly safer. They can be scored by computer, and the person being reviewed is presented with aggregate data.

Fairness is an issue, too, when it comes to customer ratings. The system must be designed to prevent bias—for example, being rated by somebody who has become a close friend. Employees may nominate customers, but management must approve. By the same token, there is a danger that a customer will hold an employee hostage to a favorable review; for example, he may threaten to give the team member a bad review unless his claim is paid immediately and in full. Utilizing statistical sampling techniques may mitigate these issues.

Because of such concerns, companies that are introducing 360-degree feedback or peer review should initially limit them to development purposes, that is, to providing information about how employees are viewed, so they can do their jobs better. That is probably the least threatening way to launch this process. Once employees become more confident that it's fair, it can then be applied to the performance appraisal process and eventually linked to pay.

## Case Study: 360-Degree Review at Gore

*Externally competitive. Internally fair.*
Those are the two standards by which W. L. Gore & Associates—the high-technology manufacturing company headquartered in Newark, Delaware, that may be best known for its all-weather Gore-Tex fabrics—guides its compensation policy. And while most companies would probably lay claim to the same standards, Gore tries to meet them through an unusual 360-degree/multi-rater review consistent with the antihierarchical, proteam philosophy of Wilbert Gore, the man who founded the company in 1958.

For a start, at Gore it would be "unfair" to have a single individual conduct a performance review. So when the "associates"—anyone who works at Gore—are reviewed, it's by an assortment of people including peers, teammates, and "sponsors" (Gore rejects the notion of "bosses"). Occasionally, external customers or others outside the company may also have a say; outside tax consultants, for example, have been asked to participate in the review of Gore's financial associates.

In addition, twice a year Gore conducts a "contribution list" process to determine compensation. It draws up lists of associates who can be compared in terms of their contribution to the company because they work on the same team or in the same function or at least in the same area. Each contribution list is circulated among several individuals, known as "inputters," who then do a simple numerical ranking. If the inputters choose, they may also make written comments (which, in turn, may be used anonymously in performance reviews).

Gore doesn't tell the inputters what competencies to use. The only directive is that people be ranked in terms of their total contribution to the financial success of the company. That includes not just their direct impact on the bottom line, but also any special skills, notable achievements, or qualities such as leadership. Salespeople, for example, are not ranked solely on the sales they generate, but on their *total* contribution to the corporation: Have they thought up new applications for existing products? Do they help others? Are their customers satisfied? And, even, do they file their expense reports accurately and on time?

The contribution lists for each group of associates are then sent to a corporate compensation committee. For each associate, a graph is produced that compares the individual's salary with his or her contribution ranking. Ideally, the higher-ranked contributors should be paid more than those at the bottom of the list. The graph shows whether that's actually the case. If there are discrepancies, Gore makes adjustments; people whose salary is lagging behind others' may receive raises, while those associates who are fairly paid may not get any increase in that period.

## Case Study: Peer Review at the Auto Parts Manufacturer

Three times a year at the auto parts manufacturer described in Chapter 3 (Case Study 2), production and packing line teams are shut down for about an hour while everybody becomes a human resources expert. Workers file into a room where they're handed a sheet listing about a half dozen of their fellow team members and the ten or so competencies considered critical to the company's success. They watch a video in which someone quickly reviews all of the competencies, then describes in detail competency number 1 and what it "looks like" in real-life behavior. "Now," says the speaker, "rate your teammates." There are a few minutes of silence while people circle the level of behavior they see most frequently in each person they're rating. Then the video goes on to describe competency 2.

The process, which takes about an hour, looks simple, but it took management several months of trial and error to get there. That it persisted in the effort is a measure of its commitment to teams, of which peer review was a natural outgrowth. Because it uses process or work teams that are more or less self-directed, there are no supervisors who are knowledgeable enough to evaluate the teams. "Coaches," who act as a resource for the teams in other areas, also manage the performance appraisal process, consolidating the input, giving feedback to individuals, and doing developmental planning: a relative rarity for hourly workers.

Management began redesigning its performance appraisal process several years ago to accommodate its growing emphasis on teams. Initially it used "coordinators"—the two supervisors per shift—to rate the teams, using competencies rather than the standard review form it had used for years. But that quickly proved unsatisfactory. When experts talk about performance appraisals, they demand two measures of reliability:

1. Does the instrument produce consistent results over time?
2. Do all of the raters rate similarly?

To be fair, as well as legally defensible, a company must be able to answer in the affirmative to both questions. In this case, however, the reliability was terrible on both scores.

For one thing, there was tremendous inconsistency in the way different coordinators rated people. The third-shift workers, for example, were universally "excellent," while on the first shift, nobody was even "good." For another, there was suspicious consistency over time. Management compared the new ratings with those conducted a year earlier, which had been based largely on skills. In principle, the two sets of reviews should have been dramatically different for a number of employees; in fact, there was an extremely high correlation. That, the company concluded, was due to bias: Many of the supervisors had already formed opinions about employees and were unwilling to change them, despite the fact that they were using a completely different yardstick based upon behavioral skills.

Even had the coordinators been willing to change their minds, human resources managers observed, doing so might have been difficult: With self-directed teams, they weren't close enough to the people to evaluate how they worked. The supervisors don't see the hour-by-hour behavior that can undermine team effectiveness, like an employee's going to the bathroom ten times a day or returning late from breaks.

So the company tried again with a pilot in which upwards of one hundred high-performing team members rated each other. This time, the results were very different. Team members could say, "It's easy for the supervisor to give somebody a good score, but I have to work with that person. You think I'm going to say they get along with others, when they're as moody as can be? No way!" So they were more honest about the ratings because they had a vested interest in the results. At the same time, any concerns that personal friendships or grudges would affect scores proved unfounded. The company found that, even if a couple of team members tried to make a deal by pumping up each other's ratings, there were perhaps half a dozen other people on the team to balance the score.

So the company took the plunge into 180-degree feedback. It decided to have everyone rate about half of the other members on his or her team. (The company believed that rating everybody on the team would be too demanding.) It was only after going through the peer review process successfully a few times that management made the link between ratings and pay. In keeping with the company's "expectations philosophy," however, the connection works more as a negative: Team members who don't meet the minimum level for competencies and skill (as well as for basic standards for attendance and safety) won't receive any increase in pay. The process is designed not to say who are the superstars, who is average, and who is below. Rather, it's to seek out deficiencies and offer remedial measures before the team becomes dysfunctional.

Every four months, therefore, team members must have a basic score on competencies and show some improvement in skills. If, at the end of a year, they're behind in either area, their coach will help them set developmental milestones. If they catch up, that's fine; if they don't, they're out. This is consistent with the company's culture as a learning environment.

## Case Study: "Hybrid" Appraisal

In mid-1994, Time Insurance, a Milwaukee-based company that provides insurance to individuals and small groups, announced to employees that it would base merit raises partly on peer review. "There was general panic," says Kathryn Thomas, vice president, health underwriting. "Many staff didn't like the idea that they'd be impacting somebody else's pay." To meet their objections, Time has adopted a hybrid approach to performance appraisal that blends peer and supervisor review, competencies and quantitative results, and group and individual performance.

Time, which had adopted process teams the previous spring, only a few months before it phased in peer review, has a total of ten teams, composed of four exempt and six nonexempt employees each. The exempt staffers are the underwriters; the nonexempt perform either of two main functions, customer service or clerical (policy assembly, mail matching, etc.). Each team is a self-contained work unit, responsible for the product from beginning to end.

In 1994, nonexempt employees' merit raises were based on the following input: one-third on individual rating, one-third on team rating, and one-third from the department performance. Of the one-third based on the individual rating, roughly half came from peer review; the other half came from the team's coach. (Each coach oversees two or three teams, a full-time job that provides sufficient information to conduct reviews.)

That equation reflected a fair amount of spirited debate. In a test of the peer-review process, which was conducted prior to formal year-end reviews, "the quality of response was excellent," says Thomas. "People were extremely serious and deliberate with their comments, and the coaches found it very helpful in putting together team members' development plans." But because employees continued to resist the notion of affecting their coworkers' pay, they continued to ask that the team's coach determine which parts of the reviews should be incorporated in the total appraisal. "We didn't use a hard number," says Thomas, "but I don't know of one instance where a coach disregarded the comments. They were good, insightful, comments. People were kind," she added, "but as time goes on, they'll feel more confident about giving candid feedback."

For the individual performance appraisal, then, roughly half depends on the coach. For nonexempt workers, that evaluation tends to be largely subjective, based on such elements as the quality of customer service. The evaluation is considerably more precise for the underwriters, because its quality audits give the company hard data on risk management—the primary competency for underwriters. The peer-review process is the same for both groups: a brief questionnaire in which each member of the team is asked to rate the others on a few competencies (teamwork, customer service) and "housekeeping" characteristics such as schedule adherence.

The process is truly a hybrid, bottom-up as well as top-down. In a semiannual employee-opinion survey, each team rates its coach. And a year after peer review was introduced for teams, it was introduced for the coaches and support staff, who now rate each other.

## Note

1. John Case, "What the Experts Forgot to Mention," *Inc.*, September 1993, p. 66.

# 6

# Increasing Base Pay

"I come to work every day."

In a recent survey that was the least inspired of the reasons that executives said employees had provided in trying to justify their request for a raise or promotion. Other gems included: "My work isn't necessarily very good, but others in the same position are making more," "My mom says I should be promoted by now," and "Hey, I'm broke."[1]

Establishing a methodical basis for increasing base pay won't necessarily spare you those excuses. But at least you'll be able to point to the steps that the employee will have to take to qualify for a raise. And that's crucial, because the approach your company takes to increasing base pay conveys a specific message to employees about what the company values, reinforces the company's culture, and can either foster or hinder team effectiveness.

A common mistake among companies changing to a team-oriented work design is to assume that only some of the available reward mechanisms—base-salary ranges, raises, recognition awards, and variable pay devices—should reflect the new orientation toward quality or competencies and skills. In fact, all of these reward elements must be aligned with the work culture, with the salary increase process being one of the more effective delivery and reinforcement vehicles. It helps employees understand what is being valued and paid for in the new work cultures and resultant team designs. It also effectively conveys the message that the organization is no longer paying primarily for tenure, but rather for performance in line with new quality, speed, and productivity initiatives and for the development and demonstration of desired new competencies.

In this chapter, I discuss some of the most common systems that companies have implemented as a means of granting team-member base-salary and wage increases. I also offer a practical how-to guide to setting up your own pay increase process and present some case studies of companies with exemplary programs.

## Approaches to Increasing Base Pay

There are three legs to the base-pay "stool," the structure that describes the shape of people's pay. (See Exhibit 6-1.) The first two—work comparison or job evaluation and market pricing—were discussed in Chapter 4. In this chapter we turn our attention to the third leg: pay delivery, or the rationale for giving team members different pay when work comparison would indicate that they are performing the same job and are being held accountable for the same results. Everybody's pay relies on the base-pay stool, but in different ways, and for some individuals the pay delivery "leg" is more important than for others.

Over the years, companies have developed a variety of other approaches, both formal and ad hoc, to increasing base pay. Some of the tried-and-true systems supporting wage or salary increases include across-the-board wage increases, step rates (seniority), merit increases based on individual performance appraisal ratings, and the acquisition of additional skills or knowledge (better known as skill- or knowledge-based pay). Paying for competencies (behaviors) is a more recent approach. Despite broadbanding, these approaches will allow the pay of individuals in the same job to diverge at a given point in time—perhaps even more than it did historically.

Other rationales, more arbitrary—and in some cases, blatantly illegal—have been based on employees' need or sex or age. Personal history, including such factors as the employee's wage in a previous job, has also been a rationale for paying some team members more than others. This is particularly true at the time the person is hired. (Even managers who are reluctant to give raises are generally more willing to *hire* at differentials on grounds that have little to do with the company's interests—a "let's make a deal" approach to compensation that, on the whole, should be strongly discouraged for the obvious legal, fairness, and cost implications. The only exception should be for individuals who bring in unique skills, competencies, or experiences.)

Clearly, certain approaches are more appropriate than others, depending on the company, the marketplace, the economy, and even the times or mood of the workforce. But whatever the approach, if it includes variations in base pay, it must be for reasons that, as noted in Chapter 4, are understood and accepted by the employees or, in

**Exhibit 6-1. Base-pay components.**

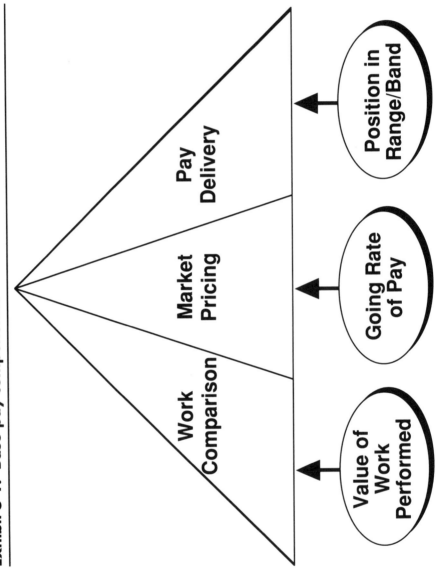

the case of a team, by the members. For example, seniority, whatever its faults—and there are many—is a more accepted basis than, say, age, for wage differentials. Of course, a different conclusion might be reached in Japan. An approach that is not accepted will lead to internal competition and divisiveness. Correctly or not, many employees see the issue of raises as a zero-sum game in which one team member's gain is another's loss, or at least his or her opportunity lost.

Finally, differences must be legally defensible. The constant threat of legal challenge makes it that much more imperative that companies develop a systematic approach to increasing base pay that is based upon established job-related criteria, applied on a consistent nondiscriminating basis and well documented.

## Characteristics of Traditional Systems

Up until the 1980s the salary increase process, while important, took a back seat to the way companies were operated. Significant salary growth occurred through promotions every few years and, even if promotions were not readily available, double-digit-increase budgets fueled by inflation provided plenty of money for all employees. Increases not related to productivity improvements were easily passed along to customers as most companies determined their increase budgets from surveying the domestic marketplace without the concern of global competition, which plays by a different set of rules.

Business's response to recent slow growth and competition has been to embrace an array of new philosophies such as total quality management and business process reengineering which have reduced corporate hierarchies (fewer promotional opportunities) and have created teams as an organizational design. This, coupled with low inflation and reduced salary increase budgets, has put pressure on management to come up with creative approaches to reward outstanding employee performance by dividing the limited increase amounts on a different basis and to adopt incentive compensation (addressed in Chapter 8). This chapter does not address issues associated with bona fide promotions. It assumes that all employees have a need to continuously learn and improve their performance as a basic job requirement in order to maintain their position.

In the following section, I describe the major approaches to base-pay increases and their implications for the various types of work cultures and teams. I conclude with a preferred course of action. First, however, I note that the different work cultures not only spawn different kinds of teams but also have their own approach to administering pay and to granting increases for members of their teams.

Parallel teams in a functional culture typically administer increases with tight controls minimizing differentiation of employees in the same pay range. Process cultures with process or work teams have medium levels of flexibility, depending upon the team's stage of evolution in recognizing individual development. And project teams in a time-based culture, which emphasize individual contribution and display minimal concern for internal equity, have the greatest increase flexibility, or the broadest bands.

The challenge in deciding upon the appropriate increase methodology revolves around the importance and role of the individual versus the team in assessing individual contribution. The first step is to understand the advantages and disadvantages of each methodology.

## General Wage Increases

This system assumes that all employees perform at the same level or that it is not feasible to assess individual contributions. Employers may also believe that differentiating base pay would damage working relationships, particularly among people working in teams; and unions—for this approach is typical of union shops—may see it as conceding too much control and power to the employers. With a system of general wage increases, everybody sinks or swims together. If the company has a good year or other employers in the area are paying their workforces more (market pricing) or a cost-of-living factor or a contract mandates an across-the-board increase, everybody may get a raise. If not, wages may be flat.

The definition of *everybody*, however, has been modified over time. Fifty years ago, the word might have encompassed every hourly worker in the company. (This approach is most commonly used with hourly or low-level salaried employees.) These days there is more concern about equity within a business unit or team. So even if the rest of the company remains at the status quo, the employees of a business unit that has exceeded expectations may receive an increase.

Apart from its obvious simplicity, the main advantage of this approach is that, as noted in Chapter 4, with process teams especially, "less is more"—the less differentiation, the better. And there may indeed be cases where, given the nature of the work, it is virtually impossible to differentiate among workers and to single out some for praise or blame. Let's consider the case of an integrated steel minimill whose main components are a melt shop and a rolling mill. If the finished steel product that comes out of the rolling mill is substandard, is it fair to blame the people who work in the rolling mill? Or the people in the melt shop, who processed raw material that did not meet specifications? By the same token, if the melt shop isn't operating up to standard due to poor-quality raw material, is it fair to penalize the team responsible for that aspect of the product?

But while the across-the-board raise may be appropriate in such cases, there are many drawbacks to this approach. A general wage increase creates a sense of entitlement among employees. People come to expect an annual increase, irrespective of how they or the company performed. More significantly, perhaps, this approach can limit the company's ability to compete for good workers while encouraging inferior workers to dig in for the duration. The employer can only hope that peer pressure will help the team weed out the nonperformers or raise their level of performance. But the bad news is that this system may be a turnoff to good performers, and peer pressure may drag down the norm.

## Step Rate Increases

This approach, where increases to the base wages are predetermined based upon the passage of time, is commonly used to administer pay for hourly and nonexempt (overtime-eligible) workers. Performance (of either the individual or the team member) does not influence the size or the timing of the wage increase. Seniority has been a common basis for pay increases for decades, particularly in unionized shops. The assumption was that the longer a worker stayed on a job, the better he/she could perform it—and that his/her loyalty should be rewarded.

But there is a basic fallacy to that belief: With the possible exception of Supreme Court justices, most people beyond a certain point cease to grow in their jobs and perform them better. Is nine years of experience one year repeated nine times? Or is it three years, three times? Depending upon the answer, seniority, maturity, or longevity pay would play a different role. Now, as the result of a few hard-edged trends—the decline of unionism, the move to a service economy, and companies' loss of interest in encouraging longtime, higher-priced employees to stay—seniority has been falling out of favor. It will continue to decline as long as higher pay is not associated with higher productivity.

## Merit Increases

Merit increases, sometimes known as pay-for-performance, are based upon individual performance ratings and are the way base-salary increases are determined for the vast majority of salaried employees in the private sector in the United States.

This approach has an obvious advantage over the two systems described above: It rewards employees for performance, not merely for drawing breath, and should thus provide more motivation when administered properly. And it may be the most appropriate approach for companies using parallel and project teams, allowing employees' contribution to the company to be measured primarily in terms of their individual performance.

But there are drawbacks, too. While more innovative programs such as skill or competency-based pay generally evaluate employees more frequently, the individual performance rating systems tend to be somewhat inflexible, rating and rewarding employees typically on an annual basis. The traditional vehicle for assessing individual performance is the performance review by one's superior—an event that, as discussed in Chapter 5, is often not only dreaded but even counterproductive. The system, by rating performance, does not explicitly encourage people to learn other skills or competencies.

More serious problems exist in companies where performance ratings are forced into a stated distribution, so that only so many employees at any given time may be rated outstanding, above average, competent, etc. This approach is condemned by the total quality movement because it pits employees against each other for performance ratings, instead of against the competition. Teamwork and cooperation are discouraged if you and I are both vying for one available outstanding rating. As indicated in Chapter 5, an employee's ability to demonstrate a competency or acquire a skill should be solely contingent upon that employee's abilities, and not upon other team members, if we truly want teams to work together effectively. A second problem deals with rater reliability—that is, will two raters of the same employee come up with the same performance evaluation? The more objective and job related the criteria, based upon what outstanding employees do more often, the more reliable the rating. (See Chapter 3 for a more complete discussion on competencies.) Finally, because—by definition—performance ratings focus on individual achievement, they can become irrelevant or counterproductive in a process culture where the emphasis is on teams and teamwork.

## Skill-Based Pay

Also known by such labels as "career ladders" and "pay for knowledge," this system determines base pay increases on the skills or knowledge a person is able to demonstrate, rather than on the specific job. In a pay-for-skills or pay-for-knowledge program, companies may certify an employee in any of a handful of ways:

- He or she passes a written test.
- He or she performs the job adequately under supervision.
- Peers certify that he or she has the skill.

Skill-based pay programs encourage employees to acquire multiple skills. This can be beneficial for employers because, not only do these employees become more flexible resources, able to perform multiple roles, but they also develop a broader understanding of the work processes. This facilitates job-sharing and self-directed work teams, and the creation of career paths in the flattened hierarchy that will become increasingly characteristic of companies as we approach the next millennium.

The downside is that skill-based pay programs require more time and attention to develop and implement than traditional pay programs. There are additional training requirements, along with the need for testing and certification processes and precise communications with employees. Furthermore, skill-based pay is cost-effective only when people with needed skills cannot be hired easily. If there is a large pool of qualified workers, then raising employees' pay for skills that are readily available can't be justified in economic terms, even if it's good for morale and flexibility. That apart, at Hay we have found that, when appropriately designed and administered, a skill-based program can achieve long-term savings that far outweigh the short-term development costs, if the program creates a learning environment that continually encourages employees to acquire new skills as the pace of technological change quickens.

In designing a skill-based program, one of the issues companies must address is what we'll call "skill inflation." If you're paying for skills, the chances are good that many of your employees will acquire many of those skills even if there is no immediate opportunity to use them. Let's say your average pay level at an insurance company claims-processing work team is 3 (claims adjudication, say) in a band with levels from 1 (opening the mail) to 5 (training new employees). (See Exhibit 6-2.) With a skill-based program, the average pay level will probably migrate up to 4 (respond to customer complaints). But if the openings at the top are limited, a company may find itself paying "4's" for level-1 and -2 work. Should everybody be paid at the highest level, or must there be openings? In other words, do you pay for the *acquisition* or the *application* of skills?

This is an area where companies need to strike a delicate balance.

**Exhibit 6-2. Skill levels.**

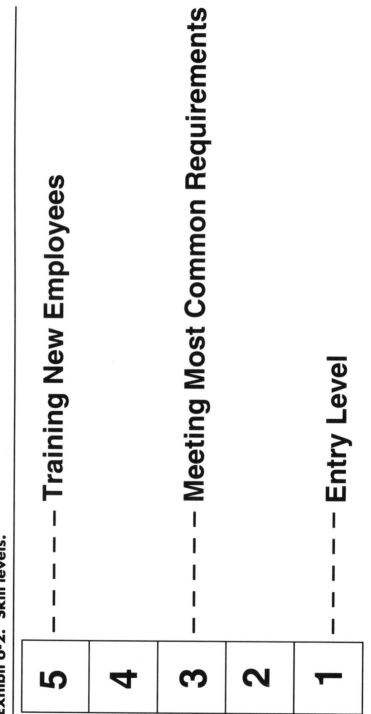

| | |
|---|---|
| 5 | — — — — Training New Employees |
| 4 | — — — — |
| 3 | — — — — Meeting Most Common Requirements |
| 2 | — — — — |
| 1 | — — — — Entry Level |

On the one hand, you don't want to pay top dollar to employees who are doing only entry-level work. On the other hand, you don't want to discourage employees from acquiring skills that will probably prove useful down the road. Unless it's prohibitively expensive, our advice is to pay for skills, up to a point—for example, pay for people who have acquired level-4 skill, but perhaps not for level 5. As I mentioned earlier, the upside is increased flexibility, assuming you can eventually take advantage of it in a positive fashion.

Which brings me, once again, to teams. Paying for skills is an approach particularly well suited to organizations with process teams, whose members have similar training and education and do similar work. Except for a new hire, there are no level-1 workers on such teams; all or most of the tasks are shared, so everyone works at level 3 or above. On process teams, skill acquisition should be strongly encouraged. The more skills shared by the more team members, the better for everyone: Productivity goes up faster, customer satisfaction increases, employees get paid more and do more interesting and varied work. Other benefits may be company specific. For example, American Meter in Nebraska City, Nebraska, hopes that by rotating tasks it will reduce the incidence of repetitive stress injury among its workers. Finally, with the acquisition of more advanced skills that are normally associated with leaders or managers, the further the team moves along the path to self-management.

My view is that skill-based pay is a worthy interim step to encouraging people to acquire skills and build teams. Over time, however, assuming a stable workforce, the company should migrate away from this approach on inputs and toward paying for competencies—which I discuss later in this chapter—and for results (use of the skills), a strategy also known as incentive compensation. That is the subject of Chapter 8. The role of each compensation element for each type of team is further discussed in Chapter 9, The Architecture of Team Pay.

## Paying for Skills: Case Study 1

In 1989 the Aid Association for Lutherans (AAL), a leading fraternal-benefits society based in Appleton, Wisconsin, developed a skill-based pay program that compensates individuals for each additional skill (or "service," in the AAL's language) they acquire and apply on behalf of their team. The pay program was designed to support the self-managed work team concept AAL had adopted two years earlier in its two large service areas: insurance product services and field administration services.

In insurance products, AAL defined some 160 different services delivered by the organization, within such categories as underwriting, policy support, team management skills, systems support, and contractual services. The field administration services teams were accountable for thirty-seven services (compensation and financing, field employment, reimbursement, etc.). AAL developed a dictionary describing in detail every service and giving its associated dollar value. Each person's job—known as a "personal assignment"—represented the total of the various services he or she performed.

AAL then developed a compensation system to support the teams. It was called Pay for Applied Services (PAS), a term that emphasized the importance of *applying* as well as *acquiring* new skills. There were four components to the PAS system: personal assignment, market adjustment (or market pricing), team performance incentive, and individual performance incentive. We will describe the first two components here. Chapter 8 contains a general discussion of incentive compensation.

There were two types of services under PAS: primary and additional. The most complex service (determined by the Hay Guide Chart® Profile Method of Job Evaluation) was the primary service. Each primary service had a market salary range which was divided into ten "performance segments." An employee's position in the range was determined by his or her experience and performance. Additional services built on an employee's base of knowledge. The combined value of the primary and additional services (called the personal assignment) determined the employee's base pay.

To illustrate, I'll borrow AAL's hypothetical example of a primary-service market range with entry-level pay of $252 per week and maximum of $312. Each performance segment is equal to one-tenth of the amount between those two points, or $6.

One way employees can increase their base pay is by acquiring new services (with the consent of their team). The value of additional services depends on their "know-how" points—harking back to the Hay Guide Charts—and other services that are already part of their personal assignment. The higher the points, the higher the monetary value. However, AAL does build in a diminishing-returns element: The first additional service is worth more than the second, third, or fourth additional services with the same number of points.

In the example, an employee is at the fourth performance segment, which is worth $276 per week. The employee also has six additional services. Three of these services have 100 know-how points, two have 87 points, and one has 76. Using the PAS matrix for additional services, we arrive at a value for additional services of $55, resulting in a base-pay total of $331 per week. Once the employee's ability to perform those additional services has been verified, the $55 is added to his base pay (irrespective of the $312 maximum on the market range).

Another way the employee can increase his base pay is by moving through the market range, as determined by his performance rating by his manager. The better the rating, the further he can move along the continuum. In the example, the employee "meets/sometimes exceeds expectations," a rating that's worth two performance segments. At $6 per segment, that represents a $12 increase in primary service pay, to $288. Combined with the value of additional services, that brings our hypothetical employee to a new base total of $343 per week.

You'll notice that such increases can take the employee beyond the maximum for that market range. When that happens, AAL gives the portion of the *performance increase* above the maximum in the form of an annualized cash lump-sum payment for that year only. The value of the primary service is now at the maximum. (The value of additional services does not change.)

One way to break out of this box is through a promotion, which moves the employee into a higher market range. An employee who acquires a service with a larger number of know-how points than his current primary service will be promoted and move to a higher market range. The new service will become his primary service, and his current service converts to an additional service. A promotion gives him the opportunity for continued base-pay growth.

Market adjustments, the other means of increasing base pay, are made to the salary ranges periodically, based on the results of external market surveys. In most cases, AAL passes along market adjustments if the employee's performance rating at least "partially meets expectations." (The only rating below that—"does not meet expectations"—would merit no increase.) In the case of this hypothetical AAL employee, if base pay is adjusted 4 percent across the board to reflect the marketplace, the value of his primary service would rise to $300, from $288.

## Paying for Skills: Case Study 2

In 1993, McDonnell Douglas Helicopter, in Mesa, Arizona, adopted a company-wide pay-for-skills compensation system.[2] The plan, which replaced a system of automatic wage progression every three to six months, made pay increases contingent on consistently learning and demonstrating new skills. Employee involvement was high: Each of the company's thirty "job families" designed its own skill-based pay system. (A subsidiary benefit of the planning process was that the company cut in half—to thirty from fifty-eight—the total number of individual job classifications within its job "families.")

---

In establishing a pay-for-skills program, McDonnell Douglas defined each of the major components. Here's its glossary:

**Skill**   A learned ability that improves with practice over time. The skills used in skill-based pay plans must be relevant to the work.

**Skill block**   The skill or skills that must be accomplished for an increase in pay. Often, more than one skill is included in a skill block.

**Baseline skills**   Those skills needed to gain entry into the job. Proficiency in all baseline skills is required before attempting a skill block.

---

Under the program, any employee in a work group for which a skill-based pay plan existed will receive a pay increase of thirty-five cents per hour every thirteen to twenty-six weeks, only after demonstrating proficiency in a relevant skill block. (For example, management rejected the proposal by assemblers that word processing be included as a necessary skill.) Each job-family group determines the timing of an employee's potential increase.

Program Structure Standards
1. Development teams consist of hourly employees and managers.
2. Skill-based pay plans must contain baseline skills.
3. Plans must be based on skills and skill blocks.
4. An official review team is set up to verify skills. At least one hourly team member must serve on two consecutive review meetings.

Skill and Skill-Block Standards
1. To merit a pay increase:

   • Skills must be demonstrated and be current.
   • Skills must meet specified quality and time standards.
   • Skills must be witnessed by at least one review-team member.

2. The skill block for the next pay-increase period must be approved by the immediate supervisor. Skill blocks must be approved and documented on a Skills Planning Form.
3. The skill block for the next pay-increase period must be identified within one month of the last increase. This is to ensure that:

   • Managers are able to assign the jobs needed to verify identified skills.
   • Managers are able to schedule training needed by the employee.

## Paying for Competencies

Paying for competencies is the newest approach in base-pay systems, although the notion of using competencies to evaluate and develop employees—primarily management-level individuals—has been gaining more acceptance.

One issue is how competencies would be "verified." In skill-based pay programs, certification is relatively straightforward; you demonstrate before your peers or supervisor that you can perform the task at hand. In competencies, it's not so tangible. It could be argued that, as with skills, a jury of one's peers is the best test, but even organizations that have experimented enthusiastically with multi-rater 360-degree (or 180-degree) peer, customer, and subordinate feedback for developmental purposes are far more reluctant to apply it to money. People need to have a good experience with 360-degree review, and the company needs to have a trusting climate, before they will feel confident about entrusting their raises to an evaluation of their coworkers.

Another issue is precisely how much impact competencies should have on pay. While its proponents—and certainly I'm among them—argue that competencies are the best predictor of future performance based upon past success, they do not represent current performance. Competencies represent an assessment of *how* individuals go about their jobs. A pay system also needs to consider *what* is accomplished. A good balance uses competencies to determine base-pay increases and reserves what is accomplished—the results—for spot cash awards (discussed in Chapter 7) and incentive compensation (addressed in Chapter 8).

Having raised all those objections, I'll note here that there is much to be said for paying for competencies. As I noted in Chapter 3, different types of corporate cultures emphasize different competencies. A pay-for-competencies program enables the corporation to align its values to base pay. By linking the two, organizations send a clear message to employees about the behaviors they expect to see.

Exhibit 6-3 illustrates the differences between a pay-for-skills and a pay-for-competencies approach. The key difference is that the skills approach focuses on demonstrations of certain knowledge, while a competencies approach pays for attributes that *predict* successful performance. In theory, a pay-for-skills plan can deliver only a fixed return on a employer's investment of compensation dollars; a broader pay-for-competencies plan has the potential to deliver a significantly higher return on that investment.

In a pay-for-competencies approach the organization would define *expected* and *exceptional* behavior. (This is similar to basic and advanced skill levels in skill-based pay programs.) Increases in base pay would be reserved for demonstration of exceptional competencies. Again, as in skill-based pay, there is the question of the "trigger mechanism" for the raise: Does the company pay people merely for *possession* of desired competencies? Or should a raise be triggered only when there's been substantial *application* of the competencies over time? How the company answers those questions is determined, as I show in the following section, by its cultural profile and its approach to teams.

## Raises and Teams

### *Parallel Teams*

The key consideration in selecting an approach to increasing base pay is how much of the person's time and energy is allocated to the team. As a rule, giving pay increases through a skill- or competency-based program is not effective for team performance, because, in a functional culture, parallel teams typically represent a relatively small

**Exhibit 6-3. A comparison of the differences: skills versus competencies.**

| | Pay for Skills | Pay for Competencies |
|---|---|---|
| **Examples** | • Equipment Operation<br><br>• Equipment Set-Up/Changeover<br><br>• Elementary Equipment Troubleshooting<br><br>• Team Problem-Solving Skills | • Customer-Service Orientation<br><br>• Conceptual Thinking<br><br>• Flexibility<br><br>• Team Commitment |
| **Emphasis** | • Developed | • Selected for and Developed |
| **Organizational Expectations** | • Fixed Number of Highest or Multi-Skill Positions | • Desire to Have All Employees Strive for Superior Competencies |
| **Impact** | • Short- to Medium-Term Performance | • Medium- to Long-Term Performance |

percentage of the employee's job with the company. Individual performance ratings may be the most appropriate approach: The company can base merit raises on the employee's performance on both the team and in his or her regular job, considering competency and skill acquisition factors. The key to success is to define in advance the priorities and time commitments to the various activities likely to cause tension for the employee, along with a process to resolve conflicts that will inevitably occur. (If the company is unionized, seniority or step rates may regulate the pay increases instead.) Alternatively, those companies reluctant to raise base pay for a temporary team role should consider recognizing members' contributions through noncash recognition and spot cash awards (see Chapter 7).

## Process Teams

For teams operating in a process culture, there is arguably the greatest variety of potential approaches to increasing base pay. Some companies favor the "all-for-one, one-for-all" general wage increase, particularly for teams composed of hourly and/or nonexempt workers. However, a more progressive mix of components may be used to determine raises, starting with:

- Skill-based pay, as a good means to get people to learn skills. Paying for skills—rewarding employees for incremental progress—is also consistent with the continuous-improvement orientation of process cultures. From there it can evolve into:
- Pay tied to demonstration of desired competencies, to ensure the presence of behaviors needed to spur maximum team performance. Paying for incremental progress over baseline competencies is consistent with the emphasis on continuous improvement. Eventually this approach may lead to:
- Peer evaluations, or 360-degree/multi-rater assessments of team members' contributions to the overall performance of the unit.

## Project Teams

Program or project teams in time-based cultures may have the greatest variation in the education and expertise of their members and, accordingly, in their base pay. Restructuring base pay for these temporary teams is impractical and unwarranted; because, as a rule, people are on (long-term) loan from different departments, there is less concern about internal equity than there is with other teams. Thus, as with parallel teams, project teams may be most amenable to individual performance ratings as a way of granting merit increases. Outstanding people may receive raises twice the size of those given to average performers; alternatively, everyone may receive a small merit increase, with the rest of the gain used to fund a team-based incentive program contingent upon achieving predefined results.

The use of a skill- or competency-based pay program in this culture is more problematic. Paying for *incremental* skills or competencies may be impractical in a culture where the emphasis is on becoming the best in the fastest way possible. Thus, rewards should be weighted toward full possession and immediate *application* of the skills and competencies that have been deemed critical to success; it is necessary to demonstrate competencies, not merely to develop them. And because these teams tend to be multifunctional, an individual would need to demonstrate competencies in a wider variety of areas before earning additional rewards.

The exception to this rule may be "permanent" project teams, such as those devoted to systems or information technology, that reform every several months as each project moves toward completion and another begins. On such teams, members may be treated more like members of process teams, rewarded for the acquisition of incremental skills and competencies that enhance the work of the team. A pay structure can be created that encourages people to become better team members and, ultimately, team or project leaders.

See Exhibit 6-4 for a summary of team-based approaches to increasing base pay.

# Increasing Base Pay: A How-to Guide for Teams

Having chosen its approach to increasing base pay, a company must still set parameters. In other words, how much? how often? Below, I offer some rules of thumb.

To have an impact, you must have a meaningful differentiation in pay. In our view at Hay, "meaningful" is at least 15 percent between levels of pay. (We'd also put a promotion at that level.)

But, what if everybody at the company is getting a raise? How do you differentiate the top performers? The superior employee should receive *twice* the increase of the average or competent employee. And the less-than-average employee—that is, the one who "does not meet

**Exhibit 6-4. Increase approaches.**

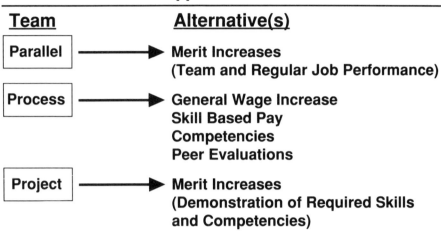

| Team | Alternative(s) |
|------|----------------|
| Parallel | ➤ Merit Increases (Team and Regular Job Performance) |
| Process | ➤ General Wage Increase, Skill Based Pay, Competencies, Peer Evaluations |
| Project | ➤ Merit Increases (Demonstration of Required Skills and Competencies) |

expectations"—gets no raise at all. See Exhibit 6-5 for effective increase recommendations.

In a competency- or skill-acquisition pay program, there is an alternative way to determine base-pay increases: on the demonstration of a competency or certification of a skill. General increases might be granted to all competent employees which, over time, maintain competitive market position and typically closely follow the Consumer Price Index. Real growth, however, is contingent on created added value. The following example at a leading service company illustrates how best to use base pay increase dollars to pay for competencies in a team environment. This organization has established varying behaviors (states of performance) from high to low around each competency, as follows:

*Performance Levels*

7    Can do all of the team's jobs acceptably or better. Does work in ways that develop new best practices for satisfaction of customers and effectiveness of the team's process.

6    Can do all of the team's jobs better than beginners, and many acceptably or better. Does work in ways that demonstrate the best practices for the effectiveness of the team's process.

5    Can do most of the team's jobs better than beginners, and more than one acceptably. Does work in ways that support and improve effectiveness of the team's process.

4    Can do all of the team's jobs at or below the same job level acceptably or better than beginners. Does work in effective ways that fill the expected role as well as the assigned job.

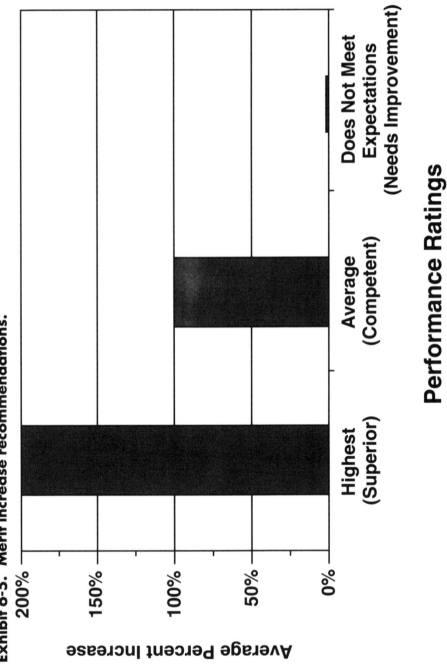

Exhibit 6-5. Merit increase recommendations.

3       Can do all of the team's jobs at or below the same job level
        better than beginners, and fills the expected role acceptably or
        better.
2       Can fill the expected role on the team acceptably or better.
1       Qualified for a job on the team and can do it at a beginner level.

To calculate base-pay increases determined on the highest-level
behavior demonstrated "often" (see Chapter 5 for additional ways to
assess competency achievement), here is one guide:

| Behavior Level | Target Pay Level (% of Band Minimum) |
|---|---|
| 7 | 300% (band maximum) |
| 6 | 267 |
| 5 | 233 |
| 4 | 200 |
| 3 | 167 |
| 2 | 133 |
| 1 | 100 |

Step 1:     Assess employee's competency level.
Step 2:     Calculate employee's base pay as a percent of pay band
            minimum.
Step 3:     Determine difference between desired actual base pay.
Step 4:     If actual pay equals or exceeds target base pay, then pro-
            vide no increase.
Step 5:     If actual pay is less than target pay and not greater than
            twice the base-salary increase budget, then provide in-
            crease up to the target level. If the difference between ac-
            tual and target pay is greater than twice the increase
            budget, then divide the difference by a factor of between
            2 to 3, and grant that amount as the base-pay increase,
            with a minimum being twice the average budget base sal-
            ary increase amount. In this case, the employee will reach
            the target pay level within two to three years if he/she
            continues to perform at the current behavioral compe-
            tency level.

Of course the minimum target base pay must be reviewed annually
to assure that the pay range is consistent with the organization's philosophy regarding market competitiveness. Band adjustments provide a basis to increase all employees' pay without having to
demonstrate a higher level of behavioral performance.

There must also be set times to evaluate employees' acquisition of skills and demonstration of competencies. Typical programs evaluate employee performance of those who work on teams as follows:

- Parallel: normal review cycle every twelve months—generally on the employee's anniversary or from date of last increase or a common date for all employees
- Process: more often than parallel: quarterly or semiannually based upon the team's maturity and time required to acquire skills and demonstrate competencies
- Project: normal review date or project milestones, which can create a sense of urgency associated with a time-based culture

## Notes

1. "You Don't Say," *Personnel Journal*, January 1994, p. 18.
2. Bradford A. Johnson and Harry H. Ray, "Employee-Developed Pay System Increases Productivity," *Personnel Journal*, November 1993, p. 112.

# 7
# Recognition Awards

"I don't get no . . . recognition . . ."

With apologies to the Rolling Stones, I'd say that's one of the most common laments of the workplace of the 1990s. When workers are asked about job satisfaction, one item that continually goes to the top of their list as a source of dissatisfaction is a lack of recognition for their contributions to the company and their impact on its results.

And in a team environment, the likelihood that contributions—by both the team and individual members—will go unrecognized or underrecognized is even greater. With their traditional orientation toward individuals, management may give short shrift to team accomplishments. Supervisors may not be aware of each member's contribution, especially when it's a self-managed team.

Yet recognition for the people who serve on a team may be more critical than for those who work by themselves, because there is also the danger that people will feel their identity has been subsumed by the team. Recognition, if handled correctly, can give people the strokes they need while increasing team cohesiveness. It can foster many of the team competencies modeled in Chapter 3: commitment, flexibility, adaptability. Positive recognition is one of the most powerful motivators managers and supervisors have, and it can cost virtually nothing—just a little time, energy, and forethought.

## Why Recognition?

One of the smartest things companies can do is to develop a systematic program of recognition of team results. This is also known as recognition and reward, or as spot cash awards, or, more exuberantly, as a "celebration" of success. By whatever name, recognition awards value contribution "after the fact"—that is, when the performance is known. That is in contrast to incentive compensation which, as I discuss in Chapter 8, provides employees with the opportunity to earn extra compensation under an arrangement that has been determined "before the fact," that is, before performance is known. And while incentive compensation typically rewards recurring performance, recognition celebrates a one-time "event," although that event might be a milestone achieved or successful completion of a project of several months' duration.

Unlike incentive plans, which are generally guided by a corporate initiative, recognition awards can be distributed at the local or team level. As a result, they can be introduced easily, quickly, and inexpensively, without layers of approval and analyses of how they fit into the corporate compensation architecture. For that reason, many companies find them preferable to incentive plans. However, because they are after-the-fact, recognition programs carry less of a front-end motivational impact than incentives. As I discuss in Chapter 9, they're not mutually exclusive.

Recognition can come in two shapes: cash and noncash. Noncash awards, which are the most common, tend to be given out for a job well done and are usually of nominal value. Jack Manes, director of human resources for North American operations of Cabot Corporation, a Boston-based chemicals company, calls the company's small tokens of gratitude—$25 and a candy-filled mug that says "110%"— "attaboy, attagirl" rewards. Cash awards can be far more substantial—although usually they're small bonuses—and, depending on the corporation, may be given only for efforts that have a measurable financial impact. There's a rule of thumb that's implicit in this difference, and that many companies instinctively follow: To recognize efforts and activities above expectations, give noncash awards. To get *results*, pay cash. (See Exhibit 7-1.)

In theory, all spot cash awards (sometimes called lightning bolts) are for achievement that exceeds reasonable expectations. Precisely what constitutes "reasonable," however, depends partly on the position of the people involved. If a manager generates a cost-saving idea, it may be said that he was just doing his job. If a support person on the team comes up with the idea, however, that's well beyond his/ her job description, and it's worth recognizing.

Does recognition work? There's strong evidence it does, judging from the findings of a 1994 Hay survey of eighty-six large U.S. corporations represented in The Business Roundtable, an association of some 200 chief executives of the largest U.S. companies. The survey sought to determine which reward and recognition strategies were effective in achieving total quality management (TQM). Of the business units surveyed, 61 percent reported that cash recognition was

**Exhibit 7-1. Recognition awards.**

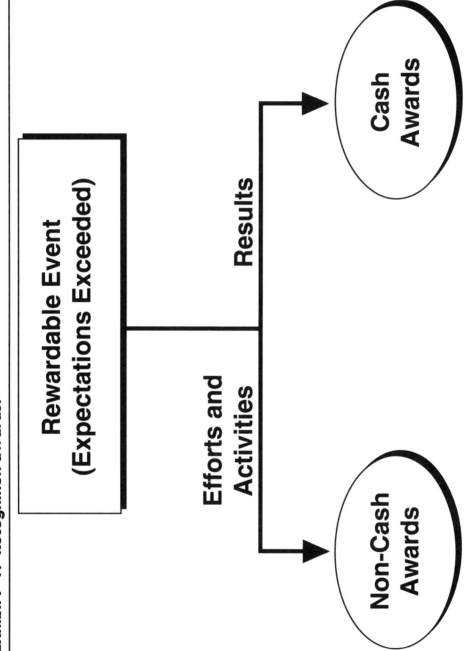

effective in advancing quality objectives among clerical/nonexempt workers, and 63 percent said spot cash was effective for hourly/production workers. Noncash recognition got even higher marks: 76 percent said it was effective for clerical/nonexempt workers, and 84 percent said it was effective for hourly/production workers. (Effectiveness at the executive/management level was much lower, while incentive compensation and performance ratings had the highest rankings.)

Moreover, the "best practice" units—defined in the survey as those units that reported specific reward practices as having greatly advanced their quality efforts—tended to reward a greater percentage of their employees. In these units, 23 percent of the hourly employees received spot cash awards, compared with only 10 percent in other units. By the same token, almost 40 percent of the nonexempt employees in best-practice business units received noncash awards, compared with only 14 percent in the other units. That number jumped to 44 percent of the best-practice hourly workers, compared with only 18 percent of those in other units.

How widespread is the use of recognition? In Hay's 1994 survey of compensation practices by nearly 600 organizations that took part in its annual compensation conferences, 38 percent reported using spot awards—more than any other variable pay program—and 35 percent said they were considering such programs.

Finally, it's noteworthy that recognition appears to be a standard feature at those companies that are acknowledged leaders. Of the early (1988–89) winners of the Malcolm Baldrige Award for Quality Management, all eight had utilized recognition award programs. And a separate recent Hay survey of fifteen benchmarked world-class companies (all of which had noncash recognition programs, and most of which also distributed spot cash awards) found that their most enthusiastic comments were for those recognition programs that supported *team* efforts.

In this chapter, I discuss the various forms of cash and noncash awards, and identify which are most appropriate for different team types. I also provide a guide to implementing a recognition program and describe in detail the programs in place at two leading companies.

## Dollars and Sense

How much should a company spend on a recognition program? How much bang does a company get for its recognition bucks? In our survey of benchmarked companies, we found considerable variation in total outlay. The budgeted cost of programs ranged from 0.3 percent to 1.5 percent of payroll, with 1 percent being typical. But some companies that are big believers in recognition spend far more. At AT&T Universal Card Services, for instance, it's 2 percent of payroll, although that amount also includes expenses like an occasional free lunch for all employees when the company meets a milestone. (For more on AT&T's recognition and reward programs, see the case study later in this chapter.)

In the benchmark survey, the size of the award also varied significantly, from $100 to $15,000, with the average much closer to the low end. However, companies that are trying to calculate the impact of the award must consider the after-tax effect. All cash awards and cash-equivalent awards greater than $25 (savings bonds, gift certificates, weekend packages, tickets to sporting events or movies, merchandise, mementos) are considered income by the Internal Revenue Service and are taxed as such. Exceptions generally exist for service and safety achievement awards, which exclude up to $400 of tangible awards, for example, service pins, jewelry or other merchandise, etc.

Some companies "gross up" the prize so that the recipient realizes the full value of the award, a practice that typically increases the cost of the program by one third. Other companies decline to do so, and some companies gross up smaller prizes but draw the line at doing so for those over, say, $100.

As with all cash awards, the impact on overtime pay needs to be considered. See Chapter 8 for further discussion.

## Noncash Awards

There is an almost infinite variety of noncash rewards that companies can hand out to recognize the contribution of employees. It ranges from the most modest—a thank-you note for a job well done—to the most lavish, like an all-expenses-paid trip for two to the Caribbean. Between those two extremes are the vast majority of noncash rewards that are sometimes unkindly dismissed as "trinkets and trash" or more elegantly described as "symbolic": plaques, T-shirts, stickers on hard hats, vouchers for coffee or lunch in the company cafeteria, pins and caps.

In their design, such items often play on the company image, strengthening the connection between employer and employee. Cigna, whose corporate logo is a tree, sends out its thank-yous on leaf-shaped note cards, while the Unisys motif is a computer keyboard. And there are the plethora of polo shirts, T-shirts, coffee mugs, and other items that are stamped with the company logo or the trademark of a product.

Companies also recognize employees by giving them the opportunity to break bread with senior management or include them in an event, such as a senior management meeting, normally reserved for the upper echelons of the corporation. For example, at The Vanguard Group, the financial services company, president Jack Brennan sits down to breakfast each month with the members of one of the Vanguard Quality Partnership teams that has just completed a project. (Vanguard uses these cross-functional, parallel teams to address issues from work-family programs to reducing copying costs.) Breakfast with Brennan in Valley Forge, Pennsylvania, may not rival the one in New Orleans, but it gives people from all levels of the company a chance to increase their visibility with top management.

Noncash rewards may also be an extremely useful way of saying "Thanks, but" for behavior that companies want to recognize but feel they shouldn't reward in the conventional sense. For example, many corporations give lip service to risk-taking by employees, but tend to look the other way (at best) if it fails. At Cabot's Atlanta location, however, there's a presentation every quarter for what the company determines is a "notable failure": a trophy of a flounder on a marble base. The "fish on a stick," as it's known, has gone to employees such as the individual who tried unsuccessfully to save Cabot money by changing its car-rental policy.

On the subject of noncash recognition, two warnings:

First, companies shouldn't confuse office Christmas parties or the Friday night beer blasts that were popular in Silicon Valley a decade or two ago with recognition. (Both of which, by the way, have been the victim of business trends as contrary as downsizing and growth, as well as a number of social changes.) While there's nothing wrong with such "feel good" events, which probably do build esprit de corps, they're too all-encompassing to convey a sense that any one group's accomplishments are being celebrated. To be effective, recognition must be focused on the team whose achievements are being celebrated.

Secondly, in designing its recognition programs, management should be sure that employees are as enthusiastic about the recognition or reward as the company is itself. If they're not, it can actually be counterproductive. AT&T Universal Card Services, for example, at one time used an air horn to trumpet its announcement of "Power of One" award winners. However, employees—who, as discussed in Chapter 8, work on an incentive plan under which their activities and results are measured daily—were concerned that the distraction would bother cardholders, thus reducing customer satisfaction.

# Cash Awards

The standards for cash awards should be higher and more exacting. In the best of all worlds, anytime a company recognizes an event with real dollars, it should be not merely measurable but productive of tangible financial gain. Admittedly, we don't live in the best of all worlds, and many companies choose to recognize actions that they believe will prove financially significant down the road.

One reason that standards should be higher is that, to be meaningful, cash awards are relatively expensive (compared to, say, that candy-filled mug). To have an impact, a cash award should generally be at least $250 and preferably $500, depending in part on the base pay of the people involved. (I sometimes use the VCR test: The reward should be big enough to buy a standard video cassette recorder for the individual.) Cash awards for teams typically can go up to $5,000 per member. However, usually it's individuals who get the largest awards.

If the company dislikes the idea of handing out cold cash, and some do, it can distribute it under another guise. Since 1986, for example, American Airlines has recognized employees with a point system, in which points translate to hard dollars (200 points are $1). Employees can earn points in three ways. They can be cited for special service by customers who are frequent fliers; they can get a "check" on the spot from a manager or supervisor for exceeding expectations, such as handling skillfully the rebooking of passengers from a canceled flight; or—the most lucrative possibility—they can collect points for proposing ideas that pay off. (For more about this program, see Chapter 8.) The points, in effect, are deposited in American's AAchievers bank, and may be redeemed by employees for merchandise, gift certificates, and travel.

Had it given money directly, says John Ford, director, World Class IdeAAs, personnel resources, employees might have confused the payments as compensation or come to view them as an entitlement. Since American deals with a number of unions, it was particularly reluctant to meddle with the compensation structure. This way, says Ford, "it's like fun money." And it's popular: Almost half of American's union employees have participated in the ideas programs.

# Recognition for Teams

The issues I've addressed generally apply to teams and individuals alike. For teams, however, there is one additional set of issues: Should all team members be recognized equally? Team members tend to say yes. Management tends to say no. The correct answer depends, as usual, on the type of team and the corporate culture. I'll discuss each in this section.

## *Recognition for Parallel Teams*

In a parallel setting, both cash and noncash awards can be used to reward the team. However, noncash awards are considerably more popular for this type of team. The 1995 Hay Team Based Pay Survey found that, of companies with parallel teams, 49 percent used noncash awards and another 16 percent were considering doing the same. In contrast, only 37 percent had spot cash awards, with 7 percent considering adding such programs.

On parallel and project teams, whose members are likely to represent different functions and layers in the hierarchy and to contribute accordingly to team results, there may be situations where different levels of reward are justified. As I've said earlier, some team members are more equal than others, and can be recognized as such. In fact, I'll go farther: They should be recognized differently. Doing so sets up a role model for everybody else in the company: "If you work in a certain way, you'll be rewarded. If you work even better, you'll be rewarded better."

However, any company that differentiates among members in its rewards must be sure that the differential is defensible—and must be willing, if necessary, to say so in public. In compensation, as also noted earlier, there can be no secrets. Take the case of a team within Mobil Corporation's U.S. Marketing and Refining Division, which was able to interpret regulations to meet and exceed certain requirements by adopting new technologies. The team saved the company some several hundred thousand dollars. For that, the team leader was awarded $3,000 and each member $1,000. Before divvying up the award, however, the division's spot award committee made sure that allocation was fully accepted by the team itself by conducting a focus group. See Chapter 10 for further discussion on soliciting employee opinions.

Whether the award is cash or noncash, it's likely to be relatively modest. For one thing, parallel teams, unlike project teams, are usually chartered for a specific task. While some parallel teams propose ideas, such as the St. Joseph Hospital suggestion teams cited in Chapter 2, far more typical is the situation where the team will be asked to research or implement an idea that has originated elsewhere, usually from management. Furthermore, because the members have full-time jobs, the expectations of success for parallel teams are not as high.

Here are three possible outcomes for parallel teams, with appropriate forms of recognition:

1. *Success* (the team's recommendations are implemented, with desired results). The company may give cash.
2. *Mixed results* (the team's recommendations are implemented but results are disappointing, or the team's recommendations are accepted but not implemented). The company recognizes the team's efforts, probably through a noncash award.
3. *Failure* (the team's recommendations are rejected). Management may "thank" the team, perhaps with a memo to all members noting their hard work.

As an example of how recognition can be used for mixed or ambiguous results, here is the real-life case of a praiseworthy team effort to rectify a decidedly unpraiseworthy team mistake. In this company, which will go unnamed, a part-time parallel team of engineers had reformulated a product. What the team had overlooked was that the reformulation was better suited to the sunny climes of the Southwest, where they were headquartered, than to the cold temperatures of, say, New England. When the product went on the market, their miscalculation became apparent immediately. For the next week, the engineers set up and manned a telephone hotline around the clock to answer customers' concerns.

Should the company recognize the engineers' hard work and good intentions despite the blunder—and if so, how? One option was to provide a spot cash award. Or should the company take a hard-line approach that would focus on results and fire the "culprits"? But there was also a middle route available, which is what the company chose. It printed up and distributed T-shirts that stated, "I survived the 'week from hell.' " It was a dubious award, but so was their achievement.

## Recognition for Process Teams

Process or work team members are equally likely to receive spot cash and noncash awards—42 percent versus 41 percent, according to the Hay 1995 Team-Based Pay Survey. (On the other hand, as I discuss in

Chapter 8, the use of cash in incentive compensation is even more widespread.)

One reason for the preference for incentive compensation is that process teams' achievements are generally a matter of incremental improvement. However, spot cash awards may be distributed to process teams in recognition of certain milestones—for example, the training of every member in a new skill, or the conversion of all the data to a new system.

Another advantage to incentive compensation for process teams is that they are less likely to create disharmony. Whether they differentiate or not, spot cash awards have a greater potential to create a sense of inequity. Somebody may feel he/she should have received more, or that everybody should have received the same. (This is less significant an issue for project or parallel teams, which dissolve when the job is completed.)

Noncash awards not only can prevent discord on the team; they can actually bring the team together. For example, an appropriate nod of recognition to a team that has met a milestone might be breakfast at a local restaurant. At LEGO Systems, Inc., teams got treated to pizza when three consecutive shifts met a certain level of production. Because it's the entire team that is being rewarded, such celebrations have to be carefully scheduled around regular work hours. Individual achievement is also possible if a suggested improvement or educational milestone is completed by a team member.

## Recognition for Project Teams

In a time-based environment, companies are almost equally likely to use noncash awards and spot cash awards—53 percent and 48 percent, respectively, according to the Hay survey. It is on project teams that the opportunity for sizable cash awards is the most substantial. If, for example, a team of scientists at a small biotech company comes up with a new therapy, their reward may be royalties in the new drug. Or a team that generates the basis for a new business unit could be rewarded with so-called phantom stock in that unit—an interest, on paper only, that would be purchased by the company at a specified future date and at a pseudo-market rate established by a predetermined formula.

However, those are the sorts of awards of which dreams are made. Far more typical is a noncash award for a team that has met expectations, or a cash award for a team that has exceeded expectations. For example, a team that has been given specific parameters for the development of a new product or service—to bring it in by a certain time, within a certain budget—and that beats either the dead-line or the price tag or both may receive a sizable cash award. As I said earlier, the award should be linked to a real financial measure. Getting to market early for a drug or computer company, for example, can have immense financial impact; getting into the stores by Christmas for a toy company can be a make-or-break issue. (See Exhibit 7-2 for guidelines on the use of recognition awards by team type.)

## Implementing Recognition: A Guide

Recognition programs are arguably the easiest of all compensation programs to implement: They can be comparatively simple, inexpensive, and nonbureaucratic. The Hay survey of benchmarked companies found that measurement criteria were typically undefined and at the discretion of management "after the fact." Still, to avoid being seen as arbitrary, and to have maximum possible impact, recognition programs need to take note of the following elements:

• *Purpose/objective.* The program should formalize the company's approach to recognizing team contributions and results that exceed expectations and support the business's strategies. It may be driven by financial or operational results, or by less tangible measures, such as customer satisfaction. In either case, it should provide a sense of celebration of what has been accomplished, and a way to communicate to employees what the company values.

• *Eligibility.* In designing their recognition programs, some companies exclude senior executives who have their own, more lucrative incentive plans; others exclude union members. The Hay survey of fifteen benchmarked companies found that, in most cases, all employees were eligible to participate. Depending on their culture, companies must strike a balance between recognizing individuals and recognizing teams. Finally, they must consider how frequently employees may be eligible for spot cash awards for different accomplishments: once a year, twice a year, or as frequently as the award is given out.

• *Program award levels.* I recommend the use of a few levels to recognize different accomplishments and degrees of contribution. Here's a sample:

1. *Appreciation noncash awards,* for recognition/extra effort, up to a maximum fair market value of $250 (grossed up so the recip-

Exhibit 7-2. Recognition approach guidelines.

| Award \ Team Type | Parallel | Process | Project |
|---|---|---|---|
| Non-Cash | Primary | Primary | Primary |
| Cash | Secondary | Secondary | Primary |

ient nets the full value). Typical awards include letters of appreciation, gift certificates, plaques, tickets to a sporting event, company insignia items (jackets, caps). In determining the types of appreciation awards within their function or department, supervisors should take the opportunity to develop forms of rewards that are meaningful to their employees.

2. *Awards for "significant financial contribution."* Cash awards, ranging from $250 to $2,500 (not grossed up), for team members whose efforts significantly exceed expectations, support the unit's efforts, and produce measurable results.

3. *Awards for "extraordinary financial results."* Cash awards, between $2,500 and $10,000, for team members whose efforts have exceptional bottom-line impact.

• *Benefit implications.* Recognition awards are not considered benefit bearing (that is, they have no effect on pension, insurance, savings plans, etc.) and are not included in salary for the calculation of overtime since they are viewed as discretionary and not based on predetermined criteria. If the goals and potential award amounts were preselected, then the overtime implications would be different.

• *Funding.* Recognition programs, unlike incentive plans, are typically funded out of the expense budget of the business unit or department, and are often stated as a percentage of total payroll. Over time, however, the financial results generated through the program should allow the more expensive awards to be self-funded. Program expenses should be budgeted annually.

• *Types of awards: noncash versus cash.* In finding an appropriate balance between the two, companies need to consider the pros and cons discussed earlier in this chapter. As for administering the two types of awards, some companies link them under the same administrative guidelines. However, since noncash recognition tends to be more modest, local, and spontaneous, it may be preferable to have two separate programs.

• *Nomination procedure.* Particularly for awards at the "appreciation" level, the nomination procedure should be as simple as possible, and teams should establish their own guidelines. For company-wide rewards, nomination procedures may be much more elaborate with peers, customers, and supervisors all having an opportunity to nominate individuals and teams for cash and noncash awards.

• *Approval process.* The bigger or more expensive the award, the higher the level it must go for approval. For an "appreciation award," approval authority should be the immediate supervisor, within the guidelines established by the function or department.

Approval authority of a $250 to $2,500 award could be the manager of the department or unit, with endorsement by Human Resources. During the initial year of the program, to establish consistency, the approval authority should probably be at a higher level until the organization acquires experience with these types of programs.

Approval authority for a $2,500 to $10,000 award is the business unit's leadership team.

• *Timing.* All awards should be given "on the spot," or as close to the event as possible, to reinforce the program's objective of recognizing and celebrating achievement. Therefore the program administrator must initiate the payroll process for a cash award before the winner is notified, and order the engraving of a plaque or trophy in sufficient time before the award presentation.

• *Award presentation.* At what decibel level management chooses to announce the award should reflect the company's culture or style. In addition, the celebration should be in proportion to the prize; the presentation of an appreciation award may be handled within the office or department, while a $5,000 cash award may call for a recognition ceremony in one of the corporation's big meeting rooms.

In either case, as guidelines for the presentation, your company should:

1. *Make this a positive experience,* which makes the winner feel proud.
2. *Personalize your comments,* referring to the key points of the accomplishment and what the winner(s) did to achieve the results.
3. *Comment on the relationship between the winner's achievement and the business strategies/goals of the department, business unit, or company.*
4. *Give an appropriate message of recognition.* Use this occasion to communicate pride and appreciation.
5. *Never present the award "in passing."* Depending on the level of the award, it should be presented by the employee's immediate supervisor or higher management. This is not the occasion to delegate.
6. *Publicize.* Arrange to have Human Resources or Internal Communications tack a memo onto the bulletin board, post the team's photographs on a "wall of fame" in the company

lobby, include an item in the business unit or company news-letter.

• *Program evaluation.* Annually, a rewards and recognition group appointed by senior management of the business unit, with people from Human Resources, should be chartered to evaluate the program against its purpose and objectives. Among the questions the group should ask:

1. Did behavior change? Were employees motivated toward new values and team contribution?
2. Did the program achieve operational improvements?
3. Does the program avoid the "entitlement syndrome"?
4. Have we achieved consistency in rewards and recognition?
5. Does the program have employee acceptance?
6. Was the program well implemented and well integrated?
7. Is the program self-funding?

## Case Study: Recognition at AT&T Universal Card

Four times a year at AT&T Universal Card Services' headquarters in Jacksonville, Florida, or its sites in Salt Lake City and Columbus, Georgia, the company recognizes employees and teams that have made a special contribution. Flowers and balloons are delivered to recipients' desks, and the president of the business unit presents plaques to winning teams. Each team member also receives a gold ring (for successive wins, diamonds are added to the rings). Company-wide award winners' pictures are hung on a wall in the lobby. "The whole day is devoted to recognizing the winners," says Debbie Patrick, recognition manager, human resources, at AT&T Universal Card Services.

The quarterly award for team achievement is one of seven company-wide recognition and reward programs at AT&T Universal Card. (Individual departments also have their own recognition programs.) And while three of those programs are limited to individual "associates" or employees, three others are open to teams—and a fourth is exclusively for teams. Candidates for that award include, in the company's words, "any cross-functional team or special project/task force group that completes a project in the prior quarter, or a functional work group team that completes a project or exceeds their set objectives in the prior quarter"—in other words, parallel, project, and process teams.

To win, the team must improve systems or processes, produce cost savings and/or customer delight (AT&T's term for quality, of which customer satisfaction is the key element), while meeting financial goals and focusing on teamwork. Up to three teams per quarter are selected. Last year, one winner was an "early identification" team, a process team whose job is to detect fraud in credit card accounts. It saved the company some $13 million. Another was a "values in practice" team, a parallel team whose assignment was to overhaul the way the company deals with employee behavioral issues such as tardiness. "Eventually we'll see cost savings due to less absenteeism, but they're not measurable right now," says Patrick.

In addition to the team award program, the other reward and recognition programs for which teams may be nominated are:

• *The President's Circle.* The highest honor AT&T Universal Card gives out, the President's Circle award is given annually to individuals and to one team—cross-functional only—that have shown a commitment to the company's values throughout the length of the project, significantly improved a process and quality, and saved money or generated additional revenue. (In 1994 the winner was a parallel team that spent about fifteen months, part-time, in relocating employees to different office areas at Jacksonville, so that the company was able to give up its lease on a three-story office building. It was estimated that the team brought in the entire project at least $300,000 under budget.) Winners get noncash awards (crystal, a watch, a gold lapel pin), an all-expenses-paid out-of-town trip (New York, in 1995), and invitations to a stream of recognition and team-building events all year long.

• *Community Involvement.* Recognizes one individual or team each month for exceptional service in the community. Teams get a pizza party, $100 donated to a United Way charity of their choice, a plaque and individual/team photo displayed in the lobby. (One recent team winner was the same "early identification" group that had won a team award in 1994. Individually and as a team, members had engaged in numerous good works, from feeding families at a local Ronald McDonald house to cleaning up the beach; for Christmas, the entire team "adopted" a local family.) Most team winners (like the group just described) are process teams whose day-in, day-out sharing of work has helped build strong interpersonal relationships.

• *Key to Quality Service.* Recognizes teams or individuals for "going above and beyond" expectations and job requirements while focusing on quality. Winning teams—usually work teams that have improved a process—receive a letter of congratulations, a plaque, a lapel pin, and a place on the company's Wall of Fame.

## Case Study: Recognition at SmithKline Beecham

As part of a corporate-wide reengineering effort, SmithKline Beecham, the London-headquartered international healthcare company, in 1994 launched a recognition program. It had two parts:

1. A *"Simply the Best" Awards program* that would annually recognize and reward efforts by teams—generally parallel or project teams—to improve specific processes, from customer relations to the use of materials. This program was designed not only to recognize achievements but to stimulate them, a practice that fitted the company's total reengineering effort. Accordingly, the program received a significant amount of attention from top management. Despite the

received a significant amount of attention from top management. Despite the massive effort involved in applying for it, the main reward for the fifteen winning teams each year would not, explicitly, at least, be financial. Rather, it would be the opportunity for team members to present their accomplishments to senior management in London or Philadelphia, the company's U.S. headquarters. However, since the winners were literally from around the world, that represented a nice "out-of-town" noncash award.

(In its first year, the awards program produced winners representing a broad cross section of countries and activities. The leader was a team in the consumer products business in Nairobi, Kenya, which had reduced by 75 percent the cycle time involved in responding to customer (retailer) complaints. Other winners included a production team in Singapore that had significantly reduced the amount of a material used in the manufacture of one of the company's top-selling pharmaceuticals, at an annual savings of some $300,000; and a team in South Africa that had provided bridging education for employees who needed to be brought up quickly to take advantage of the new opportunities for people of color.)

2. *A "grassroots" recognition program* with innumerable ways of recognizing workplace behavior, tailored to the variety of sites and businesses in which SmithKline Beecham operates. Like the "Simply the Best" Awards program, the grassroots program began with the notion that what should be recognized were efforts that went toward meeting customers' needs. However, it was far less formal and more varied. Some of the rewards were for individuals, others for teams; some were ad hoc, others more highly structured. Starting with the shortest time frame, they included:

- *Frequent on-the-spot recognition*
  —Thank-you notes.
  —Coffee break/lunch vouchers for the company cafeteria.
  —Premium parking space.
  —Discount coupons for local products and services, such as movie tickets. Notes, vouchers, and coupons could be given by managers to employees, or by employees to each other as a token of thanks or recognition.
  —"Dress-down" days—employees within a team or business unit can dress casually one or two days per week if the unit has met sales and profit targets.

- *Monthly recognition*
  —"All-hand" plant meetings that all employees may attend.
  —Team updates/sharing best practices: meetings where teams update management and each other on the status of projects.
  —Visits to another plant or facility in another sector of the company.
  —Invitations to attend meetings of the steering committee, normally restricted to management.
  —Customer (internal/external) contact: structured activities, such as focus groups and surveys, that permit interchange with customers.

- *Quarterly recognition*
  —Opportunities to make project presentations to the steering committee of the unit or factory.
  —Visits to vendors.
  —Visits to customers.

- *Annual recognition*
  —Team-sharing events—for example, an annual event in which each team publicly reviews its achievements for the previous year.
  —Fun/education events.
  —Special holiday celebrations.
  —Community service activities.
  —Vendor day—vendors meet with management/purchasing to discuss quality.
  —Zero defects day (culmination of yearlong campaign).
  —Quality day.

# 8

# Incentive Compensation

"Pay is not a motivator."[1]

That comment, from no less august an authority than the late W. Edwards Deming, the father of total quality management, may seem a heretical way to open a chapter on the merits of incentive compensation. But what I'd like to do here is confront its opponents head-on.

It's become fashionable lately to argue that paying for performance is actually demotivating. In his book *Punished by Rewards: The Trouble with Gold Stars, Incentive Plans, A's, Praise, and Other Bribes* (Houghton Mifflin, 1993), Alfie Kohn has argued that workers, rather than being inspired to work better or harder, may in fact work less well when they see themselves working to get a reward. Driven by extrinsic motivation (money) rather than intrinsic motivation (the inherent interest of the work), they lose interest in what they are doing and increasingly perceive work as drudgery.

The trouble with that argument is that it presumes an either-or situation—either you motivate employees (ineffectively, says Kohn) with money, or you motivate them with fulfilling work. Fortunately, it is not an either-or. What Deming was saying, I believe, was that pay cannot be a substitute for a sense of empowerment or interesting and varied work—the very elements that many companies hope to encourage through the creation of teams. Nor can money be a substitute for good management.

By the same token, however, enlightened management cannot be a substitute for money. In fact, money *is* a motivator—a powerful one. Business has always recognized that fact, but traditionally it's reserved incentives, like a great many other goodies, for senior management. Arguing that lower-level workers aren't similarly motivated is not only ivory-tower, it's elitist. I believe that perhaps 80 percent of any employee's activity is dictated by his or her customers, supervisors, peers, and subordinates. It's that remaining 20 percent that we seek to influence through incentives.

Why, then, *team* incentives? The answer is simple: They're the logical extension of paying for teams. Incentives work best when they reward performance that is within the control of the employee. For team members, that means team performance. Kohn has said that rewards create unhealthy competition among workers, but this is less likely to be the case if an entire team is rewarded together. In fact, incentive plans that reward superior team performance should help engender feelings of teamwork, reinforcing team members' sense of accountability and mutual dependency. That is particularly true of process teams, which work together over the long term to achieve the kind of incremental improvements that incentive plans typically reward.

If pay motivates, then, the next question is: *How much pay?* In other words, how large should the incentive be? To be meaningful, the payout should be at least a month's pay. That represents true discretionary income. Hay surveys show that, on process teams, incentive opportunities and payouts typically range between 5 and 10 percent of employees' pay when their base pay is competitive with the marketplace. However, the variation below and above that is great, depending in part on the level of base pay or how much pay is at risk. Finding the best balance between base and incentive pay will be addressed in detail in Chapter 9.

In this chapter, I review the numerous design elements required by a good incentive compensation plan, and then offer illustrations of plans at several companies. Such plans are becoming increasingly common. The Hay 1994 Compensation Conference Survey of nearly 600 companies found that 21 percent already had group or team incentive plans in place, and another 24 percent were considering adding them.

## Designing an Incentive Plan

There is no ideal, one-size-fits-all incentive compensation plan. As organizations evolve from a traditional functional culture, adopt different types of teams, and have varying levels of experience for different periods of time, the application of incentive compensation needs to be customized.

At the same time, all team incentive plans should define a number of basic elements:

1. *Eligibility*—who qualifies for the plan
2. *Participation*—the level at which each member is potentially rewarded
3. *Measurement*—quantifying the criteria used to determine payouts
4. *Goals*—determining how target levels of performance are established and updated
5. *Funding*—paying for the plan payouts
6. *Timing*—the length of the measurement period and when payouts occur
7. *Benefits*—the impact of incentive payouts on salary-related programs such as pension and insurance coverages
8. *Administration*—how the plan is managed
9. *Evaluation*—criteria used to evaluate plan success

This section describes in detail each of these elements and how they may vary from one type of team to the next. But first one point needs to be made: Plans must be relatively simple in design so that they can be readily understood by all employees. It's a cliché to say that communication is important, but in incentive compensation it's a cliché worth repeating. The best-designed plan will only produce random results if employees do not understand what they are supposed to do differently as a result of the plan.

## 1. Eligibility

Every member of the team should be eligible for the plan. As a rule, it's bad business to exclude anybody, even if the team feels that person isn't contributing at the same level to the team goals; to do so is likely to worsen the problem. The single exception to that rule is managerial-level employees who qualify for a separate management incentive plan.

Still, plans should indicate *when* someone becomes eligible or loses eligibility. For example, new hires may qualify only after a three-month probationary period, while employees transferred from another area of the company may be paid on a prorated basis for their time on the team. A prorated payout also applies to people leaving the team for a variety of reasons: transfer to another department, company downsizing, retirement, disability, or even death. However, people who are fired or who are on disciplinary probation on the last day of the plan's measurement cycle are not considered contributors to the results for that period and should not share in the rewards.

## 2. Participation

Determining *how* a plan pays out is a crucial design element. Should all team members receive the same opportunity or payout amount? Or the same percentage of their base pay? (For hourly and nonexempt workers, by law, overtime must be factored into determining payouts. If workers receive the same payout amount, then the premium wages for overtime need to be recomputed, assuming the payout was included in base pay. Alternatively, if payouts are determined as a percentage of pay, then that percentage must be based on wages and overtime earned during the measurement period.) Or should team members be paid on the basis of their contribution to team results? There are a great many variations on the theme. Hay's 1995 Team Based Pay Survey shows that, of the companies that responded, nearly one-third favor the same-dollar-amount option, another third use the same-percentage-of-pay option, and the final third base payouts on the assessment of each member's contribution to the team's success.

There are arguments to be made on behalf of each of these options. The equal-pay and equal-percentage approaches have the not-to-be-discounted advantage of simplicity. Using assessment of individual contributions can add significant complexity, as companies must use one of the performance appraisal methods described in Chapter 5. But the most important determinant of which approach should be used is the type of team being compensated. (See Exhibit 8-1.)

For process teams—where the goal is to minimize differentiation among members, particularly if they all perform the same or similar tasks—a plan that pays equal dollars to all members is the obvious choice. A same-percentage-of-pay plan reinforces differences in base pay, which may be undesirable—particularly if those differences are a historical function, reflecting the fact that people joined the team at different times and performed different tasks or worked in different areas. On the other hand, if differences in base pay reflect different skills, competencies, and contribution to team results, then taking an equal-dollar approach diffuses the impact of those differences, thwarting the intention of the overall compensation structure. In that case, a payout based on same-percentage or relative contribution is more suitable. That's particularly true for project teams, which are typically formed by drawing on people from a wide variety of functions and levels and thus reflect a wide variation in base pay. If, as is the case with some projects, the plan has a substantial payout, it would be unfair to reward nonexempt technicians and product de-

**Exhibit 8-1. Incentive compensation participation.**

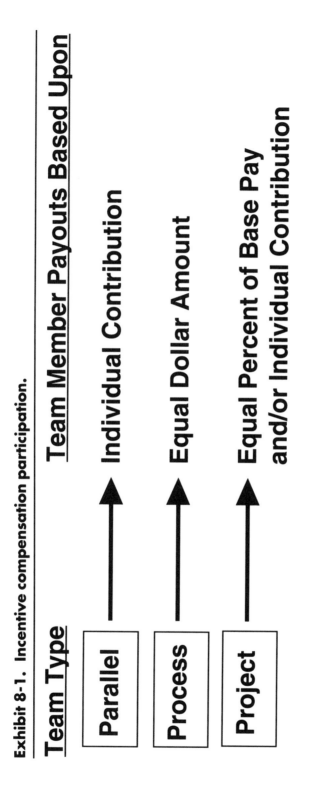

## Team Type

| | Team Member Payouts Based Upon |
|---|---|
| **Parallel** → | **Individual Contribution** |
| **Process** → | **Equal Dollar Amount** |
| **Project** → | **Equal Percent of Base Pay and/or Individual Contribution** |

signers with the same lump-sum payment if they contribute at different levels.

Another complication revolves around hybrid teams with full-time and part-time membership. Should all members have the same opportunity? One suggested approach is to determine each member's opportunity in advance for full or partial shares of the potential incentive award. For example, full-time members would receive 100 percent shares while part-timers would be eligible for one-quarter, half, or three-quarter shares. This would eliminate any bickering at the end of the measurement period while minimizing any misunderstandings in advance. In the event that an inequity occurs, management through a recognition program also has the opportunity to make amends through the granting of a spot cash award.

In general, I'm not an advocate of incentive plans for parallel teams: The danger is that they will create conflict between the members' regular jobs and their team jobs, with employees working harder for the higher bidder. When they are used, however, the most equitable plan is for a payout on the basis of individual contribution. Let's take the hypothetical case of a cost-reduction team. The financial member of the team may devote a lot of extracurricular time to doing cost analyses, while another member just shows up for meetings. Similarly, on an employee suggestion team, one member may generate the idea while the others just nod their agreement. Relative contributions need to be recognized—but preferably, I repeat, through noncash rewards.

## Case Study: Incentives and Parallel Teams

While incentive plans and parallel teams generally don't mix, an exception to that rule is the employee suggestion team. Many organizations have found that such teams, with their explicitly limited scope, have enhanced employee enthusiasm and corporate profits without creating conflicts.

For example, the team proposal system installed at St. Joseph Hospital in Lancaster, Pennsylvania, in 1991 was used to jump-start the organization into a team approach to solving problems and culture change. Some 75 percent of employees voluntarily signed up for the seven-member teams. (Seven is a widely used number because it provides enough people to collect ideas from a variety of perspectives, but keeps the groups small enough so that everyone gets involved.) And the one-year program yielded some nice savings for the hospital and employees. The biggest accepted proposal was for an encoder for the medical records department, which saved the hospital an estimated $250,000 per year—and gave each member of the team that had the idea a minimum of $7,500.

How much of the savings from proposals should be shared with employees is one of the first elements that must be addressed in designing this type of team incentive plan. As a rule, we at Hay recommend about 20 percent of the total savings or revenue gain. On a seven-member team, this gives each team member a 3 percent share, or about $300 on a $10,000 suggestion. In most programs, if a proposal affects the quality of service but no savings or revenue can be directly associated with it, the company should set a fixed level of reward.

American Airlines does the math somewhat differently. As mentioned in Chapter 7, the airline has a company-wide recognition program that uses a point system to reward employees. But the vast majority of points come from "IdeAAs in Action," a company-wide employee suggestion program that rewards people with about $10 million each year in incentive payouts. Although teams generate only 10 percent of the ideas, they account for half of the savings.

When the airline launched the program, it corralled people onto teams—an approach that quickly proved unpopular; members worried about "free riders" who didn't pay their way. Now the teams are self-formed, and points are shared equally by all team members, regardless of whose idea it was. The team gets 10 percent of the savings, up to a top award of $50,000 worth of points; if an idea saves $500,000, the team shares $50,000 in points. The airline distributes an additional 2 percent of savings to other employees involved in implementing the suggestion. "We typically recognize between ten and fifteen people on any idea we approve," says American Airlines' John Ford, director, World Class IdeAAs.

With incentive compensation designed that way, the idea process becomes evolutionary. For example, when smoking was still permitted on most flights, one of the mechanics suggested eliminating one of the four ashtrays traditionally built into a three-seat configuration. Another team suggested taking out both aisle and wall ashtrays, which resulted in $500,000/year in savings.

## 3. Measurement

There are two main ways to measure team results: financial and operational. Financial measures tend to be "bigger," encompassing profit and loss (measured either company-wide or in terms of the team's contribution) or revenues. Operational measures are typically productivity-based and can include a wide variety of factors: cost per ton of steel produced, transactions per hour. Cycle time (the amount of time it takes to produce a product or service) is a favorite: the length of time to process a claim, to answer the phone, to produce a specified product.

As the basis for team incentives, financial measures have several drawbacks. For one thing, an individual team can't control the big financial picture, or the corporate-level decisions that will affect their microfinances. An underwriting team can control the pricing of its premiums, for example, but it can't affect payouts on claims, which are handled by a separate team. For another, an individual team may have just enough control to distort the company's financial picture.

Using the same example, our underwriting team may opt for only minimum-risk policies, as a means of improving their own bottom line. However, the effect of writing fewer policies is to raise the average cost per policy and thus reduce the company's profitability. Thus, the company will need to craft a plan with multiple financial measures, for example, total revenue as well as profits.

Operational measures, by contrast, tend to be more firmly within the team's grasp or its "line of sight." "Financial measures generally measure performance above the facility level; operational measures generally work at or below the facility level," the American Compensation Association noted in its 1994 study of performance-based reward, conducted by the Consortium for Alternative Reward Strategies Research. Ultimately, however, operational measures need to be calibrated back to financial measures, for example, payroll savings from processing more transactions per hour. Otherwise, companies may be paying out when the profits aren't there or rewarding high productivity that's actually counterproductive. Our hypothetical underwriters, for example, may be so intent on productivity—as measured by, say, volume of premiums—that they make costly errors. How does the company prevent them from sacrificing quality or accuracy for the sake of a measure? It needs to input an additional measure, a penalty ranging from 50 to 200 percent of the premium for substantial errors detected internally or externally, respectively.

The effort to improve customer satisfaction—a growing focus of all companies, but particularly those with a process culture—also generates ambiguous productivity measures. As mentioned in Chapter 5, it's easy to confuse customer service and customer satisfaction; in fact (and unfortunately), one doesn't inevitably guarantee the other. Consider the real-life case of a package-delivery company that ordered its customer service employees to answer all telephone calls within two rings. The problem was that, in their haste to answer the phone, clerks often rushed customers when phone traffic was heavy. The results dissatisfied customers. Again, as with our underwriting firm, the company needs to introduce a "modifier": adjusting the size of the reward according to the results of a periodic customer-satisfaction survey. In a customer-driven company, customer satisfaction is a make-or-break measure: If it declines, so should the incentive pool, even if productivity rises. Satisfaction is measured in terms of whether the team meets or exceeds customer expectations, with the standard increasing each year—that is, the team must exceed the level it met the previous year, to be rewarded.

Project teams in time-based organizations typically use another threshold: time. Their goal is to complete the project (get the product to the market, reengineer a process, convert the information system, put up the building) on time but within budget, thus linking operational and financial measures. Incentives can be structured to encourage speed, increasing the size of the pool by, say, 10 percent for each month that the project is ahead of schedule, and reducing it by 20 percent for each month it falls behind. Here, too, the company may need to add "modifiers" to ensure that quality isn't sacrificed in the interest of speed.

One all-important exception to the rule that operational measures must tie in to finances is safety, a critical factor—particularly for manufacturing companies—that is beyond financial quantification. Safety is an absolute: A company may mandate that for every lost-time accident, for example, the size of the pool falls 10 percent, regardless of productivity gains. (And a member with a *personal* lost-time accident may find his award decreased by 50 percent.) Another possible exception is cycle time. There may be cases where, for reasons that aren't readily quantifiable, it's valuable to expedite a process, get to market faster, and so forth. See Exhibit 8-2 for a summary of incentive plan objectives.

## 4. Goals

Any incentive plan's goals must be realistic and fair. Beyond that, however, you have considerable flexibility, in terms of the performance on which to base the goals, the "trigger" or threshold point you set for beginning payouts along with the target and maximum award levels, and the use of different goals for different teams.

Goals can be based on either "historical" performance—that is, how the team has performed in the past—or projected (or budgeted) results. There are pros and cons to each approach.

The most immediate advantage of the historical approach is that employees can readily accept it: They've met that target before, they know they can do it again. They're likely to have little problem with a plan that "freezes" the base period—probably the previous year—and pays them incentive compensation for any improvement over the base period. Management, on the other hand, isn't likely to welcome the idea of being frozen at a low base level and may well prefer to determine incentive payouts on performance against this year's budget, which reflects current (rather than historical) realities. But since management sets the budget, employees may balk.

One popular compromise is a historical approach that includes ways of increasing the base level—widely known as "raising the bar." The most direct method is to increase the base period and give

**Exhibit 8-2. Incentive plan objectives.**

| | Prevalence* |
|---|---|
| Financial Performance | 41% |
| Productivity | 37 |
| Customer Satisfaction | 35 |
| Quality of Goods or Services | 30 |

*Does not add to 100% since companies have multiple objectives.

Source: Hay 1995 Team-Based Pay Survey (U.S.A.)

employees a one-time payment to compensate them for lost incentive opportunity. This is a problematic solution, because employees and management will inevitably disagree over the size of the buyout. The better solution—one that companies can live with, year after year—is a *rolling average*, in which an organization uses as a basis the results of several previous measurement periods, thus raising the bar by increments each cycle. Process teams, which strive toward continuous, incremental improvement, are well suited to this approach.

A rolling average works this way: Let's say the team produced 10,000 widgets in year 1, 15,000 widgets in year 2, and 20,000 widgets in year 3. The average for the three years is 15,000. In year 4, the team produces 25,000 widgets and receives incentive payouts for exceeding the threshold (average of years 1, 2, and 3) by 10,000. In year 5, under the three-year rolling average, the threshold has risen to 20,000 (average of years 2, 3, and 4), so if the team produces 25,000 widgets, it's rewarded for the extra 5,000. Eventually, as the example indicates, the payouts may reach a point of diminishing returns without increased productivity, process and/or technological changes. Management may decide not to pay incentives at stagnant productivity levels, or may select different criteria to measure productivity as a basis for incentive compensation.

On the other hand, let's say that the company then introduces new technology that doubles virtually overnight the rate at which it can produce widgets. In year 6, the team produces 50,000 widgets. How are the workers rewarded? The company has to steer a careful middle course, giving the workers an incentive to deploy the new technology without forfeiting its own profits by giving them a windfall. If its incentive plan is based on its budget, management can "ramp up" the goal, gradually raising the bar while passing along some of the profit to workers. While ramping up is a budgetary approach, in this case, companies that pay on a historical approach may also ramp up, renegotiating a new frozen base or a new rolling average. An approach that will garner the greatest goodwill and take advantage of the technological improvements would overpay initially in order for the company to realize its gains faster. Fairness, equity, and reasonableness are the keys.

Now that you've got your base level of performance, do you start paying out as soon as production exceeds it? Where do you set your threshold? As indicated earlier, and as the graph in Exhibit 8-3 shows, you have a few payout formula options. You can take a straight-line approach (A), making an equal incentive payment for each additional widget produced. Or you can start paying out at a certain "trigger" point, when production exceeds a specified level;

**Exhibit 8-3. Incentive compensation payout formula.**

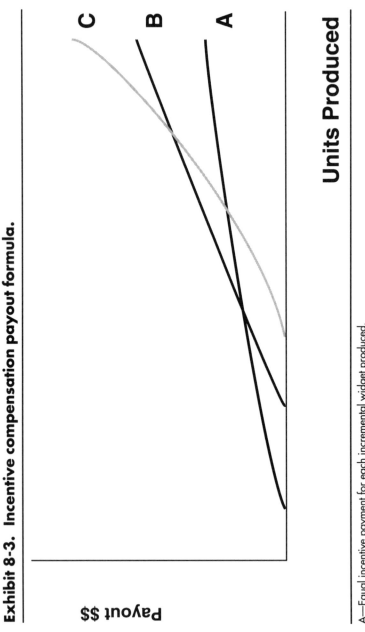

Payout $$

Units Produced

C
B
A

A—Equal incentive payment for each incremental widget produced.
B—Payout "triggered" when production exceeds specified level, hence higher per-widget payout.
C—Incremental payout geometrically rises when specific production level exceeded.

with this approach (B), companies tend to have a higher per-widget payout. Or, finally (C), you can pay more, per widget, above a certain production volume, in recognition of the fact that your overhead has been absorbed and consequently each additional widget has greater economic value.

Which curve on the graph you choose is a function of the compensation architecture your company has developed, as I discuss at length in Chapter 9. For now, however, note that if the worker's base salary is comparatively low or he/she has substantial pay at risk, the threshold should be pegged lower to improve his opportunity to catch up through incentive compensation. By the same token, if the base salary matches the market's, then the threshold can be set for average or above-average performance—that is, line B or C.

So now you have a basis for establishing goals—but goals for whom? Just as there is no one-size-fits-all incentive plan for teams, a company may need to establish a range of goals to fit teams that are doing essentially the same work but have different levels of experience, pay, and performance. Not to do so creates inequities that can be destructive to teamwork: A goal that's realistic for the top-performing team would probably be unattainable for the poorest performer. On the other hand, if you set completely separate goals for each team, you may be penalizing the high-performing team for having a strong track record.

The challenge is to craft a payout formula that will be fair and flexible enough to provide incentives for all teams. (But not all *types* of teams; while the issue is relevant to process teams, it would not arise with project teams, which have different milestones.) To illustrate, let's go back to the underwriting team—as it happens, one of four in the firm—described earlier. Because each team's total compensation expense was different, reflecting its size, members' experience, and performance, a productivity measure of labor cost per premium dollar was developed. Without normalizing the various team results, it appeared that the best-performing team was the third most productive while the worst team looked second best. After adjustments, the highest-performing team naturally had the lowest cost ($4.50) while the worst-performing team had the highest ($7). A payout matrix was devised to accommodate all four teams (see Exhibit 8-4). Goals were twofold: absolute cost per premium dollar, and cost improvement percentage.

Under this formula, the worst team will get only 50 percent of its target award if it has no improvement in productivity, and 100 percent if it reduces costs per unit by 15 percent, which also results in an approximate $6 cost per premium dollar. On the other hand, if the

**Exhibit 8-4.   Incentive payout matrix.**

**% of Target Award**

| Cost Per Premium Dollar | Cost Increases | 0% | 10% | 15% | 20% | 25% |
|---|---|---|---|---|---|---|
| | | | **Cost Improvement Percentage** | | | |
| Greater Than $7.00 | 0 | 0 | 0 | 0 | 0 | 0 |
| $7.00 | 0 | 50 | 63 | 75 | 88 | 100 |
| 6.50 | 0 | 63 | 75 | 88 | 100 | 150 |
| 6.00 | 0 | 75 | 88 | 100 | 150 | 200 |
| 5.50 | 0 | 88 | 100 | 150 | 200 | 225 |
| 5.00 | 50 | 100 | 150 | 200 | 225 | 250 |
| 4.50 | 75 | 150 | 200 | 225 | 250 | 275 |
| 4.00 | 100 | 200 | 225 | 250 | 275 | 300 |

highest-performing team simply holds the line, it will receive 150 percent of the planned payout; if it has a 15 percent improvement in cost per unit, it will get approximately 250 percent (cost per premium dollar declines to less than $4), and for 25 percent improvement it can reach the maximum of 300 percent. Thus, while the worst team has to run faster just to stay even, the payout formula is designed to encourage everybody to work better and overall not pay out additional monies for the department's productivity if aggregate performance is unchanged.

## 5. Funding

With the important exception of safety and, potentially, of cycle time, all plans should be self-funded—that is, the plan should pay for itself. While it may be a nice gesture, it's bad business to pay incentive compensation for results that are more or less what they were before the plan was adopted. A corollary is that the pool of available funds should be determined by *quantifiable* measures; you can't pay for hypothetical or intangible improvements.

Most companies contribute to the award pool at a rate— depending on the level of base pay—anywhere between 20 percent and 40 percent of value added. However, while value added sets the parameters of the pool, other, more qualitative gains may come into play as *modifiers*. In a plan in which payout is set at 25 percent of productivity gains, for example, the payout may be increased or decreased by 50 percent, based on customer satisfaction. That way, the company's maximum exposure is 37.5 percent of hard-dollar improvements.

Companies can and often do blend various measures to create the pool. For instance, at an independent refiner in the Southeast, 25 percent of the production gains and cost savings above threshold levels goes into the award pool. While employees don't have to exceed the performance threshold in both areas to earn a payout, the combined results determine the amount that goes into the pool. If the company doesn't meet its production target, 25 percent of the *loss* in production is applied against the 25 percent of any cost savings above threshold to determine the amount that goes into the pool.

## 6. Timing

In brief: The shorter, the better. Shorter measurement periods and faster payouts motivate employees more and, particularly when they've put pay at risk, are fairer. At the same time, there are a num-

ber of good reasons—starting with the obvious one that frequent payouts can create an administrative nightmare—to use longer time
frames.

For a start, certain information, particularly financial measures
such as profit and loss, are available only quarterly or at year-end.
Furthermore, shorter time frames can lead to distortions in payouts.
A flurry of policy renewals can result in a fat payout in the first quarter of the year, for example, followed by a demotivating slump in the
second quarter. The shorter the time frame, moreover, the easier it is
for employees themselves to manipulate the results. An employee
responsible for maintenance who's looking for a nice payout in January could defer taking equipment out of service and wait until February, assuring a payout even if it shortens the life of the equipment.
The longer the period being measured, the fewer the variations and
the smaller the opportunity to play games.

In some organizations, on the other hand, shorter measurement
periods work better. Daily measurement may in fact be most appropriate for some process teams, in either production or service companies (see AT&T Universal Card Services case study in this chapter).
In such cases, shorter measurement periods prevent a new member
from being penalized for, say, joining halfway into a bad quarter.
Furthermore, the shorter the time frame, the less opportunity the employee has to "sandbag" one measurement period in hopes that the
next one will be better. Each day starts anew: If the team didn't meet
its goals on Monday, it can start all over on Tuesday. (Alternatively, if
the team met or exceeded its goals on Monday, it must do it all over
again on Tuesday.)

Varying the time frame isn't the only way to prevent manipula-
tions or distortions. Some companies hold money back, paying out
20 percent of the projected annual incentive in each of the first three
quarters, and the balance at the end of the year. Employees whose
pay is on the line, however, may resent the fact that they—rather than
the company—are assuming the risk. Another approach, although
rarely used, is to carry forward the impact of a bad measurement
period. At the independent refiner, for instance, if performance is
down during a quarter, that will carry forward to the following quarter, or quarters, and offset against any positive results before a payment can be made. But even this company sets a cap: a maximum
negative award of $500 per employee, to be carried over from one
quarter to the next.

The payout should be made as soon as possible after the measurement period is completed. However, a plan may measure more
frequently than it pays out, particularly in situations where measure-

ment occurs daily (as in the case of AT&T Universal Card) or weekly. The most common plans pay out shortly after the measurement period, but it's not uncommon to see plans measure monthly and pay quarterly or, particularly when they use financial criteria, measure quarterly and pay annually. Apart from the administrative cost, a reason to aggregate payments is that frequent payments can dilute the impact of the award. If the payout comes to $1,500 a year, for example, a monthly check, after taxes, might be less than $100—and that's generally perceived to be too low to be much of an incentive.

## 7. Benefits

To the extent that they're an add-on, incentive payments should not be included in the company's calculations of benefits like pensions, savings plans, group life insurance, long-term disability or sick pay. But if they are part of a compensation architecture in which pay has been put at risk, then the payout should be considered for those programs. Otherwise, the company is essentially giving with one hand and taking away with the other.

There are of course compromise positions when there is pay at risk. One I suggest often is to modify the insurance benefits to provide coverage including any pay-at-risk amounts by changing covered earnings definition. Retirement and capital accumulation inclusion can be split; include total earnings (base pay and incentive awards) for savings, profit sharing, 401(k), and similar defined contribution plans while excluding incentive awards from defined benefit pension plans because of the long-term costs associated with pension funding requirements.

## 8. Administration

The administration of an incentive plan is usually the responsibility of the business unit. You generally won't find corporate human resources volunteering for the assignment due to their existing workload. The plan's administrators must monitor eligibility and set participation levels, help determine goals, keep records, forward the data to the payroll department, and arrange for payment. In some companies, self-managed teams may keep the books, but they'll still have to be audited.

How the payout itself is handled is one of the issues the plan's administrators must address. Should it be combined with the employee's regular paycheck? Or do you cut a separate check? That has greater impact but increases the administrative burden. One option is to put both amounts in the same check and insert a separate statement calling attention to the payout. A worksheet showing each participant how the award was calculated is required in all cases.

Tedious as they are, such details are an important measure of the plan. A well-designed plan that can't be administered efficiently, and doesn't pay out accurately, is poorly designed.

## 9. Evaluation

If results merit a payout at the end of the plan's first quarter or year, it's tempting for the company to conclude that the plan is working. Unfortunately, that would be jumping to conclusions. It could be that employees are motivated because they've become the temporary center of attention—the well-known Hawthorne effect—and not by the incentive opportunities themselves.

A well-designed incentive plan contains strategies to determine whether employees have in fact changed their short- and longer-term behaviors and activities as a direct result of the plan, and whether the measures and other design elements are appropriate ones. Focus groups provide one of the best methods companies can use to survey employees about the plan: Do they understand it? (Have them explain it to you!) Do they believe they can have an impact on results? What specific actions have they taken to affect results? If there was no payout, then a postmortem is even more crucial. For more information about evaluating a plan, see Chapter 12.

# Plans That Fail

For many managers, the big question mark is not whether incentives work, but what happens if and when a plan doesn't pay out. Some executives are afraid their employees will mutiny the first time they miss the target and forfeit the payout. I believe that, if the incentive plan is a good one and has employee buy-in, people will in fact be much more tolerant than many executives expect. But for employees to tolerate zero payout, base pay must be competitive and employees must be able to live without a payout and take accountability for plan results. Companies get into trouble when there are unfulfilled expectations about plan payouts.

Still, research has found that, to be motivational, there must be a minimum payout. If there's no payout in the first year and management believes employees have done everything right, they might consider making spot cash awards. Management may have its own reasons to support an incentive plan even if it isn't literally paying off. If the company can point to any indication that the plan has increased employee sensitivity to costs or otherwise led people to behave differently, then the plan may be rated a success at top levels. But not at the bottom: When an incentive plan fails to pay for a prolonged period—say, two or three years—it must be viewed as a failure.

At that point, I'd say there's no incentive plan in place, and the company had better go back to the drawing board to redesign key elements, including measures and goals.

## Case Study: Incentives at Hallmark

Like many companies in the 1980s, Hallmark Cards, Inc., was a traditional organization, where work was organized around functions, and employees focused on activities within their own organizational unit. As the company entered into the 1990s, business conditions began to change requiring Hallmark Cards executives to assess how work was organized. Rapidly changing consumer tastes, more convenience shopping (especially in mass merchandising stores), and increasing comfort with technology were some of the drivers affecting the company. To respond to these changes, Hallmark Cards created an organization that centers around key business activities and processes allowing employees to work horizontally as well as vertically within the organization.

As a result of this new organizational structure, numerous teams have been created to serve various internal and external customers. About a half dozen of these teams, called retail focused teams, were created to concentrate on specific segments of the retail market: grocery store chains, drug stores, mass merchandisers, and the like. These *process* teams are not only made up of employees from sales and marketing, but also finance, information systems, logistics, customer service, and administration.

To align pay with the new organizational structure, Hallmark Cards has been experimenting with various team-based incentive concepts. These concepts are designed to measure performance against various performance factors that are most applicable for each team. Operational measurements (such as retail, measured quarterly), profitability goals (assessed against annual targets), and customer satisfaction considerations are utilized. Monthly team meetings are normally held to discuss progress, how well the team is performing against objective, and the potential incentive payout (paid quarterly).

To be more precise, one team, which is focused on a single mass merchandising customer, has a ratio of fixed-to-variable pay, which varies with the employee's status. (However, all employees regardless of their status are measured against the same criteria.) For employees in exempt positions, it is 90 percent fixed, 10 percent variable; for employees in nonexempt positions, it is 95 percent fixed, 5 percent variable. Actual payouts begin with 80 percent achievement of established goals, earning 0.5 times the target or pay at risk amount. One hundred percent performance earns the target amount, and 125 percent earns 3.5

times the target. Thus, a $25,000-a-year customer service representative who has put 5 percent at risk receives a salary of $23,750. If the team hits the target, the employee breaks even at $25,000. But the employee can also top out with an incentive award of $4,375 ($25,000 × 5% × 3.5) for total annual earnings of $28,125 ($23,750 + $4,375).

In its first year, another team also agreed to take a 5 percent reduction in base pay in exchange for the possibility of incentives. Although the plan paid out, it was almost discontinued the following year by a dichotomy on the team. While some employees who were more of the risk-taking nature were in favor of the plan, others were not. "The culture of the team is an important consideration in the design of any incentive compensation plan," says Jeff Blair, compensation and performance management director. "Placing money at-risk will definitely impact the type of person attracted to the team and possibly the culture of the work group." The result was a compromise, with pay-at-risk reduced to 2.5 percent of base salary for all team members. As Blair indicates, "To maintain a team environment, management should be careful in excluding certain employees from the program."

Employees are not the only people who are ambivalent about incentive compensation; so are a number of managers. Some Hallmark Cards managers welcome the advent of incentive compensation more than others, says Blair. "It depends on your management philosophy and how a manager intends to use incentive compensation. It is a management tool designed to drive performance, requiring time and commitment from the manager." In fact, fewer than 10 percent of Hallmark Cards employees currently participate in an incentive compensation program. To maintain internal equity, incentive-eligible employees have lower salaries than employees without incentive opportunities.

Another issue with which managers are having to grapple is the need to balance incentive plan targets with business unit targets. Managers are understandably reluctant to penalize employees with an aggressive plan. Yet, Hallmark Cards' view is that incentive plan targets should correspond to business unit targets, which are meant to be aggressive. "A target must be achievable, or the plan will not work," says Blair. "But it can not be a slam dunk. It has to be a stretch."

Administratively, Blair notes, maintaining the incentive plans are also a stretch. Because Hallmark Cards has little turnover but lots of movement within the company, plan administrators frequently prorate the payout of employees. Hallmark Cards measures performance and pays quarterly because it believes it's more fair and motivating. But, says Blair, "These things start getting expensive when you consider the amount of time to maintain the program, required system modifications, and other administrative details."

Overcoming such problems can be a nuisance, but, so far the plan is working. Employees have earned more than their target incentive every year, and the company appears to be getting a good return on its investment. And, Blair notes, team leaders have seen "some very positive behavior changes on employees' parts," from the initiation of new marketing concepts to better utilization of time.

## Case Study: Piloting an Incentive Program

Two years into its effort to introduce incentive pay at Trigon Blue Cross–Blue Shield (formerly Blue Cross–Blue Shield of Virginia), the main lesson has nothing to do with the efficacy of one measure or goal over another. Rather, says Scott Amos, manager, incentive compensation, of the Richmond, Virginia–based company, "The bottom line is that changing the thinking of employees at all levels to a risk-and-return scenario is much more difficult than anticipated."

Based on a handful of process-team pilots, Amos says, Trigon's conclusion was that employees ultimately have to arrive at an acceptable risk-and-return mix by themselves. Indeed, the most successful pilot—a cross-functional group of some sixty people from operations, marketing, underwriting, and other areas who had been working together as a process team for a year—was an exercise in democracy. It held numerous meetings to debate the pros and cons of incentive compensation and to choose objectives, and adopted an incentive plan only after the vast majority of members voted to do so. In the spirit of team decision-making, the few who opposed it remained on the team to give it a chance.

The team put money at risk in two ways. The base salary ranges were reduced across the board by 5 percent—that is, every salary grade range and midpoint fell 5 percent—and 1 percent was pulled out of the annual merit increase. In return, the team incentive opportunity varied from zero to 15 percent of base pay, roughly a 1-to-3 ratio of risk to potential return.

The team had two financial measures—administrative expense reduction and enrollment growth—and a third, operations work-flow measure that had resisted management's best efforts in the past. The two financial measures were each defined in terms of achievement beyond an existing "stretch" target; for every 1 percent beyond the aggressive target for administrative costs, for example, employees would receive a specified payout. Because self-funding was difficult to measure for the work-flow objective, Trigon used a multiplier of the financial component award for superior work-flow results. It was important that in all cases the plan was self-funded.

It's too soon to tell how well the plan has worked, but at least one area has borne immediate fruit: In the area of teaming individuals to focus on operational goals, says Amos, "we saw immediate results as soon as incentive opportunities were attached."

## Case Study: Incentive Pay-by-the-Day at AT&T Universal Card

At AT&T Universal Card Services, incentive pay was used to help introduce not only a new product and service, but a new company. The telecommunications firm's consumer-credit-card subsidiary, established in 1990, was built up from 300 to 3,000 employees in just twelve months (it currently employs 4,000), with a heavy reliance from the outset on quality, customer service, and productivity.

The incentive pay program, known as the AT&T Excellence Award, was designed to distinguish the new card from others in the crowded consumer-credit market, partly through an enormous amount of performance measurement. More than one hundred different individual and group measures are reported on *daily*, giving employees in the company's operations center immediate feedback on performance in such key areas as responsiveness to customers and speed and accuracy of information processing. Measures fall into three main categories, weighted to reflect the company's priorities: customer-centered, each worth three points; business-centered with a customer impact, two points (for example, the computer system goes down); and internally centered, with no customer impact, one point (the payroll department sends out the wrong checks to employees).

When total performance on any given day falls below the goals agreed upon by employees and management, managers are informed the following morning. They are expected to file a report to the chief operating officer by noon detailing the causes of—and solutions for—the problem. Quarterly summaries reinforce the process.

The plan offers a maximum opportunity of 12 percent of base pay paid quarterly, one month after the quarter ends, to all nonexempt employees; base pay is at market levels. (Exempt employees are eligible under different plans, but are judged by many of the same measures.) In a typical quarter, employees meet approximately 75 percent of the established objectives—that is, on 75 percent of the working days, they achieved at least 96 percent of the available points for that day. For that, they get a payout of about 75 percent of the maximum possible incentive award. In 1994 the total incentive pool amounted to 9 percent of nonexempt payroll.

While the plan was evidently working—in 1992 AT&T Universal Card Services won the Baldrige Award—the company in 1994 decided it needed a better measure of customer satisfaction. Through telephone surveys, it added a measure called "voice of the customer" that determined about a quarter of total incentive payout. After a year the company decided that measure wasn't good enough. So in 1995 it substituted "action of the customer," which measures growth in receivables outstanding—the biggest driver behind the profitability of a credit-card company. AT&T Universal Card can monitor this figure almost by the second, and so can employees: There is a digital readout monitor at each of the company's three sites.

And AT&T Universal Card also made other, more fundamental changes to the plan. Specifically, says Ira Walter, director, compensation, human resources effectiveness and HR information systems, "we felt it was a stretch for any given employee to relate their own performance to company-wide performance. We wanted to create more motivation, and to do that, we had to shorten the line of sight."

So in 1994, management began testing a different incentive plan with a "team" of some 300 process collection and recovery employees: the people who try to collect unpaid bills. While the employees continued to get two-thirds of their potential incentive awards from the Excellence Award program, one-third was now funded through a plan that was more tightly linked to the work of the team.

That plan used two measures that, like the others, were tallied daily and paid quarterly: productivity, based on the dollars collected on unpaid bills, compared to past performance; and quality, also known as Total Customer Delight. The company quantified quality by measuring "customer impacts"—defined as the times an action such as an inaccurate statement or bad telephone manner negatively impacts the customer—and set a goal of a specified number of impacts per 1,000 contacts. If the team fell below that target, yet beat its productivity target, it could receive a payout of up to 3 percent of base pay.

Walter expects that such plans, tailored to process teams, will become more common as AT&T Universal continues to experiment with incentives. Although it won't abandon its company-wide Excellence Award, that program may eventually account for only half of incentive payouts, with other, more customized team plans making up the balance.

# Note

1. "Carrots, Sticks, and Self-Deception," *Across the Board*, January 1994, p. 39.

# 9

# The Architecture of Team Pay

The whole is greater than the sum of the parts.

Probably you've been hearing that all your life. If you work with teams, we hope you've come to recognize its truth: People working together can achieve more than the aggregate of what they can do alone.

That's equally true of pay. Compensation consists of numerous components, or building blocks. Together, they constitute an architecture. The total architecture can support productive employee behavior or, if it's inappropriate, encourage behavior that's counterproductive. So the architecture is critical because of the message it sends employees.

In the previous chapters, I've discussed the four main components of pay—base pay opportunities, increases to base pay, recognition awards, and incentive compensation—and the multiplicity of ways they're calculated by organizations. I've treated each in isolation. In this chapter, I show how the component parts can be brought together in a compensation architecture that motivates teams. At the same time, I show how, as a lever to sustain team performance, one component may be more powerful in one cultural context than in another.

Each team type has its own architecture. There are four factors that must be addressed within any compensation architecture: value, process, activity, and results. As I've suggested through the funnel motif in Exhibit 9-1, each factor "trickles down" into a different reward alternative:

**Value** refers to the way an organization's values work, creating the opportunity for pay. It is by means of valuation, generally through work comparison, that the company determines initial pay opportunities, for example the salary range or band.

**Exhibit 9-1. Team reward alternatives.**

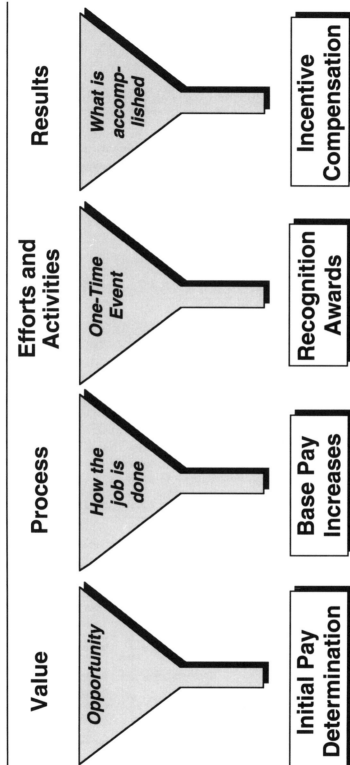

**Process** describes how the job is done, and determines which skills and behavioral competencies should be rewarded with base-pay increases.

**Activity** refers to one-time events, particularly for parallel and project teams, that should be recognized and rewarded by the organization.

**Results**, the capstone of the compensation architecture, are the means by which the organization evaluates ongoing performance in order to establish variable pay. Incentives are a function of the results of the team, generally a process or work team. At the same time, as observed in Chapter 8, the results should also be a function of the incentives.

## Architecture for Team Types

In this section, I model the compensation architecture for each of the three team types: parallel, process, and project. There is no single, one-size-fits-all team compensation architecture. As the discussion that follows and Exhibit 9-2 indicates, some components of pay that are fundamental to one team type may be largely irrelevant to another. And as the case studies illustrate, there is a vast range of combinations and permutations of the different reward alternatives.

However, there are two key issues that differentiate one team compensation architecture from another. One is the extent of commitment by the worker to the team. Members of teams that are part-time

**Exhibit 9-2. Team pay architecture (focus).**

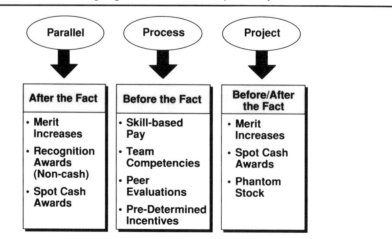

| Parallel | Process | Project |
|---|---|---|
| **After the Fact** | **Before the Fact** | **Before/After the Fact** |
| • Merit Increases | • Skill-based Pay | • Merit Increases |
| • Recognition Awards (Non-cash) | • Team Competencies | • Spot Cash Awards |
| • Spot Cash Awards | • Peer Evaluations | • Phantom Stock |
|  | • Pre-Determined Incentives |  |

or temporary—even if temporary is a year or more—bring their own compensation package to the team. Members of teams that are full-time and permanent—that is, process or work teams—draw their blueprint on the job. Hence, different architectures.

The second, related issue is the time frame chosen in awarding variable pay. Does the company establish compensation in advance of performance (before the fact) or pay for results "on the spot" (after the fact)? For members of process teams, a plan that explicitly defines the rewards for performance, *before* the fact, is considered the most motivating. For members of parallel or project teams, with their divided loyalties and different levels of contribution, a plan that rewards performance *after* the fact may be the safer option for the organization. Again, different cultures, different architectures. (See Exhibit 9-3 for prevalence of different compensation components by team.)

## Architecture for Parallel Teams

As noted earlier, what distinguishes a parallel team from other teams is that it is part-time. The team may be temporary—formed to solve a particular problem within a matter of weeks or months, after which it is dissolved—or it may be permanent, requiring its members to convene periodically, year in, year out. It may be cross-functional, representing different skills and levels within the organization. Or, less often, it may consist of employees who do more or less the same full-time job. In either case, the parallel team involves only a partial and limited use of its members' time. The members have other jobs within the company that make an equal or a greater demand on their time.

Therein lies one of the key issues in designing a compensation architecture. Conflict is almost part of the job description for people who serve on parallel teams. The team's members typically have at least two bosses: the individual who leads or supervises their team, and a different individual to whom they regularly report. Because of an incontrovertible law of nature—that one body can't occupy two spaces simultaneously—the challenge in designing a compensation architecture is to get employees to order their priorities right.

### Helping Henry Hapless (Hypothetically)

Let's take the hypothetical case of a Henry Hapless, who works eight-to-four producing widgets. Henry gets named to a safety team that meets every month for an hour or so. His boss and coworkers

**Exhibit 9-3. Team compensation prevalence.**

### Parallel

| | |
|---|---|
| Merit Increases | 54 % |
| Non-Cash Awards | 49 % |
|    Considering 16% | |
| Spot Cash Awards | 37 % |
| Pre-Determined Incentives | 16 % |

### Process

| | |
|---|---|
| Merit Increases | 74 % |
| Pre-Determined Incentives | 46 % |
|    Considering 16% | |
| Non-Cash Awards | 41 % |
| Spot Cash Awards | 42 % |

### Project

| | |
|---|---|
| Merit Increases | 71 % |
| Non-Cash Awards | 53 % |
| Spot Cash Awards | 48 % |
| Pre-Determined Incentives | 25 % |
|    Considering 15% | |

Source: Hay 1995 Team-Based Pay Survey (U.S.A.)

don't begrudge that amount of time. But then Henry gets assigned to a quality-control team to investigate why some widgets don't meet specifications. That team's agenda is more urgent, so Henry is summoned to meetings every week for several hours at a time—sometimes on the very morning that Henry's supervisor, who's becoming increasingly disgruntled, has also called a meeting.

From a pay perspective, there are several levers the company can use to motivate Henry and reduce the conflict, and others that could demotivate Henry or exacerbate the tensions he feels. Base pay isn't a factor here: Henry and the rest of the quality control team are all at different pay levels, and a short-term, temporary assignment isn't going to change that. However, Henry might merit a larger-than-average base-pay increase if he performs well on the team and if his regular job doesn't suffer.

The problem is that his full-time supervisor may well be unaware of what Henry has done on the team. Furthermore, the time frame for the team assignment may be out of alignment with the timing of Henry's performance appraisal. To ensure that Henry gets the credit he deserves, the company needs to develop a performance management system that takes into account his work on the team (and also must provide guidelines for the amount of time Henry should allocate to it). Still, because the parallel team is peripheral to his main job, Henry shouldn't expect a raise predicated on his team performance. At best, he might get a superior performance rating and possibly a new assignment.

But the bigger question is: Should Henry's total compensation be reconfigured *before* the team begins its work? Or should it be limited to an after-the-fact reward? And, a related question: Should Henry and his teammates get cash, or dinner and a plaque? In answering these questions, companies have several issues to consider.

Let's say the company agrees up-front to pay the team a stipulated amount of cash for each defect-free shipment of widgets in the six months after it implements its recommendations. If it's a significant amount of cash, Henry may be persuaded to spend more and more time on quality control, to the detriment of his full-time job—not to mention his role on the safety committee. The performance management process may state explicitly that Henry's first priority is his job, and the safety team may have been told that their work is important, but the compensation architecture is sending a different message. And, as I've maintained throughout this book, money talks. Unless the team's assignment is to come up with money-saving or revenue-generating ideas—the employee proposal or suggestion teams discussed in Chapter 8—I advise against predetermined incentives for parallel teams.

So, no before-the-fact rewards. Of course, that doesn't preclude paying cash for perfect widgets after the fact. But here the issue of cash raises a different problem. Coming from different functions and levels within the company, Henry and his teammates have all brought different types of skills and competencies to the endeavor. Arguably, too, some have voluntarily put in a lot of time while others have merely punched a clock. Should everybody be paid equally? Interestingly, in most cases the team tends to say yes; management says no.

My recommendation is: Go with the teams. If cash is the reward, it's better to pay everybody the same lump sum than to differentiate and create disharmony. Giving everybody the same percentage of base pay can also accentuate differences, particularly when team members come from different levels of the hierarchy and represent a wide range of pay. On the other hand, if one or two individuals have clearly been ahead of the pack, and the distinction is acknowledged by the rest of the team, then it's legitimate to recognize their superior performance with a bonus greater than their peers'. In fact, it would be bad management *not* to do so.

If the foregoing sounds like an argument against cash, well, that's a fair conclusion. I admit there are times when cash may be the best way of rewarding teamwork, specifically, as I indicated in Chapter 8, when the team's work has yielded real financial gains above expected performance and the company wants to make a point of rewarding such efforts. And if you want to make distinctions among team members—for example, rewarding a secretary or other clerical worker who's made an unexpected contribution—cash is undoubtedly the best vehicle. In general, however, I believe that noncash awards, after the fact, are most appropriate for recognizing the work of parallel teams. A group dinner, a group outing or presentation—such rewards are a conflict-free means of recognizing the value of the team's work.

Judging from the results of the Hay 1995 Team-Based Pay Survey, many companies have come to the same conclusion. Of the 230 companies surveyed, 49 percent said they offered noncash awards to their parallel teams, another 16 percent were considering doing so, and 37 percent offered spot cash. Only 16 percent paid predetermined incentives.

## Case Study: A Cigna Parallel Team

For three months in 1994, a parallel team of corporate compensation specialists at Cigna, the Philadelphia-based insurance company, worked together to plan and run a training session on team pay for the company's human resources generalists. Part of their work involved putting together a case study based on a real-life situation at the company's group insurance division, which sells group life, accident, and disability policies.

None of the team members were led to expect extra compensation for their efforts. But after the successful event, everybody was "recognized" by the group insurance division. The team members each received a recognition gold "leaf" (the Cigna logo being a tree), which could be redeemed for a Cigna watch. Even the people who'd attended the session received plain leaves, for their contribution to the discussion of the case study. "It was particularly nice because it was instant recognition from the people we'd helped," says William A. Faris, assistant vice president, corporation design and education, who directed the team.

In addition, one member of the team received a cash award: A staff member who had worked exceptionally hard to make the conference a success. Not coincidentally, this person was also the most junior member of the team. For the other members, who were more senior and better paid, the extra effort went with the territory; for this professional, it was above and beyond the job description. At the same time, the spot cash award was too modest to be controversial: several hundred dollars in gift certificates. "It was more of a way of saying thank you, than trying to assess the value of the contribution," says Faris.

## Architecture for Process Teams

The process team—sometimes known as the work team—is a full-time, permanent team whose job, as the name suggests, is to do the day-to-day work. Not only are such teams rarely cross-functional; they usually consist of people doing similar work with comparable training and education. Like the culture that produces it, the process team is driven by an emphasis on quality, and it typically advances in incremental steps rather than quantum leaps, following rules that have been preestablished, that is, before the fact. Members need to know up-front what is expected of them and what they, in turn, can expect from the organization. Their compensation architecture must be designed accordingly.

For a start, base-pay increases are a key building block in the compensation architecture of the process team. To function effectively, the members of process teams typically must be able to do each other's jobs and to work together well. That means upgrading skills and knowledge, on the one hand, and behavioral competencies on the other—those personal qualities or traits that shape the way individuals approach their jobs and interface with other team members. Even if members of a process team are "broadbanded" into only one or two bands of pay, as discussed in Chapter 4, they still might be paid at different levels because they have different skills and have demonstrated different competencies. Team members grow at different rates. The only stipulation is that they all have the same opportunity to grow and be rewarded.

Paying for skills and competencies, then, lays the groundwork for the compensation architecture for process teams. To encourage cross-training—for example, bringing everybody up to a level where they can perform three or four of the team's five processes—the company may have a pay-for-skills program that will result in individual base-pay increases. Assuming the workforce is stable, most members will acquire the requisite skills for their teams over a period between, say, six months and three years. But competencies can be an area of continuing focus and reward.

As noted in Chapter 3, teams typically pass through four stages, as members' competencies emerge and develop: (1) forming (confusion and orientation), (2) storming (conflict and turmoil), (3) norming (recognizing the importance of their roles as members of the team), and (4) performing (working together, regardless of formal assignment, to improve overall team performance). In the performing stage, all members have at least an average level of competencies, and some have progressed to the excellent levels characteristic of leaders. In tandem with pay-for-skills, companies need a pay-for-competency program that will help maintain their teams at the performing stage.

Thus, while merit increases are a common element in most team compensation architecture (54 percent for parallel teams and 71 percent for project teams, according to the Hay 1995 Team-Based Pay Survey), they are most prevalent (74 percent) among companies dealing with process teams.

### Determining Raises

How do companies determine raises? That depends on the nature of the teams. As Chapter 6 indicated, there are several comparatively objective ways to measure the acquisition of skills. Judging members' progress in a dozen or so competencies is more difficult, and the issue may be finding the most appropriate person or persons to make those judgments. If the team has relatively close supervision, then there is probably a leader or manager in place who can assess performance. If, however, the team is self-directed, then the company may decide to use one of the multi-rater or peer feedback approaches to performance appraisal described in Chapter 5.

At the end of the day, of course, companies aren't really paying for the acquisition of skills or competencies by individuals: They're paying for production, whether of goods or services, by the entire team. The real goal of the process team is to produce more with the same resources, or the same with less, and to produce it faster or better—in other words, to improve productivity and quality. That's where variable pay, in the form of predetermined incentives, comes in. Because success is measured in terms of operational results directly under the control of the team, incentive compensation opportunities for those results is the lever most likely to motivate process teams. Organizations recognize this fact. In the Hay 1995 Team Based Pay Survey, 46 percent of companies had incentive compensation for their process teams—between two and three times the percentage for project or parallel teams—and another 16 percent were considering implementing it.

### How Much Incentive?

But it isn't enough to say that incentives should be included in a team's compensation architecture. The question is, How much incentive? Or, given that the opportunity for incentive pay should result in above-average compensation if the goals are reached, what's the best balance between fixed (base) pay and variable or incentive compensation (also known as pay-at-risk)? To get the balance right, a company needs to ask itself two more questions: How competitive are its base wages? And, how good is the team's relative performance—that is, how productive is the team relative to comparable teams at other organizations?

As Exhibit 9-4 shows, there are four possible ways to answer those questions. Where you, as an employer, fit on the matrix should determine how you structure your incentive compensation. Let's say, for a start, that you're paying base wages that are higher than the average for the community you're in, yet your productivity is below average. To offer incentives and at the same time get out of the "overpaying" square, you need to put pay-at-risk. Alternatively, let's say you're paying average wages and have above-average productivity. Since your productivity is already high, you can afford to offer incentives in the form of an "add-on" rather than by reducing base pay.

Once you've determined the balance, or ratio, that you want between fixed and variable pay at target performance, the next question is: How do you get there? Let's go back to the company that's in perhaps the most undesirable position in Exhibit 9-4: overpaying. To make the transition to incentives, it has three choices:

1. It can cut wages to market or below-market rate (putting that amount "at risk" by transferring it into the incentive pool).

**Exhibit 9-4. Pay versus performance matrix.**

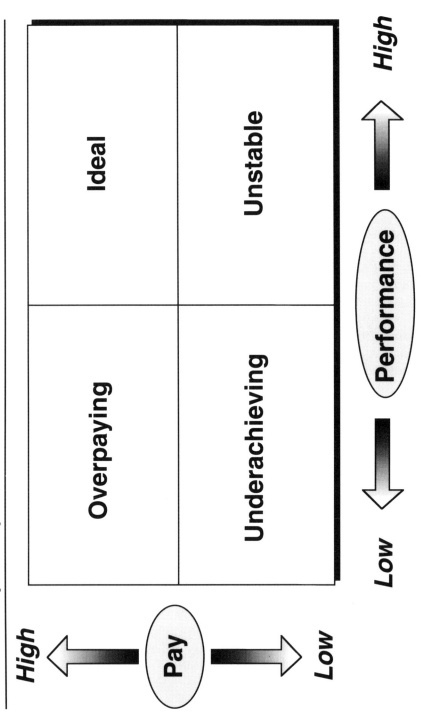

2. It can add incentives on top of base pay (the "add-on" mentioned earlier).
3. As a compromise between choices 1 and 2, it can reduce or eliminate altogether the future years' increases to base pay, redirecting that money to incentives (and eventually bringing down base pay to market or below-market levels).

In this case, option 3 is generally best. Since the company is already overpaying, an add-on is out of the question. And, unless the company is in a crisis, cutting wages is also out of the question because it would probably create a hardship for employees, many of whom have already allocated every penny of take-home pay. Merit raises, however, are fair game. Employees may be eagerly anticipating an increase, but they can't lay claim to it in the same way they can to actual wages. Furthermore, using the merit raise as a transition to pay-at-risk gives companies considerable flexibility. Depending on its pay and incentive levels, the company can eliminate the raise entirely; or reduce it, giving employees half or a quarter of the planned increase; or eliminate it selectively, freezing the wages of average workers while giving a smaller merit increase to the top performers. Lump-sum payments can also be made in lieu of base-pay increases to ease the transition.

It's at this point that the company must decide precisely how much it wants to offer as an incentive and—the flip side of the question—how much it is willing to put at risk. Incentive pay should be large enough to be meaningful. For most employees, that translates to approximately 8 to 10 percent of income, or about a month's pay. Companies, and employees, may be reluctant to put the full 10 percent at risk, however. Employees have to be able to live with zero payout at those times that they don't meet the plan goals. Otherwise, when the going gets tough, the tough get going: If there's no payout, the more marketable employees will start bailing out unless base wages are reasonably competitive or—as sometimes happens—management comes through with money to close the gap.

To hold on to employees when incentives fail, a company usually has to fix wages above the 25th percentile (bottom quarter of the market.) That may sound miserly but, in fact, a close look at the numbers reveals there's not that great a span between the top and bottom. Someone earning $30,000, for example, would earn plus or minus about $2,500 if he moves to the top quartile (75th percentile, or $32,500) or to the bottom quartile (25th percentile, or $27,500), according to Hay's Industrial Compensation Database. On the other hand, if productivity is below average—harking back to our "overpaying" company—then pay should also be below average. The company can peg base wages at the 25th percentile and, to the extent workers meet targets, use incentives to bring up total compensation.

As the company and employees gain more experience with the incentive plan, and assuming that the experience is positive, their propensity to assume risk may grow. At General Motors' Saturn plant, for example, employees put only 5 percent of pay at risk when the plan was launched in 1992. Currently it is 10 percent, and in the future, as its self-directed work teams mature, the company says that 20 percent of pay will be at risk. (Admittedly, even with a comparatively high percentage of their pay at risk, Saturn employees, who are members of the United Auto Workers, have a fixed base pay well above the average for their area, outside of Nashville, Tennessee.)

## Case Study: A Hallmark Cards Process Team

Unless there's a financial crisis, as noted earlier, cutting base wages is one of the steps companies are *not* supposed to take when they begin offering incentive pay to employees. But that's precisely what Hallmark Cards did in 1993 for the team it established to serve a single large retail customer: It subjected all team members to pay cuts between 5 and 10 percent. Because at that time there was only one such team—and even today there are only a sprinkling of process teams around the company—Hallmark Cards felt it would have been unfair to have significantly higher pay opportunities (base pay and incentive) for those employees who happened to be on the team than for those who weren't. External competitiveness was already secure—one of the major employers in Kansas City, Missouri, Hallmark Cards was already paying above-average wages—but internal equity also had to be guaranteed.

It was somewhat easier for Hallmark Cards to take that approach because the company had a history of adjusting base wages when it moved people from administrative jobs (where there was no opportunity to earn a bonus) to sales (where incentives were the norm) and back again. But at the same time, Hallmark Cards also took steps to ensure that team members couldn't lose, at least initially, under the incentive plan. In the first half year of the plan, members had the opportunity to earn the greater of two amounts: their base salary or the calculated payout under the plan.

The incentive plan was thus integrated into Hallmark Cards' total compensation architecture, an architecture that is being realigned in some other ways with team goals while retaining some traditional components. For example, Hallmark Cards had determined base pay by using traditional Hay job evaluation technology (Guide Charts) to evaluate individual positions and establish salary ranges. With its evolution toward teams, Hallmark Cards adopted an alternate Hay job measurement system based upon a process culture, and integrated the new system with salary bands. However, the company retains merit raises to reward individuals and continues to base them on performance appraisals by the team's leaders, who are from management, rather than by peers.

Most nontraditional was the incentive plan, which was tied not to Hallmark Cards' business per se but to the retail sales of the team's single customer. Payout began when performance exceeded 80 percent of the target, or goal. At 100 percent of target, the plan was "self-funded" and team members "reearned" the full amount of their pay-at-risk. The payout formula was capped at 3.5 times pay-at-risk, when performance reached 125 percent of target. For the four managers on the team, the calculations were slightly different, but determined on a consistent basis.

If an employee was to leave the team and be reassigned within Hallmark Cards, his or her base salary would be restored to the full amount—that is, the 5 percent or 10 percent pay-at-risk would be added back to base pay.

Finally, Hallmark Cards realigned one more component of its compensation architecture: recognition. Spot awards were considered particularly important for those people who weren't eligible for the incentive plan because they weren't dedicated to the team full-time but who nonetheless contributed to the team's success, for example, an employee in manufacturing who spent 10 percent of his or her time producing cards for the team's customer. "From an architectural perspective, you've also got to reward those nonmembers," says Jeff Blair, compensation and performance management director. Noncash spot recognition, such as parties, were the favored method.

## Architecture for Project Teams

A couple of neighborhood kids offer to shovel around your house after a snowstorm. Do you negotiate a flat fee in advance? Do you give them a bonus if they do a good job? If so, do you tell them in advance what the bonus will be, or do you just hold out the possibility? And, since they're nominally a team, do you pay the youngster who shoveled the driveway (he did a better job) as much as the one who shoveled your walk (it was more work)? Or do you pay more to the kid who brought both shovels?

Faced with so many choices, you might well decide to do the shoveling yourself. But corporations don't have that option. If they want to tackle a major project—whether it's the creation of a new product or service, the reengineering of a process, or the installation of a new information system—they generally have to appoint a project team.

In most respects, the project team is the antithesis of the process team. Members are committed full-time, but only for the duration of the project, and the shorter, the better. For project teams, which typically operate in a time-based culture, time is of the essence. Members come from different functions and levels of the organization, and the team receives direction from multiple or diverse sources. These teams may also be more fluid than either parallel or process teams. As the project advances, the makeup of the team may change, with some members leaving and others coming on board. And for some members, the assignment may be risky. While most return to their previous or similar work, in rare cases people may find they've worked themselves out of their jobs.

Having said that, I'll quickly note that there are projects, and then there are projects. Some people, such as design engineers or systems analysts, work on projects full-time. When one project is finished, they move on to the next. That is the nature of their job. I am not suggesting that companies develop a project team compensation architecture for these people. Rather, they need to be evaluated and compensated as employees whose full-time, permanent jobs involve membership on project teams.

When their merit raises are being determined, for example, management should evaluate these employees partly on their team competencies and their contributions to the team, but also on individual skills and attributes. To the extent they exceed expectations, they may receive an occasional spot cash award; for a good job, they may also receive noncash recognition. But building a systematic recognition and reward component into the compensation architecture, merely because they work on projects or on teams, would be unwarranted. In fact, that could create a sense of unfairness among other individuals who pursue their work alone.

When it comes to realigning the compensation architecture, the kind of employee I have in mind is one who has been taken from a permanent assignment to work temporarily on a reengineering or product development team—for example, the team assembled by Chrysler to come up with the Neon. On such teams, while an individual's manager may recommend a nominal pay increase based on team performance, base pay and merit increases tend to continue to play their customary (preteam) role. The real variability comes from spot cash awards—and, occasionally, incentive plans—based on the success of the team.

As the Hay 1995 Team Based Pay Survey indicates, 53 percent of the companies with project teams included noncash awards as part of their compensation architecture, and 48 percent also used spot cash awards. Contrast that with the use of predetermined incentives: only 25 percent for project teams, compared with 46 percent for process teams at the time of the survey (and potentially going up to 62 percent of the companies if all those considering incentives adopt such plans).

In Chapter 7, I discuss at length the various types of awards, cash and noncash, that companies use to recognize the work of teams. As part of a company's compensation architecture, these award programs can offer enormous flexibility. Companies can specify the number and value of awards to be given annually, but they have more freedom to bend their own rules than in the case of, say, an incentive plan. They can take an awards program for individuals and offer it to teams. If they are offering a cash award, they can stipulate that all of the money should be shared equally, or that the money should be distributed according to performance, or that every team member should be rewarded but star performers can get more. For example, when it was rebuilding a number of its gas stations on turnpikes, Mobil's U.S. Marketing and Refining division had a project team examine how stations could keep some pumps operating during construction. The entire team received a cash reward, but there was a bonus for the individual member who came up with the idea, checked it out with local authorities, and had the tenacity to follow it through to completion.

### A Risky Business

The earlier discussions on parallel and process teams noted that differentiating among team members is a risky business. (That explains the clear preference for noncash awards in the survey.) While they're not risk-free for project teams, such differentials are more generally accepted. One reason is that project teams may be dealing with sums of far greater magnitude, so that everybody can feel handsomely rewarded and there's still enough left over for a bonus or two. Another reason is that, when you're dealing with sums of that magnitude, the individual who's made a significantly greater contribution is likelier to feel shortchanged (as well he should) unless he receives more cash. As stated earlier, the key criterion is that the rewards pass the "public" test—that is, the company must be ready and willing to defend the differential if it becomes public.

Now, what about "before-the-fact" rewards? While they're not a building block in the compensation architecture of project teams to the extent they are for process teams, they are still sometimes used to reinforce the essential charter of the project team: Do it within budget, on time. And because the project team is a full-time job, the introduction of incentive compensation doesn't create the potential for conflict that can arise with parallel teams.

But there are other drawbacks. While the advantages of getting to market by Christmas may be obvious, for example, the financial benefits of getting a process reengineered one month ahead of schedule may be less clear or quantifiable. Another concern is that events may overtake goals, making the incentive goals obsolete. Let's take the real-life case of a project team tasked to increase the company's field representatives' access to information. While the team studied the problem, the technology leaped ahead, the price of computers plummeted, and the company was able to buy every sales representative a laptop and cellular phone. The project came to a successful conclusion, but entirely irrespective of the team's efforts. Next time, the company might try to "crystal ball," building certain technological advances into the incentive plan. Still, only hindsight is twenty-twenty.

A more fundamental problem with incentive opportunities for project teams arises if the project is relatively open-ended. Where the goals are clear—a Neon at a specified level of price and performance—incentives may be appropriate. But if the goal is something amorphous—say, to reengineer the product design process—it's harder to set targets, let alone pay for them. In theory, the company could define a goal as a 20 percent decrease in cycle time, for example. The danger of setting that target is that it becomes the end point. As Alfie Kohn, the archenemy of incentives, would say, "Set the limits and people will stop there." In this case, he's right: Instead of reengineering the process, the team may take an incremental, TQM approach.

A possible alternative—albeit generally for the upper corporate echelons—is phantom stock, a component of compensation architecture to which I briefly alluded in Chapter 7. Depending on how it's structured, phantom stock can be either an "after-the-fact" reward or a "before-the-fact" incentive. Either way, not only does it represent a substantial reward, it can also help create a sense of entrepreneurship among employees.

Where does phantom stock come into play? Let's say a company has formed a high-powered team to develop a new venture. It's a high-risk, high-reward proposition. If the venture fails, the team members may not have jobs waiting for them. On the other hand, if the venture succeeds, the members may be given the equivalent of stock in the new undertaking. Most companies don't want to give away real equity. Hence the development of phantom stock, paper shares that mirror the equity growth of the new venture as if it were publicly traded. The company may defer the details until the venture has been launched, or it may agree up front on the size of the payout (for example, 10 percent of the "equity" for the entire team) and how to value it (a multiple of the venture's earnings three to five years hence).

## Case Study: A London Life Project Team

Spot cash awards or incentives? London Life Insurance did it both ways.

In 1993, the London, Ontario, company set up a small team to begin reengineering the way it processed customers' orders for certain savings products. The team's charter was to dramatically reduce order processing time and unit costs. "We didn't have a compensation contract up front," says Steve Warren, vice president, organizational effectiveness. Throughout the design phase, the insurer gave out some ad hoc spot cash awards based on the team leader's recommendation—to recognize members' creativity. At the end of the prototype stage, all team members received a $1,000 bonus (spot cash award) to celebrate the successful completion of the first key phase of the project.

Then began the second stage of the project: implementing the design. About a half-dozen new people were transferred from their jobs to join the original members. They represented various grades—from upper-level clerical to entry-level managerial—in Systems, Human Resources, the head office, and the branch offices. The project plan called for them to be working together for the next eighteen months and that while they'd get their regular year-end salary review, no raises were guaranteed and no additional compensation was given to join the team. This time, however, based on feedback received after the initial phase of the project, a more structural compensation plan was put in place.

What emerged was a hybrid incentive plan that blended before- and after-the-fact architecture. The team settled on a conceptual design: that if milestones were achieved, everybody on the team receives a payout, and some members would get more than others according to their contributions. The team leaders determined the individual variation (guided by a scoring system they developed). For its part, London Life decided how much money it would put into the incentive pot: $175,000, or some 10 percent of the estimated annualized benefit of the project to the company. But it didn't disclose the amount up front. "Members knew it was significant," says team leader Annabelle Mackey, "but they didn't know how much. There was a little bit of 'trust me' there."

And because it was a time-based project, London Life laid down clear deadlines. In Phase I, the reengineered procedure for opening new accounts and processing new orders for tax-deferred retirement investments had to be up and running by early 1995, when Canada's tax code made such investments timely. But just meeting that date wasn't enough. For the next few months, until the deluge of orders stopped, London Life monitored the redesigned process to make sure it worked. Phase II called for redesigning the process for customers who already had accounts with London Life and wanted to transfer between funds or engage in other account management activities.

The incentive plan was structured to pay out 60 percent of the $175,000 at the end of Phase I, and the balance at the end of Phase II, if the targets were met. There was nothing in the plan for payouts below that amount if the deadlines were missed. For both phases, says Mackey, "we set incredibly aggressive stretch targets."

The team met its Phase I goals. They decentralized the work, paving the way for shutting down the processing center at headquarters, moving technology to the regional offices, and retraining employees there. And they slashed cycle time, defined as the amount of time that elapses between the customer placing the order and receiving confirmation that it's been carried out. Before reengineering, cycle time was up to three weeks. Now, in effect, everything occurs instantaneously. Unit costs were cut in half.

The two team captains structured the payout. They established a baseline award for all members of $1,500 net for meeting the Phase I target. (Due to Canada's high income tax rates, London Life routinely grosses up all awards.) They also awarded additional bonuses—up to $5,000—to individuals who'd made exceptional contributions to the team. The head of the business unit determined the incentive payout for the team leaders themselves: $10,000 apiece for Phase I.

London Life didn't disclose the specific sums, but "we were very public that some members got more and some less," says Mackey. Members were pleased with the size of the payout, she says. The company also hosted a dinner for the team. Finally, team members were "empowered" to recommend bonuses to a few individuals who weren't full-time members but who, as advisers or in some other capacity, had made a significant contribution to the project.

The experience made London Life a believer in incentives. Says Warren, "Now we're looking at a greater use of team-based pay and variable pay, to reinforce our emphasis on teamwork and pay for performance."

# 10

# Implementing Team Pay—Phase I: Feasibility

Now you have the conceptual guidelines for team-based pay. But how do you go about making it a reality for your company?

Much like the pay programs themselves, developing and implementing a program is a process with almost infinite variation. No two companies are likely to take the identical approach or to arrive at the identical result. That's not to say that any one approach is necessarily superior to another, or most likely to produce the best results. However, I will make one unequivocal statement: The best-laid plan will fail without adequate attention to the planning and implementation process. In years of guiding companies through this process, I've observed the failure of well-designed programs and the success of mediocre programs. In each case, the results have been due, in large part, to the process by which the program was crafted and put into place.

In other words, the process by which an organization produces and introduces a program is more important than the program itself. If the program is imperfect, it can always be fine-tuned. (I use that word advisedly: Programs should be given a chance to work, and any changes should be evolutionary, not revolutionary.) But if the fundamentals aren't there, it's unlikely that enough corrections can be made in a program to save it.

In the rest of this book, I identify the factors that can make or break a program. Some of this information has already been touched on in previous chapters, but will be addressed here in greater detail and as part of a logical process to effectively implement a program. Because it's so critical, however, I'm mentioning one of the factors now: In my experience, the programs with the greatest likelihood of

189

success are those where there's buy-in at all levels of the corporation. I'll return to the important issue of buy-in in several steps of this process. For now I'll note that, in any compensation program, there are a great many stakeholders whose buy-in is important:

- The members of the team(s) who will be immediately affected
- Other teams doing similar work that may be candidates for team-pay programs
- Teams supporting or serving the team with the new pay system
- Ultimately, all employees
- The administrative/human resources staff, who may be responsible for administering the plan and overseeing compensation
- Management, which seeks a motivated workforce, low costs, and satisfied customers and shareholders
- Customers, whose concern is that the plan improve "your" ability to meet "my" needs

I've defined three major phases associated with the creation of an effective team-based pay program: *feasibility, design,* and *implementation.* The phases are broken down further, into thirteen steps (see Exhibit 10-1). For a plan to succeed, every step must be followed. The entire process, up to the point of rolling out the plan, may take as much as eighteen months or as little as six months, depending on the plan's complexity, the extent of change, and the time it takes to get management approvals. If the process takes much longer, it tends to lose its momentum. But it's impossible to dictate precisely how much time and energy an organization should devote to each step. That varies with the needs of the particular organization. Suffice it to say that this is a journey and you need to have your ticket punched at each stop.

In this chapter and the next two, I discuss each step in detail, with examples drawn from companies with which I've worked. In Phase I, the subject of this chapter, I describe the four steps that must be taken to determine the feasibility of a team-pay program. That involves acquiring a thorough understanding of the business, the wants and needs of management and employees, the impact of the current compensation program, and the company's ambitions for the new plan. The objective, by the end of Phase I, is to have defined a common ground for management and employees, and the broad outlines of an appropriate compensation program.

**Exhibit 10-1. Implementing team-based compensation (Phase I).**

## Methodology

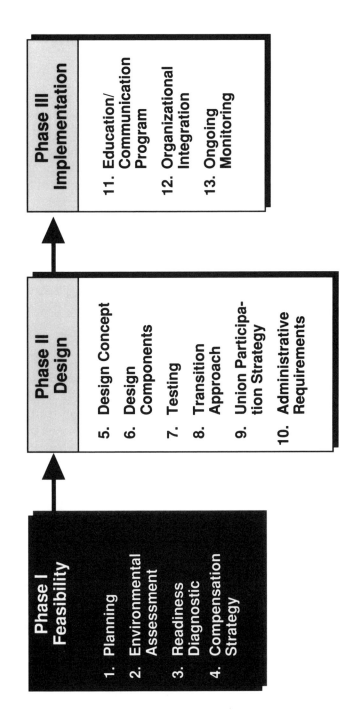

**Phase I
Feasibility**

1. Planning
2. Environmental Assessment
3. Readiness Diagnostic
4. Compensation Strategy

**Phase II
Design**

5. Design Concept
6. Design Components
7. Testing
8. Transition Approach
9. Union Participation Strategy
10. Administrative Requirements

**Phase III
Implementation**

11. Education/ Communication Program
12. Organizational Integration
13. Ongoing Monitoring

# Step 1: Planning

*Objective: Define purpose and process.*

It's only fitting that the process to create a team-based pay program should begin with a compensation design team, and that's precisely the case: The organization must establish a parallel team whose task is to plan, design, and ultimately implement the program. This team should have between seven and ten members, with good cross-functional representation from headquarters and field offices (if applicable), and from both staff and line positions. In the best-case scenario, this is a team consisting primarily of managers responsible for most of the employees who will be affected by the new program. While the planning teams for human resources-related issues are typically dominated by corporate staff, the credibility of a compensation program depends on line managers' playing a key role. At the same time, staff functions (Finance/Accounting, Systems, Human Resources) that are required to support the compensation program should be represented.

This is a team *limited* to managers. While employee views will be solicited periodically during the process (see Step 3), it's unwise to give employees a role on the team during this conceptual stage. In fact, it's probably illegal to do so. A decision by the National Labor Relations Board in 1993 in a case known as *Electromation, Inc.*, held that a company that involves employees in a group dealing with "conditions of employment," such as wages and rates of pay, may have unwittingly created an "employer-dominated labor organization." Whether the company's intent was good or bad, it may be perceived as seeking to circumvent unions and found guilty of "unlawful employer domination."

Every team needs a champion or sponsor, and a team taking on a project of this magnitude needs a powerful champion, ideally a respected member of senior management. A 1994 study of performance-reward plans by the American Compensation Association (*Organizational Performance Rewards: 663 Experiences in Making the Link*) found that 63 percent of the initial plan champions were from top management, with only 21 percent from Human Resources, and the balance mainly from line management. "Hopefully, 'championship' does not mean simply issuing a directive to 'get us one of those plans,' " the study's researchers noted, "but rather a top management team that is involved and supportive throughout the process. The role of top management as champion reinforces the finding that these plans are designed to improve business performance."

## Creating the Team Charter

The champion's or sponsor's first order of business is to charter the compensation team, thus laying the groundwork for the entire undertaking. The charter sets forth which areas come under the team's purview and which are out of bounds. Is the entire compensation program under revision? Does that include benefits? (If it's a business unit that's seeking to create a compensation plan, benefits—which tend to be centralized—may be untouchable.) Does it include fixed as well as variable pay? Such parameters must be established up front. As I note later in this chapter, however, the parameters may be redefined by the harsh realities of corporate life, as the process evolves.

The charter should also detail the structure of the compensation team, its accountabilities, and the resources that will be allocated to it. Whom does the team report to? Who needs to approve the new programs? What's the budget? How much time should members devote to the team? That's a bit like asking, How long is a piece of string? Such projects have an inexhaustible demand for time and energy, and the charter must set limits. Otherwise, members run the danger inherent in parallel teams: They may invest too much time in the team project, to the detriment of their regular jobs. But the charter should recognize that the demands will be significant. The typical compensation team meets three or four days or more a month until the project is completed. A team that meets less than two days per month will probably be unable to get the job done in a reasonable time frame because too much time will be lost bringing members up to date, and not enough time will be devoted to the project.

The team leader should be someone who has respect, influence, and time. Unfortunately, those attributes rarely occur in the same individual; while a senior line manager may be the best candidate for the job, he may not have the time to spare. One possible way to lighten his load is by appointing a staffer, perhaps from Human Resources, who coordinates the members' work, gathers information and conducts or oversees any statistical analyses, and makes sure that nothing slips through the cracks between meetings of the team. Some resources can be bought from consultants, but much of this work requires an intimate, "who's who" knowledge of the organization, possessed only by an inside manager. The appointment of such an aide to the team may also be specified in the charter.

What's the timetable? As I indicated earlier, such projects typically take anywhere between six and eighteen months. The longer the agenda—that is, the more components of the compensation architecture under review—or the more radical the changes contemplated, the longer the time frame; the more focused the agenda or the more modest the changes, the shorter the timetable. Typically, organizations that are overhauling their compensation architecture may be doing so as part of a general reengineering program and want to get it done as quickly as possible. They may also have a fixed deadline for implementation—for example, the first day of a new fiscal year. To meet that deadline, the plan must be introduced to employees months earlier. If, for example, a company proposes to put pay at risk by freezing merit raises, it has to give employees at least three months' warning or it may have some very disgruntled employees as reasonable base-pay increase expectations go unfulfilled.

To meet the timetable stated in the charter, the first task of the compensation team is to draw up an action plan. Each step has its own timeline, and each action within a step must be scheduled carefully to avoid unnecessary delays. Some actions can run concurrently; others must be consecutive. The team and team leader determine which members are accountable for which actions.

## Step 2: Environmental Assessment

*Objective: Identify the business characteristics that impact pay.*

In essence, this step asks, "By changing the compensation architecture, what do we want teams to do differently?" To answer the question, the compensation team must develop a thorough understanding of the industrial and economic issues faced by the company, the company's business strategy, and what leverage the company has to affect the way employees work.

Is your company in an industry that's growing, or in one that's declining? If it's declining, you may not have the potential volume growth on which to base incentive payouts without reducing employee head count. Is the industry cyclical? That's important, because all measures of financial performance will depend on the company's position in its cycle. If you're on the upward curve, you may evaluate your workers by different performance measures and calculate their base pay differently than if you're heading down. Is the company sensitive to interest rate fluctuations? To changes in technology? All those factors should be considered in deciding how—or whether—to restructure your compensation program.

How your company is positioned within the industry also affects its approach to compensation. Pay must be aligned with business strategy, but it has to reinforce it, too. For example, if your company's goal is to be a low-cost producer, then the measures used to evaluate team performance and set team pay should all have a cost compo-nent—more barrels of crude oil converted into usable products per man-day, more claims processed per hour. Price, not product differ-entiation, is key if you're in a very functional culture and you share Henry Ford's approach when he had just introduced the Model T's: "Any color you want, as long as it's black." If, on the other hand, you're in a service industry, then the pay system must be aligned with customer satisfaction. Or if your company's goal is to be lead-ing-edge, with high margins on new products, then cycle times may be the most appropriate measures for team performance.

As you've undoubtedly realized, such considerations are geared toward identifying the culture of the company, which, as I discussed in Chapter 9, helps determine the compensation architecture. But there are also more nuts-and-bolts questions for which the compensa-tion team needs answers. For example, it must evaluate the current business measurement and reporting systems that are already in place. No compensation program can outstrip the available measures; nor should any company create *new* measures of performance spe-cifically for pay. If such measures don't exist, they're evidently not relevant to the company's day-to-day operations, and fabricating them to support a compensation program is not only expensive, it's foolish. On the other hand, if new performance measures are gener-ally needed, this may provide the impetus to create them.

## The Issue of Leverage

Let's say our compensation team has established that the company is strongly customer-oriented, and that it has all the measurements in place—customer satisfaction surveys, retention figures, etc.—to eval-uate a team's performance. The next issue that our compensation team must address is *leverage*: What can the company do differently to affect employee behavior, that is, to get employees to perform as the company wants? Incentives may be the wrong answer if people don't have the necessary skills or behavioral competencies. In fact, instituting payouts for unattainable goals would merely frustrate em-ployees.

One way to tackle this issue is to evaluate the various initiatives offered by the human resources department, such as its training pro-grams. Since training tends to define the upper limit of employee capabilities, the compensation team may evaluate whether the limit could be raised—that is, employees could do more—through more and better training. Alternatively, better technology may be the key.

It's not enough to give word processors more instruction if, for example, the hardware itself is the rate-limiting factor.

The compensation team can also do some number-crunching to get a dollars-and-cents appreciation of leverage. Let's consider the case of an industrial gas company, where a process team is tasked with supplying portable cylinders of oxygen, nitrogen, and the like to customers. The team fills the cylinders, carries out whatever labeling and testing are mandated, and inspects equipment. The team's leverage is based on the number of cylinders it fills. The range of performance per team member varies between 150 and 200 cylinders per day. If all team members fill 200 cylinders per day, with an average profit margin of 25 cents per cylinder (assuming there's a market for the extra production, that's an incremental $12.50 [50 cylinders × 25 cents per cylinder]) for the company per day, or potentially $3,125 over the course of a year. Multiply that by 10 members per team, and 200 teams, and pretty soon you're talking about real money ($3,125 × 10 members per team × 200 teams = $6,250,000 per year).

The question is, How can you raise the team to that level of productivity? We know that technically it's feasible, because some members are already working at that level, while others are below the average. Our compensation team must try to account for the different levels of productivity. If it's a matter of improving skills and/or competencies, then the answer is more training. On the other hand, maybe the work processes need to be reengineered to eliminate nonproductive time. But if everybody already has the requisite skills and competencies, and the work processes are well designed, the lever may be motivation—specifically, predetermined incentives.

The nature of the workforce is another variable that our compensation team must consider. Is it unionized? (See Step 9, in Chapter 11.) Is turnover too high to maintain the needed talent pool or too low to allow promising employees to advance? If turnover is too high, a compensation plan that includes rewards for long-term service might be appropriate. On the other hand, if it's too low, the company might reconsider whether it's overpaying base wages. What are the demographics of the workforce? A younger workforce may be more receptive to pay-at-risk and incentives, while an older workforce or a workforce with many single mothers may be risk-averse.

### Management Interviews

Last, but certainly not least, the compensation team needs to conduct a series of interviews with all the senior managers responsible for the business(es) whose compensation structure is under review. In a

company, this typically means the chief executive officer's direct reports. In a business unit, it's the senior management. If, for example,
the subject is the compensation program for teams of underwriters at
an insurance company, our compensation team should interview the
chief operating officer, the chief administrative officer, the chief actu-
ary, and the directors of claims, marketing, and underwriting.

As a consultant, the question I frequently ask managers is: If you
could wave a magic wand and get employees to do something they're
not doing, what would it be? During interviews with management—
typically lasting an hour or two apiece—I find the question remark-
ably effective at eliciting information that describes the gap between
current and desired environments. Good managers have an almost
intuitive feel for what their employees are doing right and what they
need to do differently. Still, if you prefer a more directed approach,
try these thirteen questions:

1. What is the company's philosophy and its impact on compensation?
2. What is the ideal relationship between compensation and organizational performance?
3. How does the current compensation system support organizational efforts toward quality, efficiency, and productivity?
4. How well does the current compensation program encourage team efforts?
5. How do you know if your teams are successful?
6. Is the compensation program effectively and consistently administered?
7. How effective is the current performance appraisal system?
8. Do team members know what's expected of them?
9. How effective are the existing training programs?
10. What team member behaviors are associated with success?
11. What workforce issues do you anticipate will impact the
    company's productivity in the 1990s and beyond?
12. How effective is the company in using compensation as a
    strategic lever for change?
13. How should team performance be linked to base pay and
    incentive compensation?

Managers' responses should reveal much, not only about the
company but about their own preferences. For example, at Hallmark
Cards, as noted in Chapter 8, some managers embraced the concept
of variable pay while others had a philosophical aversion to the idea
of creating a risk-taking atmosphere. The compensation team should

be alert to such differences in style, which can affect buy-in and the scale of implementation. By synthesizing management responses with other findings, the team can begin to build a model of what measures and goals are important for the company.

# Step 3:  Readiness Diagnostic

*Objective: Gather baseline data regarding employee perceptions of current processes that relate to the successful implementation of a pay system.*

In the previous step, the compensation team interviewed management to identify the key environmental characteristics that could affect the choice of a compensation program. In this step, the compensation team must interview employees as well as management to assess the internal environment, that is, the cultural readiness of the organization for possible changes in its reward systems. Not only does the readiness diagnostic help determine whether changes in compensation are likely to work, it also pinpoints those areas that need special attention before a new program is implemented.

The team's diagnostic tools may be a management questionnaire and either an employee survey or focus groups, or both. Later in this section I discuss their pros and cons and offer a sample employee questionnaire. In either case, however, the framework for the diagnosis will be four critical issues:

*1. What is the focus of the company?* The issue is actually twofold. First, is there an individual or a group orientation? Even when employees work in teams, the organization may be more oriented toward measuring and rewarding individual performance. Second, does the company have a clear and consistent direction that it communicates to employees? Since compensation should be aligned to corporate strategy, employees need to know and understand that strategy.

*2. How demanding is the company?* Again, two related issues. The first involves the perceived pressure for performance. To what degree does the company hold employees accountable for meeting goals and reaching high standards of performance? Second, are employees encouraged to use their initiative to experiment and take risks to improve the way they work? If, for example, employees say that poor performance is tolerated, the company may not be ready for an incentive plan in which the total compensation of a team is reduced by the inappropriate behavior, lack of quality results, or laziness of one member. Peer pressure may bring everybody down, not up.

3. *Are people able and willing to change the way they work?* Trust and commitment are at issue here: Do employees trust the company and management? Are they motivated by achievement? Or by the fear of making mistakes? A low level of trust and a weak achievement orientation indicate that employees will respond cautiously at best to initiatives aimed at improving performance. They will be particularly concerned about placing any portion of compensation at risk.

4. *How effective are the key performance measures?* Again, the issue is twofold. First, how valid is the company's performance appraisal process? And second, is the current compensation system competitive and equitable? It is also important to consider whether employees believe that pay is tied to good performance. If employees are skeptical about the performance appraisals, they may distrust a compensation program that purports to link pay to individual performance assessment.

## Successful vs. Troubled Plans

You may think that the above analysis is purely theoretical, but in fact, the diagnostic framework has a direct bearing on the success or failure of a company's compensation program. When Hay Research for Management asked human resources executives to evaluate their company in terms of the diagnostic framework and the success of its compensation program, it found a strong cause-and-effect connection between the two. Exhibit 10-2 shows the spread on each issue, between those companies with successful plans and those that rated their plans troubled. It's noteworthy that compensation per se was one of the least significant issues compared with such areas as performance measurement, trust, and encouragement of initiative.

## Sampling Employee Opinion

As indicated earlier, it's at this step that the compensation team actively seeks feedback from employees as well as management. If it chooses, the team may also ask management to respond to the questions from the viewpoint of a "typical" employee. This may result in two readiness diagnostics, with some telling differences.

There are two main ways to sample employee opinion directly: the employee survey and the focus group. They serve different needs. The survey, which typically takes three months to prepare, distribute, collect, and analyze, obviously reaches a much wider audience—the entire payroll, if that's the company's target—and is thus the most cost-effective way of amassing large amounts of data. (The data can

**Exhibit 10-2. Readiness diagnostic: difference between successful and troubled plans.**

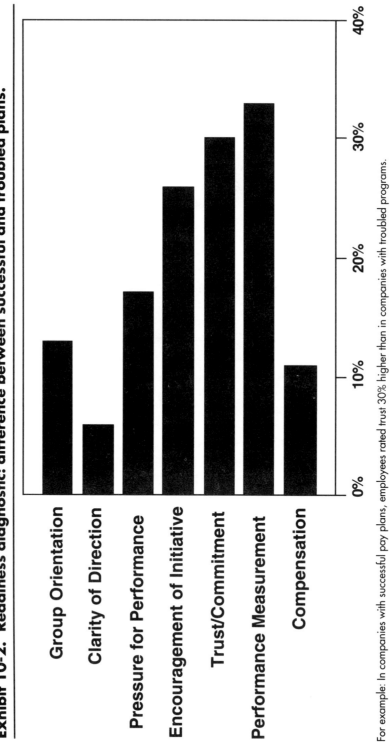

For example: In companies with successful pay plans, employees rated trust 30% higher than in companies with troubled programs.

*Source:* Hay Research for Management (U.S.A.)

be useful not only for ascertaining employee opinion but also for facilitating comparisons with other companies and to measure progress over a number of years.) It can be a highly effective way, too, for the company to trumpet the fact that it is considering an overhaul of its compensation program.

For that reason, a company that wants to go slow—using pilot teams for testing compensation changes, for example, rather than rolling out the plan to the entire organization—may prefer to use focus groups. Not only are focus groups less intrusive than surveys; they also provide the qualitative information that isn't usually forthcoming with a pencil-and-paper questionnaire. For instance, people can be asked what they would do differently to be more productive. And unlike surveys, focus groups are a resource that's easily tapped: Hallmark Cards, for one, reconvened its focus groups from time to time during the period it was revising its compensation architecture, to sample employee opinion.

Perhaps the best solution is a compromise: Begin with a survey, to get the big picture of *what* people think, and follow up with focus groups to see *why*. In either case, employers must be mindful of the *Electromation* decision. While companies are allowed to seek feedback in the form of employee surveys or other communications, it should be obtained unilaterally, without the promise or suggestion that management will negotiate with the employees regarding the information obtained. And companies must make clear to employees who participate in focus groups that the employees are speaking on their own behalf rather than as representatives of a group of other employees.

Below is an abridged version of a typical employee survey that a compensation team might distribute at this point. Most of the questions offer the respondent a numbered range of responses, from 1 ("very good" or "strongly agree") to 5 ("very poor" or "strongly disagree").

1. Based on your experience here as well as what you may know of all other companies, how would you rate your total cash compensation (base pay, overtime, incentives)?      1  2  3  4  5

2. Do you feel that your pay is fair in relation to that of others who do the same type of work within the

| | | | | | |
|---|---|---|---|---|---|
| Company | 1 | 2 | 3 | 4 | 5 |
| Your team | 1 | 2 | 3 | 4 | 5 |
| Other teams | 1 | 2 | 3 | 4 | 5 |

3. How do you rate your overall understanding of the company's pay policies and programs?                                   1  2  3  4  5

4. How strongly do you agree or disagree with the following statements?

   I am provided with sufficient information on pay policies and procedures.                                      1  2  3  4  5

   Pay at the company (base pay, overtime, incentives) motivates me to work hard on my job.                        1  2  3  4  5

   Current pay policies support the company's mission and beliefs.
   1  2  3  4  5

   The company explains the reasons behind changes in compensation policies and programs.                          1  2  3  4  5

   The current pay system at the company encourages employees to work together as a team.                          1  2  3  4  5

5. Which of the following statements represents the way your pay is currently determined?

   ☐ Mostly on the overall performance of the company.
   ☐ Mostly on the overall performance of the business unit.
   ☐ Mostly on the performance of my team.
   ☐ Mostly on my individual performance.
   ☐ Other (please specify) _____.

6. When the company gives out information about pay policies and procedures to employees, how do you feel about it?

   ☐ I can always believe it.
   ☐ I can usually believe it.
   ☐ I can believe it about half the time.
   ☐ I can seldom believe it.
   ☐ I can never believe it.

7. How strongly do you agree or disagree with the following statements?

   My job makes an important contribution to the success of the company.                                         1  2  3  4  5

   I have a good understanding of my job responsibilities.
   1  2  3  4  5

I have enough authority to carry out my job effectively.

        1  2  3  4  5

Teamwork among employees is very important to the company's success.         1  2  3  4  5

The company is interested in employees' ideas for improvement.

        1  2  3  4  5

I have sufficient control over the factors that affect the end results (output) of my job.         1  2  3  4  5

8. How strongly do you agree or disagree with the following statements?

I am proud to work for the company.         1  2  3  4  5

I understand the company's five-year business plan.

        1  2  3  4  5

I understand how the company will accomplish its five-year business plan.

        1  2  3  4  5

The company insists on high-quality work by its employees.

        1  2  3  4  5

Employees are expected to meet demands for high levels of performance.         1  2  3  4  5

Poor performance among employees is usually not tolerated at the company.         1  2  3  4  5

Employees are encouraged to take reasonable risks in their efforts to increase the effectiveness of the company.

        1  2  3  4  5

When things go well in my job, my contributions are often recognized.         1  2  3  4  5

9. Employees' pay at the company *should be* based upon performance.         1  2  3  4  5

10. If performance factors are considered in determining pay, pay at the company should be based upon:

☐ An employee's individual on-the-job performance.

☐ The performance of the employee's team.

☐ The overall performance of the company.

11. "Above-average" performing employees at the company should receive better pay increases than "average" performers.

        1  2  3  4  5

12. How would you rate the company on each of the following, based on your experience here as well as what you may know of other companies?

Cooperation between members of your team.     1   2   3   4   5

Cooperation between members of *different* teams.

                                                     1   2   3   4   5

Listening to your problems, complaints, and suggestions.

                                                     1   2   3   4   5

Responding to your problems, complaints, and suggestions.

                                                     1   2   3   4   5

Your opportunity for advancement.                  1   2   3   4   5

Your job security.                                        1   2   3   4   5

Providing you with a stable income.              1   2   3   4   5

## Readiness Follow-Up

By the end of the diagnostic process, the type of compensation plan best suited to the organization is becoming clearer. The diagnostic process will have documented the corporation's culture, as perceived by employees. By sampling employee opinion, it will have initiated the communication process that will become a critical step later in the undertaking.

Finally, it will have revealed areas that must be addressed before a new compensation program can be designed, let alone implemented. The priority now is to close the gap, if it's sizable, between the cultural requirements of the compensation system and the actual culture of the organization. Harking back to the readiness diagnostic described at the beginning of Step 3, the company may need to:

1. *Improve focus.* Team-building exercises and meetings will strengthen the company's team orientation. If they are not apparent, the company must clarify its objectives and make sure they are known to employees.

2. *Encourage accountability and innovation.* A program of performance-linked incentives will not necessarily foster new ideas if the current organizational culture does not support new ideas or penalize poor performance. The new compensation program should include active steps to change the culture, making it clear that poor performance will not be tolerated while above-expectations performance will be recognized and rewarded. Managers and supervisors must be held more accountable for managing performance in their units.

3. *Gain greater employee trust and commitment.* A lack of trust or commitment to achievement may impede the team's effort to implement a new compensation plan, or it may force a change in the plan itself. For example, a company hoping to introduce incentive compensation may reconsider using pay-at-risk for the first year of the program. It can use that time to prove to skeptical employees that the goals are achievable and that the new plan is not a veiled attempt to reduce pay. Efforts to win back employee trust will take time and require persistence, but they are critical.

4. *Measure performance more effectively.* A performance-reward compensation program will be well received only if the performance measurement process has credibility. The company may need to develop a valid employee performance management/appraisal process. Employees' view of compensation may be improved through a stronger link between performance and pay, and an external competitiveness policy.

Once the employee readiness process is completed and before any actions are undertaken, it is necessary to communicate the results of the survey and/or focus groups to all affected employees. At a minimum, summary results along with management reaction and any future plans impacting compensation need to be circulated. Employee meetings would be even better. Such communication is crucial to help create a positive atmosphere and reasonable employee expectations.

There is a rule I firmly believe: *"The greater the compensation change, the more soaking-in time required before employees can actively embrace and accept the changes mandated by the new program."*

## Step 4: Compensation Strategy

*Objective: Define the specific characteristics of the performance-reward structure: a framework for compensation decisions.*

This is the last cornerstone that must be laid before our compensation team can get down to business: designing the plan. Still, it's a critical step: It is here that the team enunciates the company's beliefs and principles about compensation. The beliefs—broad statements about the organization, culture, and strategy—form a basis for consensus, a sort of corporate mission statement (or, put less elegantly, management's gut views) about compensation. The principles are a blueprint for action, an articulation of what compensation *should* do, in an ideal environment, to support team performance. See Exhibit

10-3 for a template of the "as is" (current environment) and "to be" (ideal environment), and how a compensation intervention can move an organization from today to tomorrow.

Our compensation team may approach this step by characterizing the company's current compensation arrangement. One method is to locate the company on the pay-versus-performance matrix presented in Exhibit 9-4. Is it paying top dollar for mediocre performance (overpaying)? Paying uncompetitive wages for excellent performance (unstable)? This exercise helps define the company's starting point. The beliefs and principles describe its ideal end point (Exhibit 10-3).

It's in Steps 5 and 6, where the actions that have to be taken to move the company to the end point are identified, that the nitty-gritty work of compensation design occurs. But it would be unfair to dismiss Step 4 as an ivory-tower exercise. In this step, the compensation team may carry out more research within the company, to refine its understanding of senior and middle management views. And it may conduct external research, benchmarking the company against leaders in the same industry or region.

A sample list of *beliefs* might state that the company:

1. Attracts and retains high-quality employees that contribute to the organization's success.
2. Encourages individual and team achievement of corporate business strategy and performance goals.
3. Encourages continuous improvement through employee involvement.
4. Is perceived as responsive, fair, and equitable.
5. Provides linkage between pay and the performance appraisal system.
6. Provides competitive base pay and total cash compensation.
7. Aligns pay with business results and team performance.
8. Provides appropriate emphasis on both short- and long-term performance.
9. Provides pay in an open, interactive process.
10. Provides pay in a simple and understandable manner.

Like motherhood and apple pie, it's hard to quibble with beliefs like these. With their statement of principles, companies begin to define the *types* of interventions they are going to take to get where they want to go, although they still paint in broad brushstrokes. A company may, for example, express a commitment to differentiating individual pay, based on competencies and skills, but it may not be willing to specify which competencies are to be rewarded or to de-

**Exhibit 10-3. Compensation strategy.**

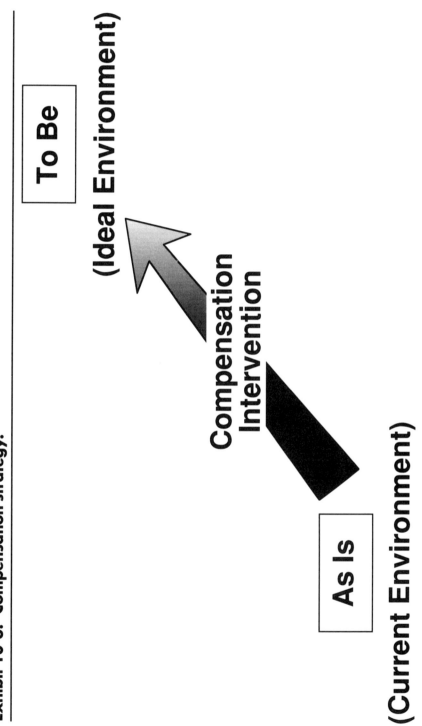

To Be

(Ideal Environment)

Compensation Intervention

As Is

(Current Environment)

scribe the skill blocks. It may endorse the concept of variable pay—specifically, incentive compensation for process teams—and pay-at-risk, but it may not be willing to specify how much pay will be put at risk, or how the payout will be funded.

The following list shows how a company interested in reforming its compensation program might describe its *principles:*

1. Compensation will be composed of a base and variable element for *all* team employees.
2. Total cash compensation (base pay plus variable) should range from below average to substantially above average, based upon achievement of incentive goals.
3. Base-pay levels will be below average when compared to appropriate industries and job markets in which the company competes for talent.
4. Increases in base pay will be based on the demonstration of skills and competencies.
5. Incentive goals are specific team performance objectives that measure continuous improvement and support business strategy.
6. Upon achievement of incentive goals, a team will receive two to four times the amount of pay-at-risk (the difference between base pay and total cash compensation at target performance).
7. Individual achievements will be rewarded through cash and noncash recognition awards.

As you've probably noticed, the list doesn't address every component in compensation architecture. The reason is that the statement of principles depends on the scope of the compensation team's charter. If the mandate is to reengineer compensation, the list of principles may provide a complete blueprint for change. But if the target is less ambitious, so is the list. For example, when Hallmark Cards decided to develop an incentive plan for its new teams, that was its exclusive focus. Unisys, which already had an incentive plan in place, refined its principles only on paying for competencies as a means to reward individual performance.

Mobil's U.S. Refining and Marketing division offers a prime example of how the process works, and the importance of the feasibility phase I've described in this chapter. Initially, division management had expressed interest in introducing variable pay as part of an overhaul of its total compensation program. But when the compensation team undertook an environmental assessment, it realized that the internal systems weren't sophisticated enough to measure what the division wanted to reward. And in any event, management became concerned that predetermined goals would limit their flexibility. Nor could they agree on which measures of success to reward. As a result, the compensation team narrowed its focus to the division's cash and noncash recognition program, to which it applied the entire process described here and in the next two chapters.

In the next chapter, I discuss the specific steps our compensation team must take to design a program. But first, it must ensure that senior management has signed off on the underlying beliefs and principles. Jumping into the design phase, without management buy-in, is one of the most common and disastrous mistakes compensation teams make. Don't start Step 5 until Step 4 has been approved and accepted no matter how long it takes. No design will please management if agreement cannot be reached on the compensation strategy.

# 11

# Implementing Team Pay—Phase II: Design

Now the work begins. In Phase II, the subject of this chapter, our compensation design team will finally design the plan.

Unlike Phase I, which was comparatively straightforward, this phase (see Exhibit 11-1) is characterized by much repetition. The team advances, reevaluates what it did earlier, retreats to make modifications or adjustments, and advances again. This "two steps forward, one step back" process may be frustrating and occasionally exasperating, but it's necessary to ensure an effective and well-designed plan.

## Step 5: Design Concept

*Objective: Draft an architectural framework that links reward to organizational culture and strategic objectives.*

It's in Steps 5 and 6 that our compensation team, having laid the foundation, actually develops all of the components and mechanics of the plan. In this step, the team makes some basic choices within its compensation architecture, drawing heavily on what it learned in Phase I. Central to its considerations, and at the core of Step 5, are two issues:

1. *The balance of total compensation dollars between fixed and variable pay.*
2. *The extent of variation in pay, if any, among team members.*

It would be politically incorrect to say that the first issue divides the men from the boys, but certainly it divides the more tradition-minded companies from those taking a comparatively progressive

**Exhibit 11-1. Implementing team-based compensation (Phase II).**

# *Methodology*

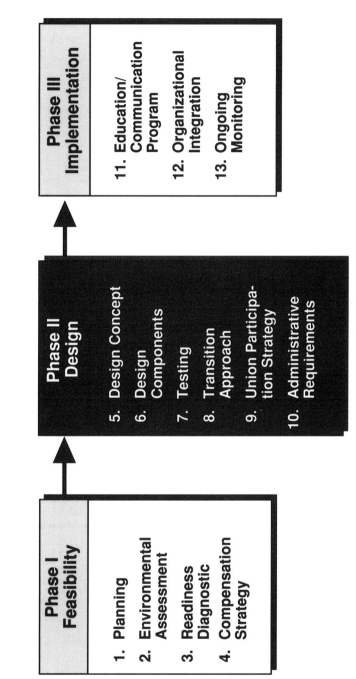

**Phase I**
**Feasibility**

1. Planning
2. Environmental Assessment
3. Readiness Diagnostic
4. Compensation Strategy

**Phase II**
**Design**

5. Design Concept
6. Design Components
7. Testing
8. Transition Approach
9. Union Participation Strategy
10. Administrative Requirements

**Phase III**
**Implementation**

11. Education/ Communication Program
12. Organizational Integration
13. Ongoing Monitoring

approach. What's at stake here is the sharing of risk and reward: The traditional companies guarantee their workers a fixed reward, regardless of performance, while the more progressive companies give workers an opportunity to earn a variable amount of compensation (contingent upon plan goals), in addition to a fixed base level. As Exhibit 11-2 shows, in the second case, workers assume some risk (their fixed pay is reduced) in return for the opportunity to earn significantly higher total cash compensation.

The balance or ratio between fixed and variable pay is an important consideration in designing an incentive compensation plan. To a degree, our compensation team will be guided by its leanings from Phase I, including the receptivity or aversion to risk among management and employees, and the statement of beliefs and principles. (While it can accept employee input, management alone must decide how much pay to put at risk. To allow employees on an individual basis to choose their risk levels could have the effect of creating an investment vehicle, which in turn might be subject to the disclosure rules of the Securities and Exchange Commission.)

Reaching a conclusion on this point requires the compensation team to determine its starting point on the pay-versus-performance matrix. Harking back to Exhibit 9-4 provides guidance on where to start incentive plan funding. On the one hand, the new plan could place a percentage of current compensation at risk, assuming that pay

**Exhibit 11-2. Risk versus reward trade-off.**

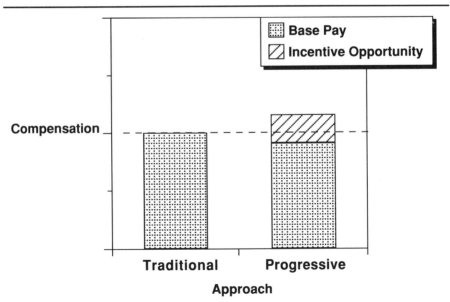

exceeds performance, and redirect the current compensation dollars into new channels. On the other hand, it could start the plan by adding opportunities to the existing base salary program. This latter alternative is usually reserved for high-performing (above-average) teams with average or below-average base pay. Between the "add-on" and the "redirect" options are a number of combinations. But whatever the choice, any additional compensation dollars should be self-funded based on costs saved or revenues generated through team performance.

Few companies today are just adding incentive opportunities without the option of reducing or slowing the growth of fixed base-pay costs sometime in the future. To do otherwise would create an unfair balance between the company and employees. In good times the employees would earn more through the incentive plan, and in bad times they would be paid the same as if no incentive plan existed; the company assumes all of the risk associated with pay-for-performance.

The second issue—the extent of variation in pay among team members—should be considered in tandem with the first because it can have a bearing on the allocation of variable pay. If, in fact, the company wants to make such distinctions among team members, it has three avenues for varying compensation: increases in base pay, incentive compensation, and/or spot cash awards. Which avenue(s) the company chooses depends partly on its beliefs and principles, and partly on the team type(s) whose compensation program is being designed. To resolve these issues, the compensation team first needs to identify the company's priorities for its future compensation program. In Step 4, it articulated the company's view of what compensation should do, in an ideal environment, to support team performance. Here (see Exhibit 11-3) it will rank in order of importance the company's realistic objectives for the plan. Only by establishing these priorities can the compensation team identify a plan that will best suit the company's needs.

If, for example, keeping fixed compensation costs down is a top priority, then we can be fairly confident that variable pay—heavily weighted toward pay-at-risk—should be a key element of the plan. If rewarding outstanding individual performance is ranked "desirable, but not necessary" or not even a plan objective, then our compensation team may conclude that group-oriented compensation and motivation for the team should be the focus of the plan, rather than merit increases and other rewards or recognition for individual team members.

As a rule, the company's priorities should correspond to the or-

**Exhibit 11-3. Plan design priorities.**

| Plan Objectives | I<br>A Primary<br>Plan<br>Objective | II<br>An Important,<br>but Secondary,<br>Objective | III<br>Desirable,<br>but Not<br>Necessary | IV<br>Not a<br>Plan<br>Objective |
|---|---|---|---|---|
| Create Identification with Company's Goals & Strategies | | | | |
| Provide Competitive Environment | | | | |
| Support TQM/Reengineering | | | | |
| Keep Fixed Compensation Costs Down | | | | |
| Reward Outstanding Individual Performers | | | | |
| Provide Outstanding Team Performance | | | | |

ganizational culture and the team type(s) whose compensation is under review:

  • *If it's a parallel team*, whose members have only a part-time commitment, the company's top priorities are likely to be rewarding outstanding individual and team performance. Variation in compensation through base-pay increases and spot cash and noncash awards is appropriate; variable pay is not a factor.

  • *If it's a project team*, whose members are committed full-time but only temporarily to the undertaking, the priorities are similar to those for parallel teams. The main differences are that the focus on individual achievement is even greater, and reengineering— particularly to gain speed, for a competitive advantage—may be an additional objective. Members of this type of team are likely to have the biggest variation in skills and competencies. Thus substantial variation in pay is the norm. Variable pay is probably not a factor but, if it is included in the compensation plan, it may allow for considerable variation among members.

  • *If it's a process team*, with full-time, permanent members, the top priority may be supporting total quality management. Keeping down fixed compensation costs, rewarding outstanding team performance, and creating an identification with the company's goals and strategies probably also rank high. Those priorities argue for team-based incentive compensation in which members should share equally: the same dollar amount for all members. (How the incentive plan is funded depends on other priorities as well, such as providing a competitive environment.) That's also true of spot awards, cash or noncash.

As for allowing any variation in pay among team members, well, that's up to the company. It can distribute incentive compensation as a percentage of pay, rather than in absolute dollars, but that rewards the highest-paid workers, not necessarily the best performers. If the company wants to differentiate by means of spot cash awards, the ground rule should be that every team member receives at least token payment before any one individual receives more. The more appropriate avenue, however, is to utilize the base-pay increase process, recognizing an individual team member's contributions measured by the demonstration of desired behavioral competencies.

## Design Guidelines

By the end of this analysis, our compensation team will have settled on a design concept for the new compensation program, and will have a set of design guidelines for the next step. In the sample guidelines, below, for a company with process teams, you'll see how the compensation team has evolved from a statement of beliefs and principles to the point where it can begin designing the compensation plan:

1. Base-pay increases will be administered with the intention of reducing variation based upon historical factors and will provide differentials based upon performance ratings measuring newly defined skills and behavioral competencies.
2. Performance ratings will be determined by a multi-rater 360-degree approach (peers and team leader).
3. All team members (salaried and hourly) will participate in an incentive plan.
4. Current compensation levels (base pay and incentive opportunities) will be maintained for current productivity levels.
5. Incentive payouts are projected to be 10 percent of total earnings for current productivity.
6. Additional compensation above current levels will be self-funded through incentive opportunities based upon improvements in measurable operational results.
7. Incentive plan goals will include: productivity, quality, production schedule (percent adherence), and controllable indirect expense as measured against prior performance.
8. Performance against incentive plan goals will be measured and paid out quarterly.
9. Incentive plan design will reduce internal base-pay inequities.
10. All team members eligible for an incentive award will receive the same dollar amount from the incentive plan award pool.
11. With the implementation of the incentive plan, the company's individual incentive (piecework program) will be discontinued.
12. All participants will be protected from loss of earnings during the first year of the incentive plan by receiving the greater of the new or average of the prior two years' incentive awards.
13. Incentive awards will continue to be excluded from any benefit program.

## Step 6: Design Components

*Objective: Design a plan reflective of the compensation strategy.*
The first task for our compensation team is to identify what it

cannot change. By now, perhaps, the team—which is undoubtedly eager to get down to business—may feel that it's sufficiently aware of the hurdles it has to jump. But my experience is that unless it identifies the assumptions and constraints that may limit its flexibility, it runs a very real risk of designing a plan that just won't fly.

For example, as noted in Chapter 9, management often stipulates that only base-pay *increases*—not current base-pay levels—may be put at risk in any incentive plan. Another rate-limiting factor may be the company's reporting and measuring systems. As noted in Chapter 10, no compensation program can outstrip the available measures; nor should any company create new measures of performance specifically for a pay program. As a political and practical matter, the last thing our compensation team wants to do is increase the plan's administrative overhead by requiring the creation of additional measures. For example, if there's currently no means for measuring a team's wastage, don't write it into the plan unless it becomes an important factor in running the business—then it will measure whether or not pay is linked to its outcome.

Having identified what it *cannot* do, the compensation team should next tackle what it *can*. The list is exhaustive. In previous chapters, I've described at length each of the components of compensation and the alternative ways by which they can be approached. Rather than covering the same ground here, I'll just note that, depending on the company's compensation strategy, the following may be on our design team's agenda:

• *Establish measurement criteria, goals, and timing.* I devoted Chapter 8 to a discussion of these design elements and others in incentive plans. In fact, they must be established for every component of pay.

Let's say, for example, that our compensation team wants to include pay-for-competencies in its new program. Assuming it's starting from scratch, it must first build a competency model, identifying those attributes and traits that are most relevant to the performance of the particular team(s) within this particular corporate culture, and perhaps assigning a value to each competency in the model. As noted in Chapter 3, this is a time-intensive process involving interviews with management and selected employees—hence the value of the action plan called for in Step 1 (Chapter 10). Then our compensation team must find a way to incorporate competencies in performance evaluation. Who conducts the appraisals, how frequently they should be conducted, and at what point competencies should actually be linked to pay are all timing issues the compensation team must decide.

• *Develop the payout formula.* In Step 5, our compensation team determined whether the company was willing to add new money to the compensation pool or wanted to put some pay at risk. In this step, the team must spell out the formula (or formulas; it's not unusual for a compensation team to develop a few plans, which they'll test in Steps 6 and 7). For example, if team members are putting 5 percent of their base pay at risk in an incentive/productivity improvement plan, what's the production threshold they have to meet to get that money back? How many more widgets per man-hour do they need to produce to max out at 10 or 20 percent of base pay? (Exhibit 8-3 illustrates several payout formulas or curves.) How many additional widgets will they have to produce the following year? What's the measurement period and when do payouts occur? (That question may not be answered until the team reaches Step 10, at the end of this chapter.)

At this point, many compensation teams are tempted to take a cookbook approach: The more you measure, the better the recipe. Avoid this temptation. It's true that some companies, industries, and team types require more measures than others, but simplicity is a virtue of any compensation plan. According to the American Compensation Association study (*Organizational Performance Rewards: 663 Experiences in Making the Link*) mentioned in Chapter 10, plans with three to five measures report better results. Below that, it's hard to be confident you've got a good reading on performance; above it, it becomes too complex.

• *Determine award levels.* The compensation team must define what constitutes an awardable activity, and how such activities should be awarded. However, compared to incentive payouts, which must be carefully formulated, recognition in the form of spot cash or noncash awards is quite discretionary. Management usually has broad latitude on the type of activity, award size (within certain parameters), and frequency. But consistency is important: You can't offer a sizable award to one team and not to another for a comparable achievement.

## Custom-Designing for Teams

Which design elements our compensation design team must address is a function of the magnitude of the program it's designing, and the type(s) of teams involved. A program for parallel teams will focus on recognition/reward, while a program for project teams may cover both recognition and merit increases; both incentives and base-pay increases may feature prominently in a program for process teams. For more information about specific team architecture, see Chapter 9.

But to some degree, as Exhibit 11-4 shows, all incentive compensation plans for teams share certain characteristics that distinguish them from company-wide incentive programs.

## Success Factors

In Chapter 10, I noted that the best-designed plans can fail if the process by which they're produced is lacking. I'll amplify that remark now by noting that certain design fundamentals are critically important, too. Over the years, I've developed a list of the key success factors in plan design, and they include both the process and the plan itself. I won't claim that any one of them can make or break a plan, but in the absence of one factor, the others will have to be that much stronger:

1. *Commitment.* Management at all levels, but particularly senior management and first-line supervision, must be committed to the design. Without team leader/manager support, it is unlikely that the new compensation plan will ever be perceived in a positive light.

2. *Focus.* A compensation plan for teams is more likely to succeed when it is clearly focused on paying for teams through incentive compensation, other shared rewards, or competencies associated with team success. When a company says it wants teamwork but focuses its compensation on individual productivity, it's sending a mixed message to employees.

3. *Measurement.* Compensation plans are most effective when they quantify what they measure—even if, in the case of customer satisfaction, that involves measures that aren't easily quantified. As noted in Chapter 8, measures can be financial (revenues, profit) or operational (output, cost reduction, attendance). The advantage of operational measures is that they generally have a shorter "line of sight": They record the performance by the team, not by the corporation, and measure "controllables," results within the team's control. The less complicated the measurement system, the better. All measurements need to be simple and straightforward. If not, they are less likely to influence behavior.

4. *Involvement.* While I earlier urged the commitment of management, employees at every level need to be involved in the design process, whether it's through surveys, focus groups, team or departmental meetings, or other mechanisms. Remember "taxation

Exhibit 11-4. Incentive compensation characteristics.

| Attribute | Company-wide | Team |
|---|---|---|
| Basis | All Employees | Small Group |
| Orientation | Accounting | Controllable Factors |
| Implication | Shared Fate | Separate Economics |
| Measurement | Relatively Simple | Relatively Complex |

without representation": If you don't elicit the views of all your constituencies, you're likely to have a revolution on your hands. The American Compensation Association study found that nonmanagement employee involvement in plans was an important factor in their success.

5. *Timing.* The shorter, the better. Employees need to see the results of their hard work in their paychecks, particularly if they've put pay at risk. So a measurement period of a quarter is better than a year, a month is better than a quarter (if administratively feasible), and payout should occur within a month after measurement.

6. *Communication.* As a corollary of involvement, be sure your communication is two-way: In addition to seeking employees' input, keep them apprised frequently and systematically as to the shape the plan is taking. I'll have more to say about this process in Step 11 (Chapter 12).

However, I'll note here that communication must continue to be an integral part of the plan after it's implemented. The American Compensation Association study found that 81 percent of the 663 companies it surveyed with pay-for-performance plans regularly communicated performance on payout measures at least quarterly, and that plans with regular communication had significantly better results. And companies that routinely shared information about business performance reported that their pay-for-performance plans achieved greater improvements in teamwork—particularly when the communications were scheduled regularly, rather than delivered at management's discretion. This assures that all teams will hear a similar message at regular intervals.

# Step 7: Testing

*Objective: No surprises!*

In Step 6, our compensation design team designed each component as a discrete entity. The plan must be tested the same way. A new approach to performance appraisal, the introduction of different skill blocks in a pay-for-skills program, an incentive plan, or recognition award program must be tested separately to see how it translates into reality (and dollars and cents). By testing, I'm referring here primarily to focus groups and pen-and-paper calculations. Pilot programs, which many people think of as testing, will be addressed in Step 8.

So, let's say you've completely redesigned your company's compensation architecture, starting with the development of a competency model that will be used in performance evaluation. Test the model on a focus group of team members, or by asking a couple of managers or supervisors to evaluate a half dozen of the teams' best and brightest. As a rule, the most outstanding performers should have the most outstanding appraisal rating.

You might think that enough evaluation has already gone into the creation of the model. However, competency models, like most elements in a compensation program, tend to be based on past experience. For example, one of my clients, which historically had little use for teams, overlooked peer collaboration as a competency. But testing revealed that the company, moving toward a time-based culture, was increasingly using project teams. If it hadn't tested the model, it would have omitted a competency that became vital to success in the following years.

While testing a competency model is a qualitative exercise, testing an incentive plan involves a lot of number-crunching on both a prospective and retrospective basis. Every plan should be modeled to determine what savings would occur at what levels of performance, what percent of those savings should be paid out to employees, and what should be reserved for the company. If, for example, harking back to the industrial gas company described in Chapter 10, each team does in fact fill an additional 500 cylinders a day, that's an extra $6.25 million a year. How much of that does the company share with employees? Typically companies pay out between 20 and 40 percent of any savings, but finding the best place on that continuum can be a tough assignment for our compensation team. On the one hand, our compensation team wants to encourage employees by sharing the gain (after all, that was the original purpose of the plan); on the other, it wants to improve the company's bottom line. Of course, the sharing percentage would be influenced by the company's current position on the pay-performance matrix (Exhibit 9-4).

Next, our compensation team must assess the likelihood that employees will achieve the payouts it's projecting. Ideally, from the company's point of view, the threshold for payout would be met at least 80 percent of the time. Calculating the probability of meeting the threshold, however, is problematic. Retrospective studies aren't that useful because, by definition, they evaluate performance before any impact the plan might have had on employee performance. Prospective studies—calculations of projected production and savings—have somewhat greater value for the company, because they at least identify the financial upside and downside of each plan. In terms of projecting performance, however, these are exercises on paper only—hence the importance of the period of transition described next in Step 8.

Testing a recognition award program poses similar problems, but, because many companies already have some kind of program in place, precedents will be helpful. Auditing the books of the previous program should provide guidance. Which activities received cash and/or noncash awards? Are those the kinds of activities and/or effects the company wants to reward in the future? Do they conform to the company's beliefs and principles? Have the existing practices motivated employees to do the right things?

In all probability, what our compensation team learns from the tests will take it back to Step 6, to revise at least some elements of the plan. It should then revisit Step 7, for more testing, before proceeding to Step 8. As I said earlier, this is an iterative process, and much of the "backing-and-forthing" occurs at this stage.

## Step 8: Transition Approach

*Objective: Integrate the recommended compensation plan with existing reward system.*

At last, it's time for our compensation team to turn its attention to launching the plan. Should it be a cautious toe in the water, or total immersion? The answer, as usual, varies with the company and type of plan. If the compensation team has made relatively modest changes to be integrated into the existing system, then a company-wide rollout is not unreasonable. And some components—notably a recognition award plan—can be introduced without a period of transition, even if they're unprecedented for the company. But when it comes to most of the design elements—incentive compensation, performance appraisals, pay-for-skills—there's a strong argument for phasing-in the initiative over the course of a year or longer, or piloting the program or parts of the program with one or more teams in a department or two.

The objective here, as it's been from the start, is to get things right. If a plan runs into trouble in the pilot stage, it's no big deal to make corrections. In fact, by piloting a plan or phasing it in, the company is implicitly declaring that it is subject to modification. But if the same plan is rolled out with great fanfare and then runs into trouble, it may be doomed. It's bad business to raise expectations you can't meet, or to create fears you can't mediate among people whose pay is on the line.

For most workers, an incentive plan that creates pay-at-risk is an alarming prospect if the transition isn't handled properly. The most direct way to introduce pay-at-risk is to reduce base pay up front by, say, 5 percent. That's quick, but brutal. A better approach is to freeze base pay, essentially putting at risk the projected base-pay increases. (One advantage of this approach is that you can still reward the best performers by giving them a smaller increment—in effect, a frost.) But this can be done only if the company gives plenty of advance notice. Three to six months' warning is reasonable. If employees expect their normal raise on January 1, you cannot, barring a crisis in the company, steal their Christmas by announcing on December 24 that you're freezing pay the coming year.

Even with three months' warning, however, eliminating raises may not be the most effective way to get workers to accept a new pay plan. An alternative approach is to give employees a lump-sum payment on January 1 that's the equivalent of a year's annual increase but, unlike an annual increase, doesn't raise their base pay. You've thus created immediate pay-at-risk (by not raising base pay), given employees a windfall, and launched the plan.

The disadvantage for the company is that, in the plan's first year, it will be paying a large sum up front, as well as accounting for any incentive payouts that the plan achieves. The double charge to earnings comes from the lump-sum payment and incentive plan accruals even though the incentive awards are paid out in the second year (assuming a calendar year measurement period). Still, persuading employees to accept a major change in the way they earn their pay has a price and, given the potential gains, a lump-sum payment may be a relatively inexpensive investment.

With modifications, the lump-sum approach may become less onerous. For example, the company can phase in the incentive program by paying the equivalent of the first quarter's base-pay increase in a lump sum up front, and in the second quarter paying out any awards earned during the first quarter. Of course, that approach is possible only if the measurement period is a quarter and the payout occurs shortly thereafter. In selecting a schedule for phasing-in incentive compensation, among the factors management must weigh are the employees' cash flow situation and the company's additional cost of compensation.

Incentive compensation plans can typically be phased in over six to twelve months, but more transition time is required for other elements of compensation. It could take two years to work through a pay-for-skills pilot, which involves training, the acquisition of new skills, and the process of becoming certified for the various blocks. A pay-for-competencies program could also take a year or two to phase in: one year to get employees used to a new performance management approach, possibly involving multi-rater/360-degree or peer review, and another year to link appraisal ratings to pay increases. Getting employees to modify their behavior could take longer still.

But timing isn't everything—the scale of the transition is important, too. Should the incentive plan or pay-for-competencies initiatives be rolled out to the entire company, or tried first in a business unit, a department, or even a team? There are arguments both ways. Company rollouts are certainly faster, and they may be fairer. At the end of a good quarter, for example, no one at a company will want to be excluded from an incentive plan that's based on financial measures (as opposed to one team's operational measures).

## Introducing Pilots

On the other hand, pilots are safer and cheaper and tend to foster a high level of enthusiasm—the phenomenon, first observed in the 1930s at Western Electric's Hawthorne Works in Illinois, that people become more motivated because they know they're being studied. (The drawback is that it may be hard to tell whether it's the plan or the Hawthorne effect that has led to better results.) Pilots also provide multiple laboratories for experimentation. A company could test its new competencies model with a project team, for example, its incentive plan designs with a process team, and its pay-for-skills program with another process team. Or if it's still hesitating between two incentive plan designs, it could pilot each with a different work team or department.

How do you choose your pilots? In aviation, test pilots tend to be the winners. The same should hold true for the departments or teams chosen to try new programs. It might be argued that using average teams will produce more-meaningful results, but the Air Force doesn't follow that rationale, and you shouldn't either. If you're trying out an incentive plan, for example, choose a team where there's more trust and higher morale. The poorer performers may need motivation or the incentive plan more, but a new program needs quick wins to make management and employees more confident.

A trial of several months or measurement periods will show where the plan needs to be modified. So our compensation team may need to retreat briefly to Step 6 before moving ahead. How quickly it advances at this point is a function partly of the corporate culture. In a time-based culture, where the premium is on speed, the tendency is to test for a quarter, then roll out company-wide. Functional cultures (with parallel teams) take a more wait-and-see approach, while a process culture may prefer to introduce change incrementally.

But first, take management's pulse. As I noted in Chapter 10, senior management must champion the new program if it's to succeed. That's another reason to pilot the program within a unit whose management is strong and supportive.

## Step 9: Union Participation Strategy

*Objective: Determine a union involvement process that will promote long-term support for plan success.*

Unions don't usually welcome new compensation programs. Pay is a union issue—arguably *the* union issue, along with job security—and labor leaders are naturally suspicious when companies seek to change the way they pay employees. That's particularly true if the change involves differentials in pay, an area that unions consider their own. But, as we've seen at General Motors' Saturn plant —where, under an agreement with the United Auto Workers, employees have 10 percent of pay-at-risk—it's possible to win over even the most powerful union.

There are a number of things companies can do to win a more favorable reception from unions. For a start, choose your time carefully. The best time to broach the subject is when contract renewal negotiations are beginning. However, it's also possible to open the contract midterm for specific issues. Trying to change compensation unilaterally, between contracts, is certain to chill the atmosphere.

At the appropriate time, then, try to involve the union in the design of the program. Whether or not that's practicable depends on management-labor relations at the company and the extent to which changes in compensation may be well received. Even if relations are good, the compensation strategy should be developed by management alone. But once the design concept (see Step 5) is in place, the process of designing the components would benefit from union involvement. That's especially true when it comes to establishing measures for an incentive plan, for example, or defining skill blocks for a pay-for-skills program to replace pay increases based on the cost of living or seniority.

Unfortunately, most companies still prefer to wait until the program is more clearly etched in stone to bring in the unions—typically in Step 11, when the plan is being communicated to all employees. And there are certain issues where companies might expect union opposition. Paying for competencies is one, because it increases the differentiation among individuals on criteria other than the traditional skills or seniority. In such cases, the company may have no option but to present the plan to the union on a take-it-or-leave-it basis. That's unfortunate, because unions are more likely to accept a program when they've had some input. Once they sign off on a program, they can be a definite help in communicating it to members.

So do try to win the union's support. That may seem obvious, but there are arguments companies can make that will give the union the rationale it needs to back change and encourage its members to accept the risk inherent in an incentive plan. The most compelling argument is that, for all its apparent riskiness, pay-at-risk may actually enhance job security because it will make the company more competitive. With an incentive plan, the company knows what its potential costs and savings are, and it may be less desperate either to manufacture overseas or to outsource.

There are also ways of structuring compensation programs to make them more attractive to unions. For example, an incentive program that creates pay-at-risk could be designed so that it measures performance retroactively—that is, the incentive plan and pay-at-risk officially start on October 1, but the measurement portion of the plan begins the previous January. That's an expensive bargaining chip for employers, but one that's likely to be more attractive to unions by almost assuring a payout for the first year. Alternatively, a company might guarantee that employees will be no worse off under the plan, for a stated period of time, by giving them the greater of their pay-at-risk or incentive plan payouts. It's probably a safe promise: Union or no union, if employee earnings decline in the long term, the company would almost certainly have to redesign or terminate the program.

## Step 10: Administrative Requirements

*Objective: Develop an administrative plan for ongoing success.*

From the first, I've underscored the need to simplify the plan design as much as possible. There are two main reasons: As I'll reiterate in Step 11, a plan must be understood if it's to be accepted. And a plan must be administered with relative ease if it's to be effective. An excellent plan is purely ornamental if it's too complex or costly to administer.

There are several administrative requirements for an effective plan:

• *Record-keeping.* This is one of the most tedious and essential administrative requirements, and the compensation plan must address who does it and what it entails. If the plan is limited to a business unit, rather than to the corporation overall, it should be administered by the unit's human resources department and audited by Corporate Accounting; corporate programs may be the responsibility of Corporate Human Resources and the chief financial officer. Records must be kept on eligibility (including new hires, terminations, retirees, those on disability, probation, etc.). Historical data on plan results and individual award payouts also need to be collected and available to management and employees.

• *Performance appraisal.* If the company is adopting merit increases in lieu of, say, a seniority system, it will need to erect the machinery for managing the performance appraisal process. Companies that have conducted traditional performance appraisals in the past will be familiar with the basic administrative requirements. However, the introduction of competency models and peer or multi-rater/360-degree review (with input from multiple sources) is likely to increase the paperwork significantly. And, at least initially, the results of a new appraisal approach should be carefully screened for any indication of inadvertent discrimination and to ensure that the results are *documented and defensible.*

• *Incentive payout issues.* What's the process for determining incentive plan payouts? Who cuts the check? How is it issued? Such questions go directly to the employee's bottom line. Because employees will rightfully demand to know, they should receive a statement with each check indicating how the payout was calculated. The record-keeping function typically performs the calculations and communicates to payroll the amount of each employee's check.

• *Recognition award issues.* Just as incentive payouts must be well documented, so should the process by which employees receive spot awards for performance. Nominating candidates and selecting the winners, presenting awards, identifying the tax implications, and keeping appropriate records are all administrative tasks.

• *Plan document.* Every incentive plan must be described in full in a comprehensive legal document to which management and employees can refer should any questions arise. This document defines all the relevant factors: eligible earnings (if incentive payouts are expressed as a percent of pay), eligibility, performance measures (definitions of exactly how measures are determined), levels of payout (payout formula), impact on benefits, and goal-setting process (how goals and formula might change from one measurement period to the next—for example, how a rolling average is computed, along with illustrations). Accountability for each of the ongoing elements (in-

## Exhibit 11-5.  Outline of a typical incentive plan document.

### XYZ Company
### Performance-Reward Incentive Plan Document

1. *Purpose.* The purpose of the Plan is to reduce waste and the costs of waste removal by giving each participating team employee a monetary incentive compensation opportunity.

2. *Eligibility.* All team members who work six or more weeks during a performance measurement period are eligible to participate, except employees who are on a formal written disciplinary action or warning at the end of any performance measurement period.

3. *Plan operation*

   a. Performance measurement periods. There will be four quarterly performance measurement periods, as follows: January–March, April–June, July–September, October–December. Payouts will occur within thirty days after the end of each measurement period.

   b. Incentive pool creation. Award pool will be generated based upon the first dollar of savings, and it will equal 50 percent of each year's savings above threshold.

   c. Threshold performance. A 10 percent reduction in costs must be achieved each year before any award payouts will be earned. Threshold is therefore defined as 90 percent of the current cost of tonnage of waste removal, and will be adjusted annually on a three-year rolling average.

   d. Participation. Award pool will be divided equally in dollars among all eligible team members. In addition, team members will be considered individually at the end of the Plan Year for a one-time spot cash award for their efforts in contributing to the team's success.

4. *Tax and benefit implications.* Awards under the Plan are compensation for federal and state tax purposes and will be reported as ordinary income in the year in which the award is paid. Payouts shall not be considered compensation for the pension, profit-sharing, life insurance, disability plan, or any other benefit plan sponsored by the Company.

5. *Terminations.* Employees who terminate employment with the Company, either voluntarily or involuntarily (other than death, retirement, or disability), during the performance measurement period will not be eligible to receive any award under this plan. Employees who leave for reasons of death, disability, or approved retirement, and who have completed more than six weeks of the performance period, will be eligible to receive a full share. Employees on long-term disability or short-term disability more than six weeks during the performance measurement period are not eligible to receive an award for that performance measurement period.

6. *Guarantee of employment.* Participation in this Plan does not in any way guarantee employment within the Company for any performance measurement period or any other length of time.

7. *Modification or termination of Plan.* In developing this Plan, the Company has in no way guaranteed payment to any employee under this Plan. The Plan shall remain in effect until such time as the Company decides to modify, amend, or terminate it at its sole discretion at the end of any respective Plan Year.

8. *Plan administration.* Company management has the sole authority to interpret the Plan, and may adapt and revise pertinent rules and regulations. Any questions of eligibility, coverage, benefits, or other matters concerning this Plan shall be resolved exclusively by management.

---

cluding interpretation and revision of the plan document) must be assigned and communicated.

With appendices, the entire document may come to a dozen pages or more. Exhibit 11-5 offers an outline of an incentive plan document recently adopted by a Hay client to indicate the categories covered. Due to space, and because every plan is different, many of the details that would necessarily be included in a typical document have been omitted.

In the next chapter, I conclude with Phase III, implementing the plan.

# 12

# Implementing Team Pay—Phase III: Implementation

This is the hardest phase, and the longest. It's no exaggeration to say that, for the company, implementing the new compensation program requires three times the effort of the previous ten steps combined (see Exhibit 12-1). For one thing, it's not only our compensation design team members who are being taken away from their regular jobs; now it's the workforce generally that must learn how the program works and undergo training and development in the techniques that will enable them to work more productively.

For another, Phase III doesn't stop with the rollout of the program to participants. In fact, it might be said that it never ends: Proper implementation requires ongoing monitoring of the program, year after year. Like companies, compensation programs are organic and must change and adapt if they are to survive.

## Step 11: Education/Communication Program

*Objective: Develop a strategy for program introduction.*

"What we have here is a failure to communicate."

That remark, spoken sardonically by a brutal prison guard in the movie *Cool Hand Luke*, has become a popular tongue-in-cheek comment whenever breakdowns in communication occur. My hope is that, by developing a sound education and communications strategy, we can prevent it from becoming the epitaph for our compensation program.

As much as any of the other steps enumerated here, good com-

**Exhibit 12-1. Implementing team-based compensation (Phase III).**

# Methodology

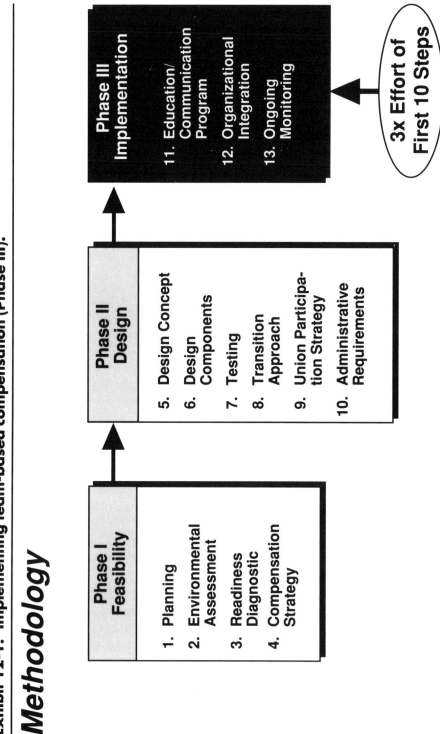

**Phase I
Feasibility**

1. Planning
2. Environmental Assessment
3. Readiness Diagnostic
4. Compensation Strategy

**Phase II
Design**

5. Design Concept
6. Design Components
7. Testing
8. Transition Approach
9. Union Participation Strategy
10. Administrative Requirements

**Phase III
Implementation**

11. Education/ Communication Program
12. Organizational Integration
13. Ongoing Monitoring

**3x Effort of First 10 Steps**

munication is integral to the success of a program. The more effectively a program is communicated to employees, the better they will understand it and the likelier they are to accept and aggressively pursue its goals. Good communication is inclusionary and empowering, too: Employees who are well informed, as a matter of corporate policy, are employees who feel that they are valued by their company and have a chance to impact its results.

Thus, as soon as the company's senior management has approved the plan design, our compensation team's next step should be to educate and communicate it to those people within the company who are affected by it. In doing so, they must address two issues: Who needs to know? And how should the information be conveyed to ensure people's immediate understanding and, ultimately, their acceptance?

If they haven't been brought into the picture thus far, the middle managers and supervisors who oversee the workers directly affected by the plan need to be brought up to speed, fast. These are the men and women, after all, who will be presenting the plan to their subordinates and answering their questions. They must be informed and supportive—particularly because, starting with this step, employees will be pulled away from their jobs from time to time to attend meetings, learn more about the program, and acquire the requisite skills and competencies. To get buy-in, then, our compensation team must emphasize the desirable business outcomes of the pay program, not just the effects on compensation. It should explain how the program contributes to business success and reinforces the company's and team's business strategy. The emphasis here is on educating the workforce as much as communicating a new pay program.

## Achieving Employee Support

Then it's time to communicate the program to employees. In general, the best forum for the initial communication is typically through supervisors and managers. Our employee attitude surveys consistently indicate that first-line supervision has the greatest credibility with a company's workers. It is also important that the initial communication be perceived as coming from top management. One way of underscoring this is by issuing a memo that is cosigned by senior management and the plant manager as well as the supervisor or team leader. This is also a good time to hand employees a brochure about the program that they can take home, read, and discuss with family and coworkers. The plan is also likely to generate questions that will be raised at follow-up meetings with management. Effective communication at this point is very much a repetitive and interactive process.

The brochure, as well as any meetings with employees, needs to open on an upbeat note. In essence, the theme is, "We're changing our compensation to support the company's vision/the new work culture/our teams," and the accent is on what the plan will mean for "you," the team member. The tone should be encouraging and empowering, not intimidating: "Here's what you can do" and "Here's how we'll help you"—not "Work harder." Above all, the writing style should be reader-friendly. As an example, here is an excerpt from the brochure issued by UCAR Carbon, a subsidiary of Union Carbide, when it launched an incentive plan a few years ago:

> **YOU MAKE THE DIFFERENCE**
>
> Every individual makes a difference to our overall business success. With [this Plan], you have a larger stake in the business . . . a good reason to look more closely at how you can help improve the bottom line.
>
> We encourage you to embrace our Vision Statement and to look at all aspects of our business and make recommendations on how we can improve productivity and the quality of our products. We are open to new ideas and new ways of doing things. Talk to your supervisor and learn more about the way your job influences other areas of our business.

The physical presentation of the brochure and any other materials that are distributed to employees is also important. These are marketing materials—after all, you're selling the program—but if they look too slick, employees may get the sense they're canned rather than the result of a multistep process by the conscientious members of the compensation team or, worse yet, that the company is wasting its money on brochures rather than paying its workers more. At the same time, the program needs to have an identity—a name and probably a logo—to give it credibility. If it's a relatively small unit of a company that is implementing the plan, an effective brochure can be created with desktop publishing. If it's a program that affects large numbers of employees, or employees in multiple locations, a brief (ten-minute) video (companion piece to the brochure) assures a consistent introduction, tone, and outline of the plan design. Like the brochure, the video should be user-friendly and inviting—not just "talking heads," but a brief philosophical statement by senior management, location shots, and employee reactions, followed by graphics that help explain the program.

## *Answering Employees' Questions*

Once the news has been broken, whether it's through a memo, a meeting followed by a brochure, or a meeting and/or a video, employees will have a host of questions. The company must allocate a generous amount of time to follow-up meetings—perhaps a series of "open houses"—where it will provide the answers. Meetings should be limited to twenty-five employees, to allow plenty of time for discussion. The compensation team, human resources staffers, and other specialists who have been involved in the process, such as consultants, may help define the agenda for these meetings and stand by, but it's the manager or supervisor who will be on the front line. Hence the need to gain their understanding and acceptance of the program.

By now, managers should be equipped with a briefing packet or binder that contains the following: the plan document (described in Step 10, Chapter 11); the employee brochure; the script of the video, if one was produced; sample forms for performance appraisals, if those are being changed; information about training programs; reference material including the company's vision statement and compensation policy (or statement of beliefs and principles); and press releases, if relevant. Because so much material is being piled on, it's particularly important that it be accessible and well organized. Transparency slides are also useful to help managers explain or illustrate elements of the program to the affected employees.

Last, but probably first in utility, is a list of sample questions managers can expect to receive, along with the preferred answers. It's critical that employees hear consistent responses. One highly effective way to develop such a list is through an employee focus group. The questions raised by participants, after all, are very likely to be the same raised at the open-house forums. (These questions are also an effective checklist to ensure the completeness of the design.) Below are listed typical questions that can be expected, organized by topic:

### Philosophy of Plan

1. Why is this Plan being adopted?
2. How are pay and business results connected?
3. I never thought of myself as being responsible for results. How am I responsible for results?
4. Are other companies putting in these types of plans?

### Performance Appraisals

5. How were the competencies developed?
6. What do these competencies have to do with the way I do my job?
7. Competencies don't seem like something I can learn, like skills; so how can I improve?
8. I've never conducted a performance review. How would I know what to do?
9. Won't my teammates find out what I've said about them?

### Incentive Plans

10. How will we know during the measurement period how the team is doing?
11. What happens if the team doesn't meet its goals for the period?
12. How are the goals determined? Will they be higher in following periods?
13. If I know my annual base rate of pay and want to figure out what I can earn in incentive compensation, how do I do it?
14. Are you going to take away my overtime? My merit raises?
15. Why can't we earn more than the maximum award level if we have a great year?

### Incentive Plans and Base-Pay Increases

16. Why won't I get a pay raise this year?
17. When base-pay raises resume (assuming lump sums in lieu of base-pay increases to create pay-at-risk), will they be less than before?
18. Suppose there's no payout from the incentive plan next year. Won't I always be out the base-pay raise I should have received?
19. Haven't merit/wage increases always been tied to profits?

### Incentive Plans and Lump-Sum Payments

20. Will I be better or worse off next year?
21. How does the lump sum compare with a base-pay raise?
22. Do I have to give back pay if my team doesn't meet its goals?

### Recognition Award

23. How can I win a spot award if I don't know what's being measured?

24. A trophy is nice but, frankly, I'd prefer the money. Why can't I get cash?
25. What types of activities, efforts, or results should be nominated for an award?
26. How do I nominate a team member for an award?

Some questions can be answered in a few words or calculations, while others require more deliberation. If competencies are a new concern for the company, for example, the manager may need to spend a lot of time helping employees understand how they are expected to achieve results. The manager or supervisor should review each competency and discuss how it can contribute to the achievement of performance goals, define specific observable behaviors the employee can display to demonstrate the competency effectively, and describe the development and training programs the company is putting in place to help employees develop the competencies.

Communication doesn't stop with a meeting or two. Other tools that might be considered after the initial communication include:

- Charts or posters showing progress toward goals in each element of the program, for example, in the number of employees receiving competency training or the percentage increase in output per manhour
- Updates in the plant newsletter
- Updates for supervisors or team leaders to give to employees on a regularly scheduled basis

Communication failure occurs more often with ongoing results than with initial plan rollout. There tends to be more energy or excitement with new plans than with maintaining the existing program.

## Step 12: Organizational Integration

*Objective: Identify and develop management and employee initiatives that will link reward programs to business strategy and employee involvement programs.*

Here's where the rubber meets the road. Now that employees understand—and, we hope, accept—the program, it's the task of the compensation team to ensure that they're given the tools to do the job. That involves asking the questions, What do you want employees to do differently? and, How can you get them to do it?

In most cases, what companies hope to change are the processes by which people work. That usually means training them, both in the classroom and on the job, in the methods, tools, and competencies that will allow them to challenge and improve the processes they've traditionally used. The goal is for employees to work smarter, not necessarily harder. And because our new compensation program is team-based, a large part of the training and development may include role-playing workshops and other efforts aimed at fostering and stimulating the processes of people working in groups or teams.

Let's say, for example, the company wants to create a team proposal system like those, described earlier, at St. Joseph Hospital or American Airlines. First, it must train employees how to turn a vague idea ("Let's turn off more lights and save money!") into a suggestion ("Let's reduce the lights in the rest rooms and save $100/week") to a proposal of how to reduce lighting, for example, install motion-sensitive switches, change the type of lightbulbs, etc. That involves training employees to think analytically, to seek information, and to troubleshoot—the competency of problem-solving. Where is there excess lighting? Do those rooms need to be so bright? What would be the costs and benefits of reducing electricity usage?

Second, the company needs to develop the ability to respond appropriately to such proposals. That may mean not only setting up the necessary infrastructure, but also training managers in competencies that would enhance their powers to influence others and their interpersonal and organizational effectiveness. In the past, management may have shrugged off an employee idea ("We'll think about it") or dismissed it out of hand ("We don't do that here"). But if the company genuinely wants a productive team proposal system, it must create a system under which any proposal gets serious and prompt attention. The company could stipulate, for example, that any proposal will receive a response within thirty days, and that there will be some further action every month until the proposal is accepted, implemented, or finally rejected.

The various competencies associated with working in teams may be a large part of any training and development program. Parallel or project teams may need training in managing—planning and organizing—a project. Process teams that are becoming more self-directed are likely to require development in many of the competencies associated with effective teamwork, as well as the leadership competencies for the new tasks—scheduling work flow, hiring and disciplining members—that are involved in running a team. In fact, we'd expect that most new recruits to teams would need competency training to help get them through team meetings: establishing agendas, imposing time limits and rules, defining mutual goals, and averting or resolving conflict.

The fundamental purpose of all this training isn't to get people to work in teams. It's to align them to the new compensation system. If the system dictates that people are going to be paid for competencies, then team members should acquire them, and some members should acquire the leadership competencies that will enable the team to be productive. If the pay system states that teams will be paid for filling more cylinders of gas per day or achieving higher scores on customer satisfaction surveys, then teams have to be taught how to look more closely at the way they work and find areas where they can make improvements. Training will raise performance levels, and better performance will raise pay levels.

How much training? It's a question of how much the company wants to change and how fast it's willing to move. A rigorous training schedule can put a short-term strain on company resources. However, if it leads to discernible bottom-line improvement, the investment in time, energy, and money is easily justified.

# Step 13: Ongoing Monitoring

*Objective: Ensure ongoing program success.*

Now that you've implemented the program, how do you know it works? That question is easily answered with another: Do people do anything differently as a result of the program?

If the answer is no, then the program is unsuccessful.

Unfortunately, it's rarely that simple.

For one thing, it's not always easy to determine whether people are doing anything differently, or whether what they're doing differently is meaningful, or whether it's due to the program. Furthermore, in the event there is a measurable change in the team's or company's results, it's virtually impossible in the short term to attribute all of it to the compensation program. Any of a variety of external environmental factors—the opening of a new market, the drop in the price of an input, price-cutting by the competition—can have far more impact than pay on revenues and profits. Even operational measures, like the number of claims processed or the tonnage of waste removed, may be more closely related to business volume than to the way people work.

## *Eliciting Employee Feedback*

But because it is important to know whether a program works, criteria for measuring its efficacy—and projected results—should be part of the design. And the first thing to be measured is communication: Do people understand the program (and do their supervisors agree)? It's impossible to evaluate a program if it's not even understood. If the answer is no, our compensation team has to return to Step 11. If the answer is yes, then our team can try to assess what impact, if any, the program has had. If it's too early for operational or financial results to be available, the first test has to be behavioral: Has team members' behavior changed? (see Exhibit 12-2).

As I indicated earlier, that can be hard to answer. But, in employee focus groups or one-on-one conversations, our compensation team and other specialists, perhaps from Human Resources, should elicit feedback from employees directly. For a start, how do they feel about the program? Have they done anything differently in their job as a result? What is it? Supervisors should be asked the same questions. Even small differences can be telling. "They're turning off the water hoses now," a supervisor at a mining company told me. "They never did that before we started to measure water usage at the team level."

Questioning can also provide specific information about the programs. At AT&T Universal Card Services, as I noted in Chapter 7, employees said that they disliked one of the aspects of the recognition program—an air horn used to trumpet the naming of the quarterly award winners—because the noise was distracting for customers. And at another company, some team members began to challenge the priorities given certain activities.

However, while such criticism is valuable, it shouldn't necessarily be heeded. Employees tend to take a shortsighted approach— "Meetings and training sessions reduce my output, which reduces my wages, so let's cut out the meetings and training"—while most companies recognize that a better-educated and -trained employee is a good long-term investment. On the other hand, if employees say they don't like the program but their behavior has changed for the better, management needs to analyze what's going on. If employees are indicating that they don't like putting pay at risk in an uncertain economy, for example, then elements of the program need reaffirmation and possible modification, and the team members probably need additional education.

## Using Financial and Operational Criteria

Longer-term, of course, financial and operational criteria can be used in determining whether a compensation plan is successful. If the company has implemented an incentive plan that rewards employees

**Exhibit 12-2. Ongoing monitoring.**

## Plan Success

**1.** Employee Understanding and Acceptance

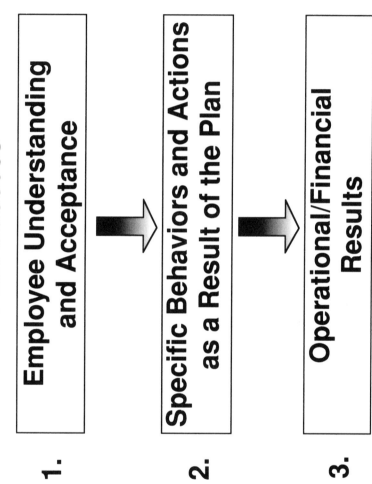

**2.** Specific Behaviors and Actions as a Result of the Plan

**3.** Operational/Financial Results

for improvements in specific financial or operational measures, those measures may be used as criteria. However, as I noted above, there is always a possibility that external environmental factors will taint these measures over the short term.

There are still more ways to measure the plan's success. Below are listed eight measures suggested by the American Compensation Association (ACA) in its study of performance and reward. A cautionary note: The study did not focus specifically on team-based pay, so some of its findings may not be relevant to teams. Furthermore, not all of the measures listed will be appropriate for every plan. Still, they offer a starting point:

### Financial Results

1. Dollar value of performance improvement per team per year (or other measurement period). While this is a good financial measure of performance, based on operational criteria, it won't apply to all plans. Some plan measures (customer satisfaction, attendance, some quality measures, etc.) and goals (greater employee participation, teamwork, greater employee identification with business results) are not easily quantified financially.

2. Payout per employee per year, reported either as a dollar value or as a percent of base pay.

3. Payout-to-gain relationship. As the ACA executive summary notes, calculating the net return on payout is as close as one can come to a net return on investment ratio. Of the plans that were able to put a dollar value on their gains—less than half of those in the ACA study—a median 134 percent net return on payout was reported. While the researchers conceded that the return does not take into account costs other than payouts, such as training, the gains were probably understated, if anything.

4. Management's satisfaction with plan results. In the ACA study, ratings of management's satisfaction with the program fell between neutral and moderately satisfied. Satisfaction seemed to be related to strong nonfinancial results rather than to the size of the payout or gain. The "satisfaction" index is especially interesting due to its bearing on program survival: The study also found that management was significantly less satisfied with programs that were subsequently terminated than in continuing plans. No surprises here!

### Nonfinancial Results—Subjective Ratings of How Much the Plan Contributed to the Original Plan Objectives

5. Improved business performance.

6. Improved teamwork, including communications, employee relations and involvement, and entrepreneurship.

7. Improved performance-reward linkage. This includes a reduction in the entitlement mentality; making labor costs more variable with organization performance; becoming more competitive with total compensation; and allocating available award funds to high-performing teams or individuals. Another factor I'd add here is a growing sense of mutual accountability among employees.

8. Improved quality of the workforce, including more satisfactory recruitment and higher employee retention.

If the results are at least as good as expected, then the company's management may relax—until the next measurement period. Monitoring should be synchronized with the program's own measures: Evaluation of a new competency model, for example, can take place only after the annual performance appraisal, while measuring financial results may occur only on the quarter or at year-end.

But what if monitoring shows that the program isn't working? Or, more likely, that specific elements need to be redesigned? Unless it's clearly a failure, the program should be left in place for a full two measurement periods, with only minor modifications. That gives our compensation team plenty of time to observe the program in action. As I noted, it takes time to detect changes in employee actions that impact financial and operational results. Furthermore, people generally don't openly embrace change—particularly when their livelihood is concerned—and the company's employees, having just come to terms with the new compensation program, however imperfect, may prefer stability to more change. It's not a good way to build trust if employees continually say that no matter what happens, they change the pay program every year—just about the time they've begun to understand it.

However, as I noted earlier in this chapter, organizations and pay programs are organic: Change is inevitable. From the time it is implemented, the program will undergo continual evolution. In fact, as the ACA study noted, "Plans are more successful when they are regularly reassessed to stay current with business strategy." The reassessment may be minor (adding to or subtracting from the competency model, tinkering with the payout formula) or more substantial (changing the basis for goals from historical to budgeted, substituting one operational measure for another). And, like the program itself, each modification will have to be tested, communicated, and regularly monitored.

# Epilogue

We are living in a period of fundamental change, including change in the way people work and are paid. Quantum advances in technology have made the world both smaller and more complex, building global networks of information while creating systems too complex for the expertise of a solitary worker. The customer is demanding, and getting, service that is better and faster—and, increasingly, the customer may be anywhere in the world.

To accommodate such massive change, many organizations are transitioning to new cultures: flattening their hierarchies, empowering their workers, and, more and more, reengineering their processes so that they are based not on individuals but on teams. Change demands change: If they have not already begun to change, compensation systems must be the next area of the corporation to undergo change.

For companies that are redefining the nature of work, it is not enough merely to modify existing reward programs. Only a thorough rethinking and restructuring of pay practices, which will align compensation (and other human resources systems, including the use of behavioral competencies) with new business strategies and cultures, will give companies the competitive advantage they need to succeed. Only those companies that use compensation and other areas of human resources as strategic tools will be able to capitalize on the tremendous potential of their employees.

Change is often painful, and it's reasonable for companies to be apprehensive about making the transition to a new culture, new employee behaviors, and new pay systems. But it *is* a transition, not a transformation: It's not necessary—or even desirable—to dismiss the entire body of compensation knowledge developed over the past fifty years. The important point is to recognize that change is also opportunity, and those companies that seize it will be ahead of the curve. Those companies that wait for others to go first will be left behind.

So be among the leaders of change. If your company is moving toward teams, identify the type(s) of teams they represent. Then determine whether the way they're being paid is aligned with the way they work. Send a message to employees that the company knows that work and pay have changed forever; that to get the results it wants, it must align work cultures, behaviors, and pay; and that to have a motivated workforce, it must pay people for performance. Experiment with different pay systems, piloting them in a department or unit or two. Keep what works, fix what doesn't, and roll out the new systems company-wide.

It's a process of continuous learning and continuous improvement, with a single objective: continuous success.

# Index